Ocean Sailing

Ocean Sailing

Robert A. James

HEARST MARINE BOOKS
New York

First published in USA 1983 by
Hearst Marine Books
105 Madison Avenue
New York, N.Y. 10016.

Library of Congress Cataloging in Publication Data

James, Robert A., 1946-
  Ocean sailing.

  Originally published: Lymington, Hampshire:
Nautical Pub. Co., 1980.
  Includes index.
  1. Sailing.   I. Title.
GV811.J34 1983   797.1'24   82-21161
ISBN 0-87851-311-6

Manufactured in the United States of America

Introduction
by Dame Naomi James D.B.E.

Anyone who, a mere six weeks after taking up sailing and only two years before setting out, decides to sail round the world single-handed, needs to acquire very quickly enough knowledge of the ins and outs of sailing to achieve that goal. As I had no former education in matters nautical—and even less inclination towards anything mathematical, the task of teaching me to sail in that time would have seemed to any would-be teacher immense.

My husband Rob, knowing that to attempt to teach me the theory of navigation in its entirety would be to distress and thoroughly depress me (and being afraid I could never grasp it anyway) showed me how to cross an ocean successfully, using the practical techniques described in this book.

After two years I had sufficient confidence—albeit somewhat misplaced in certain directions as experience showed—to find my way through many miles of ocean besides some coastal waters and to arrive at my final destination. Rob learnt something through my experiences, too. Having omitted to make quite sure that I had understood the difference between latitude and longitude scales, (although as I'd reached Australia by this time I had to conclude that it couldn't be so terribly important) he has now, I'm glad to see, been careful to point out in his piece on navigation which scale to use when measuring one's distance run! And so for many other important—although perfectly simple—aspects of navigation and boat handling which one needs to know to cross an ocean.

Now that I've graduated from cruising single-handed to racing I have encouraged Rob to get this book written as quickly as possible, so that I can take a copy with me on future races across the Atlantic, and hence discover more about how to sail faster, better and always with safety.

Contents

Acknowledgements

I am grateful for the tremendous help I received from a number of people in the preparation and production of this book.

My thanks go to Erroll Bruce who not only suggested I should write an instructional text but who was then faced with the unenviable task of editing the book once it was written.

While the book is based mostly on ideas stemming from my own experiences there are areas where I needed and was given advice. I wish to express my thanks to Dr Robin Leech for his excellent section on health, and to the following people who acted as 'sounding boards': Butch Dalrymple-Smith (yacht design), Dereck Kelsel and Dick Newick (multihulls) and my wife, Naomi (single-handed sailing).

I am very grateful for the family effort in correcting my manuscript. This was carried out jointly by my parents, John and Georgette James, and Naomi. I am especially thankful to my mother for her tireless typing.

An enormous amount of work went into the production of the numerous diagrams. My sincerest gratitude is due to Rob Jacobs for his skilful drawing.

Finally I am indebted to the Controller of Her Majesty's Stationery for permission to reproduce pages from the Nautical Almanac; to the US Naval Oceanographic Office for permission to reproduce pages from the Sight Reduction Tables; and to the following people for their photographs: Dr Robin Leech, Max le Grand, and Malcolm Sykes.

Preface

Trans-ocean sailing is easy to learn. The coastal sailor will find a logical extension of what he already knows and the novice will find it easier to master than inshore sailing. Out of sight of land one has more space and more time to get to know the sea in all its moods. There are no lee shores, rocks, tidal calculations or tricky harbour entrances to contend with.

It is a mistake to believe that only the most experienced yachtsmen can successfully cruise or race across an ocean. A lifetime could be spent learning all there is to know about the sea, but how much of this is really essential? Here lies the purpose of this book.

From knowledge gained in many voyages, including two circumnavigations under sail via Cape Horn, I have sorted out what one actually *needs* to know to prepare for, and undertake, a long ocean voyage. The book covers the *practical* aspects of every stage of a trip—choosing the yacht, planning the route, shipboard routine, sail handling systems (cruising and racing), safety and survival procedures, navigation, food, health, repairs and maintenance and advice on a few special hazards. Also included are chapters on multihull and single-handed sailing.

I hope this book will help a lot of people discover the joys of ocean sailing, without too many learning pains.

Entries for the 1977 round-the-world race placed emphasis on speed.

1 The Yacht. Choice and Preparation

The great challenge of sailing a yacht across an ocean is attempted, and achieved, far more often today than it was ten or twenty years ago. A feat that at one time was only possible with a specially designed or adapted craft is now more commonplace, due to our greater knowledge of the sea and because of the general seaworthiness of standard boats. One of the factors in this greater knowledge is the advent of trans-ocean racing. The Cape Town to Rio de Janeiro race was the pioneer. It has now been eclipsed for endurance by the Whitbread round-the-world Races and similar events. A great deal has been learned from these races.

All the yachts in the 1973 round-the-world race were cautiously prepared. Those with unlimited funds were able to design and build specifically for the trip. Chay Blyth with the magnificent *Great Britain II* and Eric Tabarly with *Pen Duick VI* were two examples. The entrants who could not afford new yachts all tended to choose strong and reliable, rather than fast, craft. The race was a success and less damage was suffered than either spectators and competitors had expected. Consequently, for the next race in 1977, most of the entries placed more emphasis on speed and less on reliability. Again there was comparatively little damage and each yacht finished the course. An indication of the confidence that this created was given by the entry list in the 1979 Parmelia race from England to Australia. While the racing division attracted 12 entries, there were many more in the cruising division, including yachts of under 12 metres in length, all happy to take the Roaring Forties route to Perth. Of course the suitability of the yacht is not the only factor in making a successful voyage; the knowledge and experience of the skipper and crew arc also important. However, in this chapter, it is the choice and preparation of a yacht that are under scrutiny.

The requirements of an ocean-going yacht are basically those of a vessel sailed inshore. The extreme weather of the 1979 Fastnet Race showed us that, rather than looking at an inshore yacht and deciding what changes should be made to venture offshore, the requirements for offshore safety should be studied, and applied to inshore craft.

Size
Is there safety in size? The answer is both yes and no. More importantly, there is safety in

strength. A strong, small yacht has a greater chance of survival in extreme conditions than a weak, larger one.

How do the elements affect the behaviour of craft of different sizes? The wind blows on large and small alike. The smaller yacht will have lighter sails, mast and rigging, but as the sail area is also smaller and the vessel itself lighter so the strains imposed are relatively similar. However the story is different when the waves, which inevitably accompany the wind, are considered. A 10-metre wave is going to appear more daunting to a 10-metre yacht than to one of 20 metres. The principle demonstrated by the ability of a two inch cork to survive a hurricane illustrates a point; while a larger object may be hitting the waves awkwardly the cork will be bobbing up and down happily. It may also be rolling over on its axis which would not be healthy, were it a yacht.

There are several cases of very small yachts successfully making ocean passages. In 1979 an american yachtsman sailed from Norfolk, Virginia, to Falmouth, England, in the 3-metre 'yacht' *Yankee Girl*, covering 3,800 miles in 54 days. While such a trip is possible with reasonable luck, the chances of surviving a bad storm are fairly small. Size helps when survival tactics have to be adopted (see chapter 6). If a yacht lies a-hull or runs off, the danger of capsize or pitchpole will reduce as size increases. The 1979 Fastnet bears this out.

The severe storm that caught the Fastnet fleet between Land's End and the south coast of Ireland caused the loss of 15 lives, as well as the loss of several yachts and the retirement of the majority. Neglecting, unfairly perhaps, all other criteria, there was a definite indication of safety in size. In the three larger classes (approx. 12-metres length and above) of the 123 starters, 51 retired (41%). In the three smaller classes the figures were 179 starters and 166 retirements (93%). All the lives lost, and the 5 yachts sunk, were from the smaller end of the fleet.

However, in normal, and even gale conditions, small yachts can hold their own. The greater limitation in choosing the size of yacht is comfort, related to the length and purpose of the voyage. While the odd trip is taken with the sole intention of getting into the record books, the more common intent is surely the pursuit of pleasure. The requirements for crew comfort, and the ability to carry sufficient stores, are different on a trans-ocean crossing compared with a coastal day sail. In a later section accommodation is discussed and it is there that the most important size-deciding factors are found.

Materials

Wood, steel, aluminium, glass-reinforced plastic, foam sandwich, ferro-cement, Kevlar and carbon fibre—whatever next? All these materials are used in boat building and all are suitable for long distance sailing. There are advantages and disadvantages to each. If racing is intended, priority will be given to the weight of the material relative to its strength. Better weight distribution can be obtained by using a lighter material, keeping weight away from where it does harm and concentrating it where needed for speed and handicapping (rating) purposes. However, heavier, cheaper materials may be suitable for a cruising yacht.

Wood. Originally the only boat building material, wood has some natural properties difficult to emulate artificially. It is still extensively used for racing yachts, generally constructed 'one-off'. Wood is expensive and needs careful maintenance. If well looked after a wooden yacht can last—Chris Waddington's *Moya* is an example, built from pitch-pine by Crossfields in 1910 she looks as though she had not yet been launched. Wood also has the advantage of being nice to live in and does not cause bad condensation down below. Two of the 15 yachts in the 1977 world race were constructed of wood, as were 3 from the 1973 race. None suffered hull damage.

Steel. Not a very popular material as it is heavy for its strength, it corrodes, and unless well lined inside, is not very pleasant to live in. It can be used to build immensely strong vessels. The yacht *British Steel* was an example. Chay Blyth chose steel for this craft which he then sailed single-handed, non-stop, east to west around the world. On his return the yacht looked in excellent condition, but several years later it became a never-ending battle to maintain her in that state. Her strength is attested to by her untimely end on the rocks of Fuerterventura. After striking a reef in rough seas she bounced for eight hours without splitting a plate before reaching the high water mark. Few steel yachts have been raced; there was only one in the 1977 world race and she proved heavy and slow.

Aluminium. Very popular for the construction of racing yachts. In 1973 there were three aluminium entries in the world race: one split her hull and had to retire. However, by 1977 there were more aluminium yachts in the world race than those of any other material. None had any problems and the biggest of them, *Flyer*, won the race. Aluminium has not been extensively used for cruising vessels as it is expensive and not ideally suited to mass production. Care has to be taken to avoid electrolysis between the hull and the skin fittings, propeller shaft and rudder bearings.

Glass Reinforced Plastic (G.R.P.). The big advantage of G.R.P. is in reducing the cost of series production, which applies to both cruising and racing yachts. Careful quantity control and new techniques of moulding have kept the material competitive in both racing and financial terms. Low maintenance requirements make it popular for cruising vessels. A new G.R.P. boat always smells slightly of fibreglass, but careful lining of the hull and deckhead can make the boat very comfortable. The life expectancy of G.R.P. is not yet known as almost everything so far made with the substance is still in existence. Osmosis (water getting under the gel coat and 'climbing' up the fibres of glass) is not common; it can be detected and successfully treated. Five series-production G.R.P. yachts completed the 1977 world race without damage.

G.R.P. Foam Sandwich. Rather than G.R.P. out of a mould, here a foam core is used to construct the hull. The core is then 'glassed' inside and out. There is an obvious advantage in the building of one-off G.R.P. yachts where the construction of a mould would be impracticable. The G.R.P.—foam—G.R.P. cross section is also stronger than a similar weight of solid G.R.P. The disadvantage is the need to fair the outside of the hull with filler to obtain a smooth finish. The possibility of water finding its way between the foam and the G.R.P. skin also exists. Nevertheless, ease of building makes this material ideal for both cruising and racing. Home construction is also feasible.

The 23-metre Gurney designed ketch *Great Britain II* was built of G.R.P. foam sandwich. She has sailed, under racing conditions, more than three times around the world and is still completely sound.

Ferro-Cement. A nice name for reinforced concrete. Mainly used by home builders, due to its inexpensive and relatively easy construction; a metal or chickenwire framework is plastered with concrete to create the hull. A disadvantage is weight; also, any concrete-to-concrete repair or join can only be done while the hull is 'green' (unlike G.R.P.). Most ferro boats look rough, but this is more a function of amateur finishing than any property of the material. Although unsuited to racing yachts one should mention the 21-metre sloop *Helsall*. This concrete vessel, nicknamed the *Flying Footpath*, held the course record for the highly contested Sydney–Hobart race for several years.

Kevlar and Carbon Fibre. Exotic and expensive but with enormous advantages for the construction of racing yachts. Kevlar has high impact resistance (it is used for bullet proof vests), and carbon fibre has high tensile strength for its weight; they can both be used to reinforce plastic instead of, or in conjunction with, glass fibres. Kevlar and carbon fibre can be combined with foam or balsa wood cores to create very sophisticated structures and impressive speed round the buoys. Nevertheless, the cost of the materials and the different requirements of long distance racing make their use unnecessary for trans-ocean voyaging.

Underwater Shape

The finer subtleties of the underwater shape of a racing yacht are the concern of the designer. He will be looking for speed within the handicapping system—the International Offshore Rule (I.O.R.)—regulated to allow yachts of different sizes to race each other on equal terms. This is the designer's problem. There are, however, certain broader design features which affect the suitability of a yacht regarding deep sea cruising or racing.

A modern yacht with a fin keel and separate rudder is perfectly seaworthy. A short (fore and aft) and deep keel is more efficient for racing purposes; a longer keel is better for a cruising yacht as its length will encourage directional stability when sailing and will make the vessel more controllable. See diagrams 1 and 2.

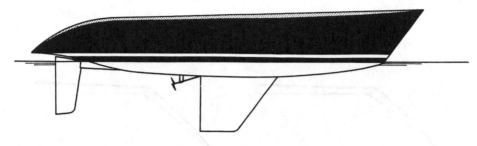

1. *A racing under-water shape.*

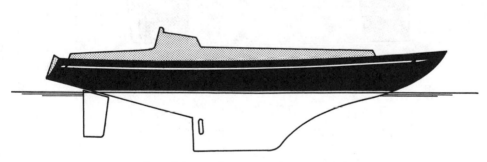

2. *A cruising under-water shape—Gallant 53.*

Rudder. Of more importance than keels is attention to the rudder: it is essential that the rudder be strong and reliable. This reliability and strength is affected by the way it is supported. If the rudder is hung on a skeg, the bending force on the rudder stock as the helm is applied, will be reduced. If the rudder is hung free, the stock must be considerably stronger. See diagram 3. The continual strains on a rudder for days on end during a long voyage can take their toll. In the 1977 round the world race *Gauloises II* lost her unsupported rudder, thus losing an almost certain victory. In the same event two other yachts had rudder problems but these were supported by skegs and survived intact until they could be strengthened at one of the scheduled ports of call. The importance of checking the rudder before a yacht is taken deep sea cannot be overstressed.

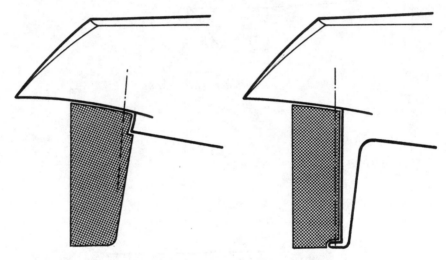

3. *Comparison of rudders with and without skegs.*

Steering Mechanism.

While on the subject of steering, attention to the whole mechanism must be given. If the vessel is wheel steered, the linkage from wheel to rudder is almost as important as the rudder itself. The system designed to take up the least space is one of rods and gearbox; however, this is difficult to repair if faults should develop.

A simpler and much better system employs wires which act on a quadrant attached to the rudder stock. See diagram 4. The wires are easy to replace if broken and nothing else is likely to fail. As well as this, and possibly more important, if steering trouble develops it is easy to see what is wrong.

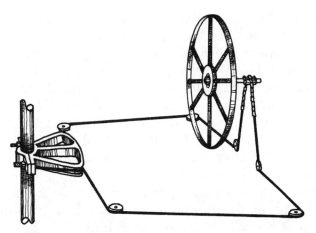

4. *Wheel, wires, quadrant—a good steering gear.*

It pays to make sure that an emergency tiller which fits on the rudder stock is carried. Before the start of the 1975 St Malo to Cape Town race the scrutinising committee, checking my entry, asked for a demonstration of the emergency steering. I tried it for the first time and found that the tiller did not fit; it was completely the wrong size and was probably designed for another yacht altogether.

Rig

Almost all inshore racing yachts are sloop rigged (one mast) as this is more efficient, especially to windward, than ketches, yawls or schooners (two masts). Racing across an ocean as oppposed to inshore the requirements are different, especially as the yacht's ability to point really close to the wind is not so important. The winners of nearly all marathon races up to 1980 have been ketches, and it is fair to say that there has always been a high proportion of two-masted yachts in these events due to the few advantages the rig does have; but the trend is now towards one mast regardless of the length of the race.

The cruising viewpoint is different. The two-masted rig makes sail-handling easier and each separate sail is smaller than on the same sized sloop. Also an element of security is achieved by carrying two masts—provided they are stayed separately. Another advantage is in extreme conditions when sailing to windward is possible with a storm jib, reefed mizzen and no mainsail. This technique is a common cruising ploy and has its place with racing ketches. Eric Tabarly used it on his very fast *Pen Duick VI*. We tried it, for the first time, on *Great Britain II* during the third leg of the 1977 round-the-world race; an easterly gale hit the fleet a few days after starting from Auckland, but using this rig we were able to outsail *Heath's Condor*, a sloop of the same size.

Another question is whether a main mast should be masthead rig or fractional rig. This means, should the forestay, and hence the jib luff, reach the top of the mast or go only some fraction of the way up as in a dinghy. The fractional rig is finding favour in smaller yachts and in those built to the International Offshore Rule. The disadvantages of the rig apply mainly to larger yachts, especially those sailed deep sea; the mast relies for its support, and the jib for its headstay tension, on running backstays which have to be made up to windward for each tack. A greater problem is the long boom of this style of rig, which tends to hit the waves on windy reaches. It is definitely not for cruising yachts, and has yet to be proved advantageous offshore.

A critical reliability factor arises with the stays holding the mast up. It is noticeable how the sizes (the diameter) of the wires vary between yachts of similar lengths, even when they are designed for the same purpose. *Pen Duick VI*, for instance, uses a forestay no more than 14 mm. in diameter, while *Great Britain II* uses a 19 mm. stay. However, *Pen Duick* has to change her rigging every 20,000 miles whereas *Great Britain II* is still using her original rig. If a yacht was designed for inshore cruising or racing and one now plans to take it across an ocean, the rigging size should be upgraded by one or two mm.

Several famous large yachts, including *Windward Passage*, *Ondine*, and *Kialoa*, were designed for long distance racing and were rigged as ketches. They have all since been re-rigged as sloops. This has been made possible by the technical advances in mast, rigging and sails which have made such massive rigs possible.

The cat-rigged ketch or schooner might also be considered for ocean cruising. These yachts, with their simple unstayed masts, wishbone booms and two-ply wrap-around sails have already achieved several Atlantic crossings. The rig is cheaper than a conventional stayed mast, is a delight to handle and is certainly fast. Quite possibly they will become the cruising boats of the future. See photo opposite.

Finally a word about halyards. The tendency inshore—especially racing—is to reduce windage at the masthead by having three halyards emerging from sheeves in the mast; these halyards double as spinnaker and genoa hoists. This is not suitable for long ocean passages because of chafe. It is better to remain with the old system of two genoa halyards, exiting over sheeves in the mast, and two spinnaker halyards that exit from the mast through double sheeves and then pass over swivel blocks hung on cranes at the masthead. This traditional system is almost chafe free.

Sail Wardrobe

Sail requirements are more critical when racing. It is nice though, to cruise with a full racing suit if such a luxury is possible. Of particular importance in long distance sailing

The Freedom rig—simple, efficient and fast.

is a measure of standby, should sails get damaged; this can be arranged either by carrying spares or by ensuring that the sails are designed for wind ranges that overlap each other. As an example, here is an extremely comprehensive suit of sails for a large (above 18-metre) sloop, setting out for a trans-ocean race.

Sail	Code	Construction		Wind range (apparent)	Notes
Mainsail	M	2 ply	8.8 oz.	0–50 knots	With 3 or 4 reefs
No 1 Genoa					
Light	IL		5.0 oz.	4–12	A third No 1
No 1 Genoa					Genoa may be
Heavy	IH	2 ply	5.5 oz.	10–22	desirable
No 2 Genoa	2	2 ply	5.5 oz.	20–28	
No 3 Genoa	3	2 ply	5.5 oz.	26–36	
Reacher	R		7.0 oz.	4–20	
Blast Reacher	BR		10.5 oz.	18–30	
No 3 Jib Top	J3		10.5 oz.		Often called Yankee
No 4 Jib Top	J4		12.0 oz	32–46	
Storm Jib	SJ		12.0 oz.	40 upwards	
Working Staysail	St		10.5 oz.	18 upwards	
Storm Trysail	T		12.0 oz.	50 upwards	
Drifter	D		2.0 oz.	0–4	In size between No 2 & 3 Genoas
Spinnaker Staysail	Sp.St		3.5 oz.	2–16	
Blooper	B		1.5 oz.	2–16	Sometimes called Shooter or Big Boy
Floater Spinnaker	F.Sp		0.5 oz.	0–4	All spinnakers
Light Spinnaker	L.Sp		.75 oz.	2–8	triradial
Medium Spinnaker	M.Sp		1.5 oz.	6–12	Plus one spare
Heavy Spinnaker	H.Sp		2.2 oz.	10–16	Plus one spare
Storm Spinnaker	S.Sp		2.6 oz.	14–20	Sometimes called Flanker Plus one spare

The details of suggested sail combinations for racing in each range of wind strength and direction are shown in chapter 5 diagram 35.

Diagram 5 shows the shape of the genoas, reachers and jibs. Under the column

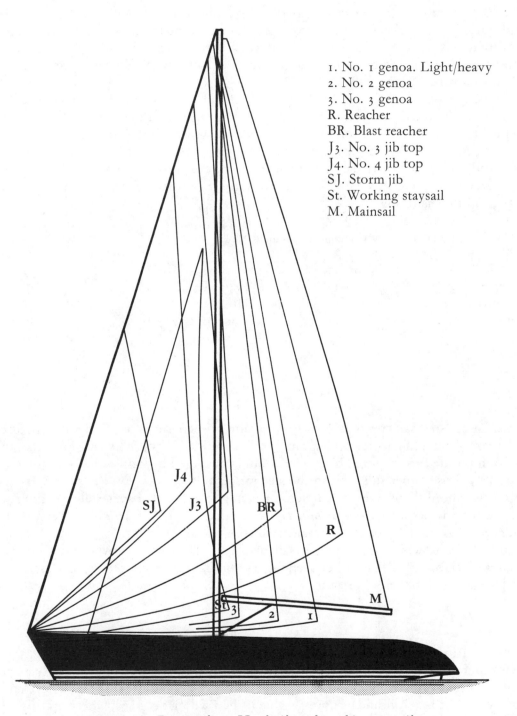

1. No. 1 genoa. Light/heavy
2. No. 2 genoa
3. No. 3 genoa
R. Reacher
BR. Blast reacher
J3. No. 3 jib top
J4. No. 4 jib top
SJ. Storm jib
St. Working staysail
M. Mainsail

5. Racing sloop. Headsails and working staysail.

Construction several sails are recommended to be 2 ply; this means that a sail is made throughout of two thicknesses of 5.5 oz. instead of one thickness of 8.2 oz. say. This process increases the cost of a sail by about 50% but, if it can be afforded, there are advantages to be gained from the resulting improved handling, resistance to ultra-violet light, and shape retention qualities.

For cruising this wardrobe can be adjusted a great deal and leaving 60% of those sails ashore is unlikely to reduce a yacht's average speed by more than 20%. For instance, one of the problems with headsails offshore is that waves will wash into the foot of the sail when it is eased outside the guardrail, which is one of the reasons why high clewed reachers and jib tops are carried on racing yachts. The cruising yacht can simplify its sail plan by carrying all headsails with high clews. A good wardrobe for a cruising yacht of any size might be as follows.

Sail	Code	Wind range (apparent)	Notes
Mainsail	M	0–40 knots	3 reefs
Trysail	T	40–50	
No 1 Genoa	1	0–14	High clew
No 2 Genoa	2	12–22	High clew
No 3 Jib	3	20–28	The working jib
No 4 Jib	4	26–34	
Storm Jib	SJ	32–50	
Staysail	St	20–34	
Spinnaker	Sp	5–10	An enjoyable option.

Details of suggested sail combinations for cruising in each range of wind strength and direction are shown in chapter 5, diagram 36. Diagram 6 shows the shape and sizes of sails. No duplicates are required because if a sail is damaged beyond repair its duty can be shared by those either side of it in the size range.

Duplicates should, however, be carried for racing spinnakers if space allows. For the round-the-world race on *Great Britain II* we carried a total of 10 spinnakers. This number, with continual repairs and maintenance, was just adequate.

A final thought while organizing a sail wardrobe for a long voyage; set up the mainsail with slab, rather than roller reefing. As will be seen in chapter 4, it is easier to use and the sail sets better as a result.

Accommodation

There is much difference between the accommodation requirements of an inshore racer and an inshore cruiser; while the former must be spartan for efficiency and weightsaving, the latter should be comfortable. When sailing deep sea, whether cruising or racing, a good interior layout will combine the best aspects of both approaches.

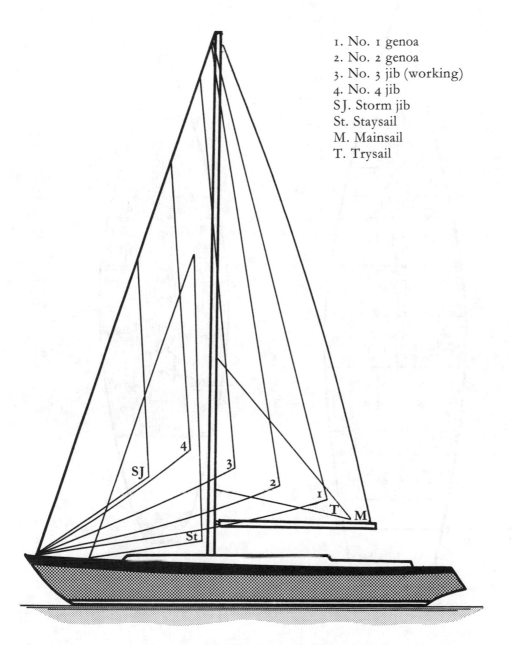

1. No. 1 genoa
2. No. 2 genoa
3. No. 3 jib (working)
4. No. 4 jib
SJ. Storm jib
St. Staysail
M. Mainsail
T. Trysail

6. *Cruising sloop. All sails.*

1. Sail stowage
2. W.C.
3. Saloon
4. Galley
5. Food stowage
6. Navigation
7. Engine
8. Work shop
9. Berths

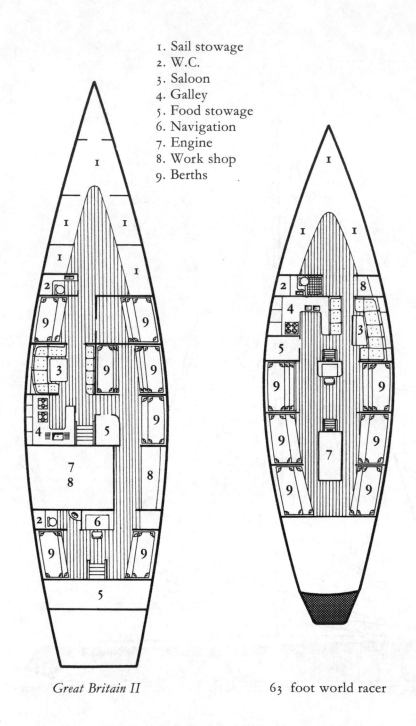

Great Britain II   63 foot world racer

7. *Accommodation plans.*

The major consideration concerns the number of bunks, and the minimum requirement will depend on the watch keeping system to be adopted (see chapter 3). There must, of course, be at least enough bunks for the total number of crew off watch. This may mean the watch coming off the deck has to take the bunks of those going on; and this 'hot-bunking' has a major disadvantage in that several of the crew will be alternating between each bunk; this causes problems of sleeping bag stowage, arguments over which bunk is best, and general time delays in watch changing. How nice on a long passage to have one bunk per crew member; you know when you come off watch that your own bunk is there ready, and no-one has dropped your sleeping bag in the bilges while you were on deck. In the 1975 Atlantic Triangle race I sailed, with 11 crew, on the 18-metre ketch *British Steel*. We had only nine bunks serviceable at sea, four of which were in the saloon. Although the arrangement worked fairly well I was determined to avoid hot bunking on *Great Britain II* in the 1977 round-the-world race; to this end I fitted her out with 18 bunks. Even though this meant building them in tiers of 3 with reduced headroom, there is no doubt that we were well off, each with our own 'castle'. If at all possible have one bunk per person, and preferably without using the saloon seats.

The size of the saloon at sea is controlled by the number of crew who use it at any one time. Unlike when in harbour, this is not the whole crew: as at any one time one watch is on deck and one watch is probably asleep. If the saloon seats between half and two thirds of the crew at a time it will be quite adequate. On larger yachts there is a disadvantage in too big a saloon. The 24-metre *Burton Cutter* had a full width saloon of almost 6 metres and this caused problems for her crew in the first round-the-world race. They had to rig ropes across it in rough weather, and had to sit on the floor to avoid being thrown around the large space. Conversely *Great Britain II*, built for long distance sailing only, has a saloon which is only half the width of the yacht. It is ideal and secure in bad conditions. See diagram 7.

The galley must be capable of providing enough food to feed the crew. Although a two-burner stove will produce enough hot nourishment for a crew of four or six, a crew of ten or more will be better served by 4 burners. The danger in a big galley is the chance of the cook being thrown around along with the food, so if space allows a U-shaped area with its opening either forward or aft is best. Inside this area the cook is within easy reach of the stove, sink, and work surfaces while secure against any violent motion of the yacht. Alternatively, the cook can be strapped in; but he or she must then be able to reach everything without moving. Although fiddles make cleaning difficult they should be placed all round the various parts of the galley; they should be very strong as inevitably the time will come when someone grabs one to prevent a fall. All the interior fittings on a yacht have to be stronger than might be initially appreciated, and certainly stronger than on a number of production boats. When running a yacht charter business I found that all manner of things were continually being broken; as our organisation was called Supersail, and our guests Supersailors, our instructions to the repairers were always suffixed 'Make it Supersailor proof'—a good maxim to follow.

The navigation area should, if at all possible, be separate from the living area of the yacht. The size of the navigation area is not critical; a full size chart table is a nice luxury but is not essential. The navigator should be able to sit, preferably on a swivel chair, and reach all the instruments, radio, and whatever other items of equipment may be fitted. At the lower end of the scale I navigate my 9-metre racing trimaran with the chart on my knees while hunched at the end of the bunk. This system is not ideal, but quite feasible.

The sail locker should be as far away from the living accommodation as the size of the yacht permits, as it is no fun sharing a bunk with a wet sail. If the layout of the yacht is traditional, having a sail locker forward with its own hatch to the deck, besides access through from the main accommodation, then fit a door or curtain to seal off the sail stowage. This will prevent spray and cold damp air getting to the saloon or bunk area while a sail is being handled through the hatch.

A separate washroom and heads compartment is essential for comfort. It does not have to be large, as regular washing is seldom a feature of long ocean voyages.

Spares and Tools

It would be impossible to carry a spare of every part of the yacht, as unless a complete duplicate vessel was towed astern there would simply not be the space. On the other hand, there are no chandlers or engineering shops in mid-ocean so it would be foolish to take no spares. A compromise must be reached. More important than numerous spares is a good tool kit, plenty of raw materials, and a good sail repair kit (see chapter 11). In general, experience has shown that less spare equipment is needed than was thought necessary in the early days of long distance sailing. On board *Second Life* in the first round-the-world race we had an enormous workshop with tools and spares taking up an area which has since been refitted as a four-berth cabin. Most of this equipment turned out to be quite unnecessary and the jumble in that vast space when the yacht heeled was uncontrollable. My reaction was to take the absolute minimum on my next long voyage. All the spares, tools and materials for a six months trip were stowed in one locker underneath one bunk. During the voyage, which was equivalent to five Atlantic crossings, we were never short of any equipment. Still, a separate workshop in a vessel gives the advantage of somewhere to stow the tools and spares, and a place to bolt a vice. The workshop need not be large as all repairs are inevitably carried out in the saloon, as that is the area with the most space, best temperature and best company.

Surveys

Before sailing out of sight of land and out of range of assistance it is common sense to check the craft carefully, giving special attention to certain key points. It is surprising how many faults, or potential faults, are revealed in a yacht by a visual examination, even if the examiner is not a professional surveyor. The vessel should be taken out of the water—if not for an antifoul, then simply so that the rudder, propeller shaft, propeller and all skin fittings can be seen. If a fault is found there may be a temptation to ignore it as 'it might be OK' or because 'it will cost a lot to fix'. But remember, a fault or weakness that appears minor while ashore or in a safe marina, will soon be found out by the first gale encountered at sea.

All the skin fittings and seacocks should be checked, not only for ease of operation, but also for the security of the pipes attached to them and for the integrity of the fixing bolts. Electrolysis can cause the corrosion of even stainless steel bolts. While preparing the 16-metre sloop *Kriter Lady* for the 1980 single handed trans-atlantic race I investigated the seacocks very carefully. As *Express Crusader* the yacht had recently been sailed around the world by Naomi James, so a bit of maintenance was due; when I looked at the skin-fitting for the engine water cooling intake I could see no nuts or bolt ends. The yacht was slipped and it could then be seen there were no boltheads either. The fitting was held in entirely by paint and friction.

Obvious faults in the rudder may be detected by simply leaning on it while the yacht is ashore; any sideways movement of the rudder stock indicates possible problems with its bearings. If in any doubt about this or any other aspect of the vessel then it will pay to have it professionally surveyed. While this is a fairly expensive way of finding out whether the galley needs painting, or how many spoons and forks are aboard, it is certainly a cheap way of finding out if the rudder is about to drop off or the hull split open.

Boat preparation is very much a question of priorities within the limits imposed by time and budget. A recent case illustrated this to me. A young Belgian couple were setting out from Dartmouth in 1978 to cross the Atlantic in an old wooden sloop. The day before their departure they asked me to check over their rigging; this I carefully did, advising a few alterations assessed from what I could see and feel. They sailed on schedule and the next communication from them was a postcard from the Azores. Their yacht had sunk under them with its mast still standing within a few minutes of either a plank springing or a skin fitting failing, and they were nine days on a liferaft before being picked up by a cargo ship. Clearly the priorities were wrong in their preparation. They are now building a new yacht out of steel.

The navigator tries for a sight in difficult conditions.

2   Navigational Planning

This is the first of three chapters on different aspects of navigation. The chapters are designed to give all the information that is needed to plan a voyage and to navigate successfully across an ocean, assuming that the reader can perform basic coastal navigation—specifically plotting bearings and laying off a course.

Firstly the navigator must decide what he is going to take on board. Consideration is given here to equipment that is essential and to equipment which, though not strictly required, is useful to have along. The preparation stage is completed with a discussion of route planning.

To explain the mysteries of navigation an imaginary voyage will be undertaken. On 22nd November 1980 the intention is to leave Dartmouth, England and sail to Barbados in the West Indies.

Essential Equipment

Charts. Two charts, North Atlantic, western part, with North Atlantic, eastern part, will be needed for day to day navigation. Plotting the course and distance steered, plotting a position from the sun, and measuring course and distance to the final destination, can all be done on these two charts. For the beginning and end of the voyage, coastal approach charts—such as Western Approaches to the English Channel, and Portsmouth to Canary Islands and Azores—will be required; their larger scale will allow more accuracy in plotting. Charts of the harbours and adjacent coastline of the points of departure and arrival will also be needed.

It is not necessary to take harbour charts of every port that may be made in an emergency. Commonsense, however, would dictate that charts of either the Canary Islands or the Azores (depending on which route is chosen—see later) are carried.

Compass. This is obviously needed to steer by, and also to indicate as nearly as possible what course has actually been steered during the day. The compass should be swung (i.e. checked on all headings) by an expert before sailing and preferably after loading all stores, as they may slightly affect the result. If for some reason the compass has not been swung, it will not be disastrous provided careful checks are kept while at sea. See chapter 7 (Navigational Day's Work).

TIME	COURSE	LOG	WIND DIRECTION	WIND SPEED	BAROM.	SAIL CHANGES AND REMARKS
0100						
0200						
0300						
0400						
0500						
0600						
0700						
0800						
etc.						

8. *A typical log book.*

Log (distance recorder). To give an indication of the speed of the yacht, and the distance sailed which is useful for plotting dead reckoning positions. An electronic log is less cumbersome—and no more expensive—than a mechanical unit trailed over the stern.

I have included the log under essential equipment as it is seamanlike to carry one, but if it should break down the failure is not serious as it is surprisingly easy to estimate speed and distance by eye. To do this, the watch leader should estimate his average speed hourly and record it in the logbook. The sum of all the hourly figures will give the day's run.

Sextant. The most reliable way to find one's position in mid-ocean is by obtaining position lines from the sun. To do this it is necessary to measure the angle of the sun above the horizon; hence the use of a sextant. There are numerous makes of sextant on the market, but the choice is basically whether to use a cheap plastic or an expensive 'proper' model. A plastic sextant has two minor drawbacks as well as reduced accuracy: firstly they are hard to use as the movement of the arc tends to be a lot less smooth than on a metal sextant, secondly they are prone to 'index error' which is a nuisance, although it can be checked and/or corrected. See chapter 8. A plastic unit makes an excellent spare, but a beginner will make life easier for himself by using a 'proper' sextant.

Chronometer. A quartz wrist watch or alarm clock is quite sufficient. The accuracy of quartz is such that daily time checks are not always needed. A good idea is to carry two watches, and by previously checking their rates of loss or gain, then comparing them daily for consistency, it will become sufficient to pick up a time signal only about once a week. An error of 4 seconds in time can at worst put out the resulting position line by only one mile.

Radio Receiver. A small transistor radio with short wave will allow time signals to be received. The BBC overseas service is very useful, as it broadcasts regular programmes and time signals world wide; the frequencies and times of transmission can be obtained from the BBC in London.

The Nautical Almanac. An almanac is a yearly publication giving details of the sun's 'position' for each second of each day of the year; this information is required for sunsight calculations. Several versions of the almanac are published and probably the easiest to use is the one produced by the Admiralty, available from all chart agents. Remember the book is yearly. For our imaginary voyage the 1980 Almanac is needed.

Sight Reduction Tables. These tables last forever. They are the pre-worked answers to the calculations required for a sunsight. Instead of getting involved in spherical trigonometry the navigator simply has to look up a table. Again, there are several versions of these tables available. The ones recommended are the marine tables, NP401, for the only reason that they are easy to come by. (The air tables are slightly easier to use, are less bulky, slightly less accurate, and are nearly always out of print).

NP401 comes in six volumes, each covering 16 degrees of latitude, 0° to 15°, 15° to 30° etc. It is only necessary to carry the volumes covering the latitude range of the proposed voyage. In our case volumes one to four.

Written Log. Many successful navigators have kept accurate records of what they are doing by using just the side of the chart, the back of an envelope or simply their mind. It is better, and a little easier, to make regular entries in a proper log book. This becomes especially important if an accurate dead reckoning position is required—such as when approaching land on a cloudy day. Only a few details need be recorded. Diagram 8 suggests a sensible log.

Drawing Instruments. Parallel rulers, dividers, pencils and rubbers are the simplest and easiest to use of all the plotting instruments.

Recommended (but not essential) Equipment
Routing Chart. These ocean charts are produced by the British Admiralty for each month of the year. They give a statistical analysis of the weather as observed over recent years for a particular month. Most importantly, they give details of the expected winds and currents ocean-wide. Also shown are the probabilities of gales and hurricanes, air

temperatures and pressures, sea temperatures and dew points, fog or low visibility, and the iceberg limits. Main shipping lanes are also marked. The value of the chart is in route planning. For the imaginary voyage chart 5124 (12), the North Atlantic—December, will be useful.

Gnomic Chart. Also very useful for route planning, as a straight line drawn on a gnomic chart represents the shortest distance from A to B. This is not the case on the mercator charts we use for navigation. See later.

Pilot Books. These Admiralty publications cover all parts of the world. Each volume covers a particular area of coastline; they are not absolutely essential, but make very good reading. They really come into their own if a yacht has to enter an unfamiliar port for which no charts are carried. Detail is given about the appearance of the shore, position of rocks, shallows and any other danger. The books are based on fairly old surveys, and despite up-dating one occasionally finds 'the well wooded slope indicates the entrance to the bay' should read 'the dense residential area. . . .'

Light Lists. Another series of Admiralty publications, produced yearly, gives the exact position and characteristics of all lighthouses, in addition to lights world wide. The light lists are of twofold value for the yachtsman: firstly, this year's light list will keep his uncorrected charts up to date; secondly, they can be used, in conjunction with pilot books, to draw charts of a harbour or coastline.

On one particular occasion I was driven back from Cape Finistere by a south-westerly gale; we decided to seek refuge in La Coruna, for which we had no chart, but we were able to draw one by plotting on a blank piece of paper the exact position of all the lights. This gave the position of the points of land, breakwater ends and harbour entrance, while the connecting detail was drawn from the pilot books. The result was quite accurate.

List of Radio Signals. More Admiralty publications. There are several volumes giving details of all radio stations, weather signals and navigation aids world wide. Volume II, the list of radio direction finding stations, is the volume most likely to be useful.

Radio Direction Finder. R.D.F. commonly used inshore is of no use at all for deep sea because of the limited range of the transmitting stations. Even 50 miles from land its accuracy is very poor—to obtain a position within 5 miles of your exact whereabouts would be good, whereas a sunsight should be within a mile or two. In the case of a yacht approaching land in bad visibility and with no sun, and there being a D.F. Station at the harbour entrance, the unit is of value.

Sun's Amplitude Table. A table used in the checking of compass error—see chapter 7. The table is printed in the various volumes of marine navigation tables, and also in some nautical almanacs (such as Reeds in England).

Tide Tables. Only really required if the departure or arrival ports are on coasts that are severely affected by tides or tidal streams. If sailing from England, the English Channel is covered by local tables. For the rest of the world carry the Admiralty tide tables for the year.

Further Modern Aids. For the yacht with reliable electric power, and the owner with a reliable bank balance, there are several electronic navigation units which are discussed further in chapter 7. Of those I would consider Satellite Navigation as the most interesting. But I certainly would not leave my sextant behind.

Calculators. Nice to have one on board as it is very useful for playing with speeds and distances, besides calculating great circle courses and distances. A calculator also makes a nice change from tables in the computation of sunsights, but do not rely on it completely though, as there is always a chance that it may fail. Use of calculators is also discussed in chapter 7.

Route Planning

The first stage in route planning is to analyse the reasons for the voyage. When racing, the objective is obviously to get from start to finish as quickly as possible. If cruising, this may still be the objective; alternatively the slower sunny route may appear more attractive. Let us assume you are required to take the quickest route; will that be the shortest? Perhaps greater speed can be achieved by taking a longer course round the favourable side of a weather pattern? How is the decision made?

In the absence of routing and gnomic charts all that can be done is to draw a straight line on the mercator (the standard) chart and follow it. This is not the shortest route—especially when sailing west to east or east to west in high latitudes. A little more sophistication is called for.

To plan the route of our imaginary voyage it is convenient to draw all the possibilities on the routing chart for December.

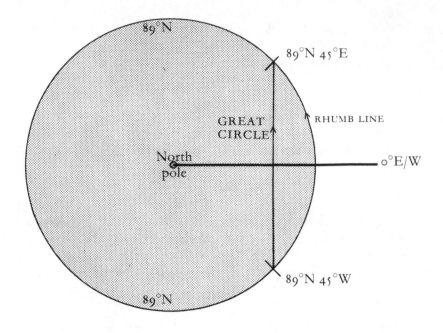

9. A simple illustration of rhumb line and great circle.

Rhumb line. This is a straight line, for instance from the English Channel to Barbados. As mentioned earlier this is not the shortest route, but is the route that would be followed by steering a constant course (232° true in fact) each day of the voyage. The rhumb line is acceptable over short distances; however it can be improved on by sailing a great circle.

Great circle. This is a circle round the world which has as its centre the centre of the earth. It is not necessary to know the detailed theory, but two simple examples may facilitate understanding. Imagine that an explorer wishes to navigate from 89°N, 45°W to 89°N, 45°E. Diagram 9 shows that the rhumb line—steering a constant east (090°)—is much longer (94 miles) than the great circle (84 miles), which entails steering a variety of courses from 045° to 135°. Another way of looking at it is to take a globe and use a piece of string to compare the distance between two points on the same parallel of latitude. The rhumb line round the parallel will be longer than the great circle found by pulling the string tight.

Whether or not the reader is convinced by the above arguments it will pay to draw the great circle course onto the routing chart, in order to compare it with the other options. To do this, begin by drawing a straight line from start to finish on the gnomic chart of the North Atlantic. See diagram 10. Now read off from the course 10 or more points of latitude and longitude; for instance two examples are 34°20′N, 40°W and 45°30′N, 20°W. Transfer these points to the routing chart and join them up. An apparently curved course is obtained, but it represents the shortest route with the initial course 249°. true. The rhumb line and great circle are now drawn.

Wind and Current Route. Careful study of the wind and current statistics on the routing chart shows that a longer voyage south of the rhumb line will probably give much more favourable conditions. The extra distance sailed may be compensated for by the greater speed obtained. The southerly route in this particular case is known as the Trade wind

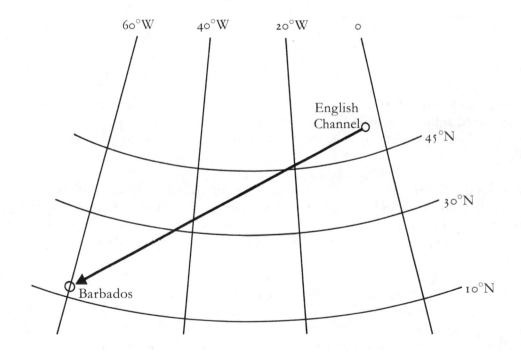

10. *Gnomic chart of North Atlantic.*

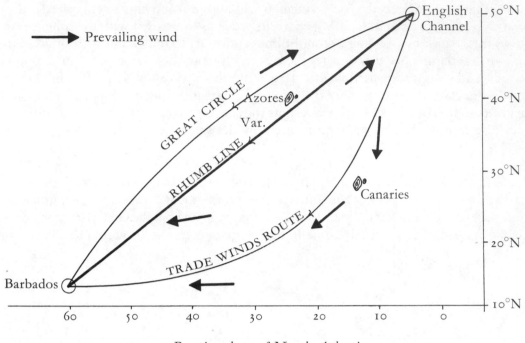

50°N

40°N

30°N

20°N

10°N

→ Prevailing wind

English Channel

GREAT CIRCLE

Azores

Var.

RHUMB LINE

Canaries

TRADE WINDS ROUTE

Barbados

60   50   40   30   20   10   0

11. *Routing chart of North Atlantic.*

route, as it was always followed by old trading ships which, due to their lack of windward ability, had little other choice. The route also has the advantage of passing the Canary Islands which could be used as a stop-off point. See diagram 11.

Best Route. Before deciding which of these three routes to take, check for any special hazards such as ice, or the likelihood of hurricanes; in our case they are negligible. The most tempting route is the southerly one as it will give a predominance of warmer weather and favourable winds. This is certainly the way to go when cruising. However it is longer.

Instead of guessing which will be faster we could divide each route into sections (ten will do) and measure their lengths (remember to use the side of the chart level with the chunk being worked on). Now, for each section, study the wind statistics and estimate the likely speed the yacht will make, and hence the time taken for each section. The sum will give the total distances and an estimate of total time that each route can be expected to take. In this particular case the distances are found to be:

Great circle	3448 miles
Rhumb line	3500 miles
Trade wind	4000 miles

There is little to choose between the great circle and longer Trade wind route. Either could be quickest.

Virtually this exact exercise was performed by each skipper for the 1978 Route du Rhum (Rum drink, not Rhumb line) from St Malo, France, racing to Guadeloupe, West Indies. I estimated the great circle would be 5% faster than the Trade wind route. In the event a trimaran, having taken the Trade route, beat by 90 seconds a monohull which had followed the great circle!

A further illustration shows the danger of being obsessed by the shortest route. The third leg of the 1977/78 round-the-world race was from Auckland, N.Z., round Cape Horn, and up to Rio de Janeiro. The shortest route from New Zealand's North Island East Cape to Cape Horn was impossible to follow as it cut down to 70 degrees south— well into pack ice. I decided to take *Great Britain II* on what I considered to be the shortest safe course. This meant a great circle to 60° South, round the parallel, and a great circle up to the Horn. About 1,000 miles before Cape Horn we were at 60° South with *Pen Duick VI* level with us but 180 miles north at 57° South. A severe depression swept across the Southern Ocean at that time. It was a bit further north, at 58° South, than usual. The result was two days of gale force easterlies heading us while *Pen Duick* had gale force westerlies following her. Needless to say she pulled out a long lead. Eric Tabarly had deliberately stayed on the slightly longer northerly route so as to avoid being caught in this way.

Back to the Atlantic voyage. Once the decision is made the chosen route should be transferred to the coastal and approach charts of the departure point and to both North Atlantic ocean charts. Of course the route does not have to be followed categorically. Day by day course decisions may be made as a result of wind direction—see chapter 7. But it is good to have an initial plan.

3 Crew and Shipboard Routine

Crew

Numbers. The success or failure of any trip depends to a large extent on the way the crew get along with their boat and with each other. The number of hands and the desired level of their skills is dictated by the purpose of the voyage, and the layout of the yacht. Ships (it is the right word to use) up to 70 metres length overall have been sailed single-handed on ocean voyages, but this is only possible if the vessel is designed specifically for short-handed sailing (see chapter 11). In the more normal world a crew is required so that a fresh helmsman is available 24 hours a day and sufficient bodies are available to keep the yacht sailing efficiently.

Whatever watchkeeping system is decided upon, it is ideal if any sail handling operation can be done by a maximum of two thirds of the crew. This will ensure adequate rest, so vital for efficiency and safety in any voyage lasting more than a few days. For a particular size of yacht more crew will be required for a trans-ocean race than for a trans-ocean cruise. For instance, when cruising a 15-metre vessel, three men on deck for a sail operation may be sufficient. The helmsman is the fourth hand and hence a crew size of six is indicated. If the same yacht is to be raced the numbers would be five on deck for sail handling, the helmsman being the sixth hand, and a crew of nine would be correct. (This yacht, inshore, would be raced by 12 crew). In fact a crew of nine is about maximum for a long voyage on a vessel of that size, due to the limit of weight carrying capacity with regard to food and water.

Smaller yachts can be cruised quite comfortably with as few as three crew if only two are normally required on deck at any one time. It is very tiring to sail any size of yacht two-handed without the aid of self-steering gear, for the obvious reason that each person has to steer for 12 hours a day, and 'all hands' will be required for any activity whatsoever. The two man round Britain and Ireland race is one of the most exhausting on the ocean racing calendar. Sailing the 16-metre trimaran *Great Britain IV* with Chay Blyth, I found that an average of four hours sleep in 24 (taken in short stretches) was the most that could be hoped for. Even if we had not been racing it would have been exceptionally tiring.

The watch below wait for a standby call.

The following is given as a suggestion for crew sizes for long distance sailing:

TABLE 1—CREW STRENGTH

Length of yacht in metres		9	11	14	17	20	24
Racing	Maximum crew	5	6	9	11	13	18
	Ideal crew	4	5	7	9	12	16
	Minimum crew	3	4	5	7	8	12
Cruising	Maximum crew	5	6	9	11	13	18
	Ideal crew	3	4	5	7	9	13
	Minimum crew	3	3	3	4	6	9

Crew skills. It would be ideal if every crewmember possessed all the skills that are required on a yacht, although fortunately it is not essential that they do. With a large yacht, where a great number of hands are needed, it is quite possible to handle sails efficiently, even if some of the crew are beginners. Provided proper instructions are given there are several jobs—such as winding a winch, or pulling the 'red rope'—that do not require skill. Basically what is needed is helming ability in enough of the crew so that alert helmsmen are always available; and, particularly when racing, a minimum of three sail trimmers, so that at any one time an experienced man or woman is on deck to control sail trim and to advise on sail changes. The rest of the crew can follow their leaders. It is interesting to note that it is only on large yachts that a skipper can get away with a percentage of unskilled labour. On *Great Britain II* in the 1977 round-the-world race I could have sailed with seven or eight skilled crew and nine or ten passengers. (In fact the crew were all proficient, some exceptionally so). However had we been sailing a 14-metre yacht, seven skilled men would still have been required, and that would mean the whole crew with no passengers.

The entry of *Second Life*, a 21-metre ketch, in the 1973 round-the-world race, was completely financed by the 12 crew and we each contributed an equal share of the costs. We were not all experts and yet our enthusiasm, and what knowledge we had, was enough to see us safely, if not brilliantly, back to England.

Following the success of that trip it was decided to finance the entry of *Great Britain II* in the 1977 world race by signing up paying crew. Due to the high cost of sailing in a 27,000 mile event it was necessary to ask for a lot of money and consequently I did not expect my crew all to be experts. 16 crew were needed with enough helming and sail trimming skill to make a decent attempt at the race. After signing on 13 crew it was a simple matter to examine their qualifications, to see if the required skills—especially three potential watch leaders—were present; if not, the remainder of the crew could have been made up from hired professionals. As it was there were, amongst the 13, at least four possible leaders, so the remaining berths were filled with extra amateurs. The result was most successful with Ian Worley, Nick Dunlop, and Quentin Wallop jointly with Enrique Zulueta, all skilfully running their watches, trimming sails, deciding when sail changes were required and organizing who should helm.

We actually needed more helmsmen than were indicated on paper before the start. To see who was best, everyone helmed during practice and during the early stages of the first leg of the race. The result was a high degree of proficiency such that, in medium weather, throughout the trip, everyone helmed; only a few dropped out of the order if conditions were difficult—either very light or very strong winds.

Personality. Living in a confined space, such as a yacht, is an excellent way to get to know someone. Unfortunately if you do not like what you find there is no easy way of escape—especially in the middle of an ocean. It is therefore a good idea to get to know your shipmates well before embarking on a long voyage. This is best done, not by meeting once a week in a pub, but by sailing together for a trial few days. Quite small incidents can be magnified out of all proportion by the intimacy of life on board. A person who snores, smokes evil cigarettes, has smelly feet, does not wash up properly after a meal, or has any of a thousand other irritating habits, can cause personality clashes.

On a big yacht life is somewhat easier; a good skipper, seeing a potential problem developing, can keep the protagonists fairly well apart simply by placing them in different watches. Conversely he should be able to recognize friendships and teamwork developing and organize the watches accordingly. If it is impossible to keep clashes from developing they must be flattened immediately by the skipper. A particular case comes to mind where, on a long voyage, the cook took a dislike to one of the crew and always served him short rations. The skipper should have stopped this happening.

There is far less likelihood of personality problems developing when a yacht is racing as everyone on board is aiming for a common goal—winning. This tends to become a factor of overriding importance and human differences can on the whole be ignored. In a case like *Great Britain II*, where the crew had invested money in the project, there was such enthusiasm to get on and do well that we had no real personality problems at all. It is generally found that crew spirit is much better on a long trip than on a short one. It is also extraordinary to note how much faster a happy ship sails.

SHIPBOARD ROUTINE

Before considering the various watch systems it pays to analyse carefully the several duties involved therein. There should be three levels of crew activity which can conveniently be referred to as on watch, on standby and on 'golden kip'.

Watchkeeping Duties

The primary function of the watch on deck is to sail the yacht. Firstly this means helming. Regardless of the size of the yacht, the size of the crew, and the length of the watch, the longest time anyone should helm without a break is one hour. This is especially true when racing. After that period, however easy the conditions, concentration will fall off. When cruising there is no reason why, provided no-one is in a hurry, helms should not stay at the wheel for longer periods. However, even when efficiency is not important, a man at the wheel for too long will get bored. Regular changes are better for morale. In heavy downwind sailing the physical effort on a wheel or tiller can become so much that one hour is too long. Cold air and cold spray can combine to make even half an hour at the helm impossible. In these conditions 20 minute spells are recommended.

Helmsmanship. It is impossible to analyse what makes a good helmsman. This skill some pick up very quickly and others never master. There are a few golden rules however that will help a beginner improve. A helmsman should keep his eyes on the horizon ahead and the waves around him. He should keep in his mind the direction of the waves and wind relative to the boat, as this is a far better indication of directional variations than staring at a compass. It is better to use a small amount of helm immediately it is needed rather than too much too late. The way the vessel rolls and the weight on the wheel or tiller should help the helsman anticipate which way the bows are going to swing. A roll to starboard accompanied by a kick of the rudder to port should be counteracted by turning the rudder to starboard. That means steering into a roll; also, when the helm is felt to push one way, push it the other. Above all, practice makes perfect and remember it helps to think about the surroundings rather than the yacht.

Sail Trimming. The second duty is sail trimming, which should be the responsibility of the watch leader. When cruising it is quite acceptable to leave the sails unaltered for hours on end provided the wind does not increase above the wind limit of those sails. Minor fluctuations in direction can be dealt with either by altering course slightly to follow the wind or by slightly over-sheeting the sails. While this course is not recommended it certainly does no harm and means that meal times or sunbathing are not interrupted too often. However, when in a hurry it will pay to monitor continually the set of the sails, also which sails should be set. This is described in the next chapter.

Sail Changes. The third duty is to carry out sail changes with or without the help of the standby watch—more of which later. In general, if a sail change involves both the watch and the standby watch, then the latter should do the easier drier jobs, while the former, having seen the situation develop, should do the harder work, especially the foredeck.

Calling the Skipper. The fourth, and possibly most important duty of the watch is to know when to call the skipper. It would be normal for the watch leader to call the skipper if it appears to him that a sail change is, or might be, needed. The watch should also alert the skipper at any set time or on the development of any circumstance for which he has previously requested a call. This sounds obvious, but there does tend to be a feeling that the skipper should be left to get some sleep if, in the eyes of those on deck, he is not needed. This is a mistake. The skipper should always be called when this has been asked. A friend of mine was skippering a yacht that was wrecked for this reason. The watch thought that they had everything under control, so they let the skipper sleep past the time he had asked to be woken. The watch had not realised that the reason for this call was that the skipper needed to navigate the yacht safely past a shallow area stretching several miles off a nearby headland.

The result of letting the skipper 'get his rest—he needs it' was the vessel striking the rocks and being wrecked. Fortunately no-one was hurt, but the lesson is clear. Personally, as a skipper I feel strongly about being called and prefer to be woken regularly, however small the possibility of my being needed. I use the motto 'if in doubt—shout'. The experience of the watch leaders is an important factor. The less experienced the more often they will need advice. Conversely, towards the end of the round-the-world race on *Great Britain II* the watch leaders were quite experienced enough to run the yacht without my help. If no sail changes were required I occasionally slept right through the night—I had the easiest job on board!

End of Watch Duties. The final watchkeeping duties are those associated with the end of the watch. Anything that needs doing regularly is best done as a watch-end duty, which ensures that it is done. As well as keeping the log by recording courses steered, miles logged and other observations, there are several other routine tasks. The bilges should be pumped. The sheets and halyards should be checked for any sign or point of chafe. All shackles should be checked to see that none are coming undone. A lot of damage can be avoided by these regular inspections.

Handing Over the Watch. Finally the watch is handed over. This is done in a fairly comprehensive way. The new watch will want to know the helming instructions—'steer 050' or 'steer 35 to 40 to the apparent wind', for example. If the yacht is close-hauled they need to know all the information about tacking headings and the desired course should the wind head or free off. If the yacht is free of the wind they need to know details of any wind variations experienced recently so that they are then better able to recognise a wind direction change as temporary or permanent. They also need to know what sails are set (it might be dark and it is easy to be mistaken), the location of the next sail up and down, whether any sail is on deck, and any other items of interest—especially any outstanding instructions about calling the skipper.

An interesting error that can occur as the result of a sleepy watch change happened to us on *Great Britain II* shortly after rounding Cape Horn in January 1978. In this case it was not a watch change itself but a confusion between myself and the watch leader. After a squally night, during which we changed from the storm spinnaker to the No. 3 jib and back three times as we sailed round the greatest cape on earth, the crew got very tired. By 0400 the wind steadied from the north-west, the waves died down and we could reach up towards the Le Maire Strait between Staten Island and Tierra del Fuego. I turned in, with our course towards the Strait of 030° magnetic being easily held.

The watch leader woke me an hour later saying he could see a gap in the land which he assumed was the Strait, and should he steer towards it. Rather than get up and look I asked: 'What course do we need to steer towards it?' The reply was: 'Thirty five'. My mind clicked over slowly and concluded that 030° to 035° was only a five degree difference so yes, it must be the Strait. I shouted up the hatch: 'Steer for it'.

Forty five minutes later the watch leader asked me to come and have a look; he thought there was something wrong. I shot on deck and saw that we were steering 350° towards a bay which had looked, from a distance, like a strait. The real strait was by then visible forty degrees round to starboard on a bearing of 030°—as expected. The error, it transpired, lay in the watch leader saying 35 when he had read from the compass the indication for 350. I, in my tiredness, had misinterpreted it. The rather indirect moral of this story is: when handing over a watch it pays to remain on deck a few minutes to check that the new shift have understood their instructions and are doing the right thing.

Standby Duties

The primary function of those on standby is to help with sail change operations. In bad or variable weather it may be necessary for the standby watch to be dressed ready to leap on deck at a second's notice. Normally though, they can be given five minutes or so warning of any approaching activity.

During the night there is no reason why they should not be asleep. It is then up to the skipper or watch leader to give the 'standbys alert' call if required. Even the odd false alarm is preferable to the alternative of waiting for hours while nothing happens.

During the day the standby watch provides the workforce for maintenance, repairs, sail mending and the other jobs covered in chapter 9. If the crew is fairly small they may also be required to undertake domestic duties as well. This depends on the watch keeping system, as will shortly be seen. But priority must be given to the work on deck; if standbys are required up top no other job should interfere.

'Golden Kip'

A term used, for the want of a better one, to describe the period or periods of the day during which a watch is not on deck or on standby. This means that they are not needed for anything short of an emergency. Their duty is to sleep without fear of being disturbed. It is important to have a watch system that allows for 'golden kip' periods as it means that, even in extreme weather when continual action is required on deck, there will always be some crew asleep recovering for their next watch. A level of tiredness that is often experienced during inshore racing, and occasionally cruising—caused by all hands continually at work—is both unnecessary and dangerous on a long voyage.

Watch-keeping Systems

There are probably as many watch-keeping systems as yachts afloat. The organisation of a crew tends to be a personal thing, with each skipper sticking to the system that he has found to work the best for him—I am no exception. None-the-less there are some observations worth making and in this section I will describe my own preference and why I find it works best.

The helmsman concentrates hard.

Two-Watch System. In the early days of sail a ship would carry exactly twice as many crew as were required to handle the ship. They were traditionally known as port and starboard watches and would rotate four hours on watch and four hours below. The length of the watches could be changed now and again in order to vary the times of day when each watch was on duty. This type of system is still used by some marathon racing yachtsmen—the French especially. The great disadvantage of this system is in having each crewman on deck for 12 hours a day, even if there is nothing to do. The converse is not always true as his 12 hours below are often broken by calls on deck when more than half the crew are needed for a particularly tricky operation.

My dislike of this system was confirmed by sailing as crewman on *Condor of Bermuda* in the 1979 Fastnet race. We were a crew of 20 and were divided into two watches of ten working four hours on, four hours off. As more than ten crew were needed for each sail change it was 'all hands' every two hours or so. This meant at least seven of the on-watch crew (there were two or three helmsmen per watch) were mostly sitting around getting cold and bored. When off watch they were continually called for sail changes. If most of the sail changes could be done by half the crew—that is without calling the sleepers, then the system would be justified.

Three-Watch System. It is much better on a long trip—and in my view would have been better in this case—to have a three-watch system. This way the whole crew, including the vitally important helmsmen, get less tired and remain more efficient, as two-thirds of the crew are always sufficient for all activity. The yacht does not go faster just because more people are watching the helmsman and sail trimmers at work. *Condor* won this particular race in record time, but I believe had the race lasted another 24 hours efficiency would have slipped noticeably.

An example of a three-watch system explains the theory. On a yacht where seven crew are required for a sail change a suitable organisation would be to have three watches of three crew each, and a skipper off watches. This way there are always three crew on deck, seven (two watches and the skipper) available for sail changes and everyone has eight hours watchkeeping, eight hours standby, and eight hours sleep per day, divided into four hour units, as specified in table 3.

G.B.II System. There was a total crew of 17 on *Great Britain II* with no full-time cook, so this task had to be shared by the crew. We needed four on deck at all times to helm and trim sails. We needed nine crew for all sail changes and occasionally twelve if conditions were tricky. To feed and clean a yacht of that size was a job for two people at any one time. How best to organise the watches?

Firstly three watch leaders were chosen. They were the most experienced people on board and were allocated one to each watch: that is, 12–4 a.m. and pm., 4–8 a.m. and p.m., and 8–12 a.m. and p.m. Their skills were too valuable to waste in the galley, so they

TABLE 2—*G.B.II* WATCH-KEEPING

Watch teams:	A Errol Peter Richard	B Jerry Di Johnny	C Terry Steve Mark	D Max John Dave
Times:	00 to 04 12 to 16	04 to 08 16 to 20	08 to 12 20 to 24	Domestics
Leader:	Nick	Ian	Henry & Quentin	
On watch: Day 1–3	A	B	C	D
4–6	D	B	C	A
7–9	D	A	C	B
10–12	D	A	B	C
13–15	C	A	B	D
16–18	C	D	B	A
19–21	C	D	A	B
22–24	B	D	A	C
25–27	B	C	A	D
28–30	B	C	D	A
31–33	A	C	D	B
34–36	A	B	D	C

Skipper/navigator: off watches.
Watch leaders to do standby with their teams.
'Golden kip' for each watch is the four hours after a watch.
Standby for each watch is the four hours prior to a watch.

continued on the same watches throughout the race. Under these three leaders there were four teams of three crew each. At any one time three of the teams would serve under the watch leaders and the fourth team would be in the galley. The watch leaders and their teams would stand watches by doing four hours on watch, four hours 'golden kip', four hours standby, four hours on watch again and so on.

After a period of three days the galley team (or 'domestics') would join a watch and the team they replaced would go into the galley. The order sheet, from the bulkhead in the saloon on *Great Britain II* explains the system.

This system allowed for 4 on deck at all times (the leader and a team of three), 9 for a sail change (the watch, plus standbys, plus skipper), and twelve if required by calling the three domestics. It can be seen by following the table, how the routine of a member of a watch team develops during the voyage. A member of team C, say, starts with nine days on the 08–12/20–24 watch, then goes domestic for three days, then 00–04/12–16 watch for nine days, then domestic again, then 04–08/16–20 watch for nine days, and so on. Note too, that for a period of three days a team of three will be on domestics. The domestics had freedom of choice as to their own interior organisation. As two cooks were enough at any one time this could be done on a two day on, one day off, or a two meal on, one meal off basis. This measure of overkill in the galley made the domestic chores easier to bear, and also provided something of a rest for the team before returning to watches.

Complicated though the system may sound it worked very well allowing for the maximum efficiency and maximum comfort. The system will work for smaller crews even if the size of the teams are reduced to two or one crewman.

System with Full-time Cook. If a permanent cook is carried, or if the crew is smaller than eight, a different system is needed. Certainly, if a full time cook or cooks can be found, the watch-keeping system is very much simplified.

TABLE 3—WATCH-KEEPING WITH A FULL-TIME COOK

Suggested system for a crew of eight or more with a full time cook.

Watch team:		A			B			C		
		—			—			—		
		—			—			—		
								(2, 3 4, 5 or 6 people per team)		
Times:	and	00 to 04			04 to 08			08 to 12		
		12 to 16			16 to 20			20 to 24		
Duties:		on w.	s.b.	g.k.	on w.	s.b.	g.k.	on w.	s.b.	g.k.
Watch		A	B	C	B	C	A	C	A	B

Skipper/navigator and cook off watches

Should the crew be less than eight in total there is unlikely to be a full time cook. In this case the cooking is simply done as one of the standby duties. If the skipper/navigator is also standing a watch (necessitated perhaps by the limited number of crew) his standby duty is to skipper and navigate.

There are of course endless permutations, but whether cruising or racing, a system requiring too many crew on deck when they are not needed is to be avoided. Strength, warmth and efficiency should be saved and available when most needed.

The cold, wet watch on Great Britain II.

Sleep

There is no reason why all the crew should not get adequate sleep on a long voyage. As can be seen from the suggested watch systems, each person will have two four-hour periods of 'golden kip' in a day. Assuming it takes 15 minutes to get out of a bunk at the start of a standby period, and 5 minutes (or less with practice!) to get into it after a watch, more than seven hours of sleep are guaranteed in every 24. Very often, at least in steady conditions, the standbys get the odd hour or two extra. This is more than adequate for maximum efficiency to be maintained.

On board *Second Life* in 1973 we used a three-watch system of four hours each. Instead of two periods of standby and two of 'golden kip' in the day, the navigator decided on one of each. This meant a crewman would do four hours on watch, eight hours asleep, four hours watch, eight hours standby and so on. The idea being to give everyone an eight hour period of uninterrupted sleep. Yet it was noticeable how, during times of steady weather, when there were no standby calls, it became natural to sleep for the first four hours of one's standby and for the first four hours of one's 'golden kip'. This was how my suggested system evolved. Incidentally, one of the snags of the *Second Life* routine showed up when, in extreme conditions, a crewman could be on deck for 16 hours at a stretch—a long time. Certainly on *Great Britain II*, the only time we were short of sleep was in port.

Meal Times

The later chapter on domestics deals with subjects such as what to eat and how much food to carry. However it will pay when organising shipboard routine to give some thought to meal times with a view especially to making life easier for both crew and cooks.

As watches are changing at 0800, 1200 and 2000 hours, these times could form the basis on which the galley works. The 08–12 watch get up early and eat breakfast at 0730 before going on watch. The 04–08 watch come off duty at 0800 and eat breakfast then. The 12–16 watch are coming on standby at 0800 and can thus join the second sitting.

Rather than have lunch at 1130 and 1200 over the watch change, it would be more balanced to have it at 1300. The watch on deck can be relieved in turn; at this time of day there is likely to be a number of crew up and about.

The system for dinner is similar to that at breakfast. The first sitting at 1930 for the 20–24 watch and the second sitting at 2000 for the 16–20 watch. The 00–04 watch are arising for their standby—if not for happy hour—and can fit into either sitting.

The navigator can help the cooks by arranging for local, or ship's, time (see chapter 7) to be set so that daylight starts before the cooks commence breakfast and does not finish until after dinner is washed up. Obviously this not always possible; clever though navigators may be they do not control the length of the day. Still, by making midday (when the sun is overhead) fit between 1300–1400, one ensures that the daylight is at its most useful time relative to ship routine.

Happy Hour

There is such a thing as a dry ship. The proponents view the weight and space taken up by carrying alcoholic drink as having a detrimental effect on the speed of the yacht. This may well be true; none-the-less the morale boost offered by the social aspect of drinking more than makes up for its shortcomings.

Carrying beer is as good a way of taking extra fluid as any. Sailing with one beer per person per day of the voyage is a suitable amount. This may not sound much but try adding up the amount needed for a crew of twelve for a forty day trip. Before the start from St Malo, France, for a race to Cape Town in 1975, the beer was delivered late to the yacht I was sailing. As at that stage we had no stowage space left the beer cans were laid evenly over the saloon and cabin floors. The only problem was slightly reduced headroom.

Carrying spirits is another matter altogether. This is where happy hour comes in. A crewman will drink his beer at any time he feels like it; the drinking of spirits, however, should be restricted to a fixed time of day — 18.30 to 19.30, before the first dinner sitting is a good time. This happy hour tends to become the high spot of the day, not because of the drink, but because of the social gathering involved.

It will probably be the only time of the day when the whole crew is out of their bunks. And I have always found it the best time to discuss the progress of the yacht and any race or cruise tactics about to be employed.

There has, obviously, to be a restriction on quantity; it would be extremely dangerous to get intoxicated on board. This danger was brought home to us on board *Second Life* shortly after rounding cape Horn in January 1974. We had a party to which all crew came except the helmsman. Two hours into this celebration we had to take down the spinnaker in a rising and heading wind. The sail change was successful but was undoubtedly unsafe and unseamanlike. Restricting each person to two or three tots per day is realistic. It is unrealistic to rely on self-discipline to gauge the size of the tots; therefore an optic or some other measure is recommended. I once sailed with a guy who was a master at getting more booze than anyone else. We had no measures on board and this fellow would always wait, without appearing to, for a big wave before pouring.

The consumption of any alcohol on a yacht has to be the subject of a reasonably disciplined system. The consequence is a greatly enlivened long trip.

4　Sail Handling and Setting On the Wind

The wellknown French yachtsman Olivier de Kersauson says 'Anything that does not make a boat go faster has no interest for me'. His views are a bit extreme, but he is certainly correct; sail handling and setting are most instrumental in getting a yacht from A to B, and therefore the most important aspect of any voyage.

The next two chapters discuss systems to be used for the setting and changing of all types of sails carried on a modern yacht. The systems are based on the special requirements of long distance voyages and are designed to combine speed, efficiency and safety, and hence are applicable to both racing and cruising. Occasional reference to the sail plans and sail lists in chapter 1 may be of benefit.

MAINSAIL

Shape control

Fullness is built into a mainsail in two ways, and an understanding of this construction will make it easier to see how the shape can then be altered while sailing to suit varying conditions.

The horizontally sewn panels that make up the sail are individually shaped by being tapered slightly towards the ends—see diagram 12. Thus when they are sewn together a bag or fullness is forced into the sail. Let us call this 'fullness 1'. Once the panels have been sewn together the leading edge of the sail is cut with a curve—see diagram 12. This has the effect of forcing more fullness into the sail. Let us call this 'fullness 2'.

If the mainsail is set on a straight mast and with little or no tension on the luff, leach or foot, it will set with the fullness that has been built into it. Although this is ideal for light or medium airs, especially off the wind, it is desirable to reduce the fullness—and hence the power in the sail—as the wind rises. How is it done? Fullness 1 can be reduced by stretching the edges of the sail. This will have the effect of drawing some of the fullness out of its centre. The luff is tensioned by tightening either the halyard or the Cunningham control. Due to the luff length of the sail and the difficulty in adjusting the

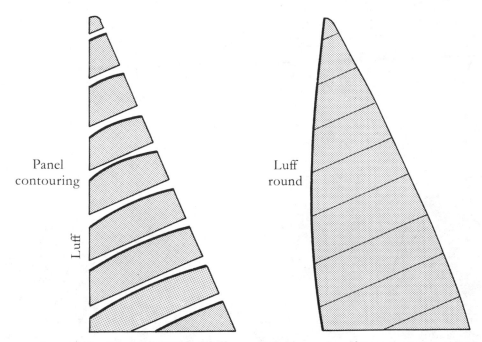

Panel
contouring

Luff
round

Luff

12. *Fullness cut into a mainsail.*

A well reefed mainsail on British Steel.

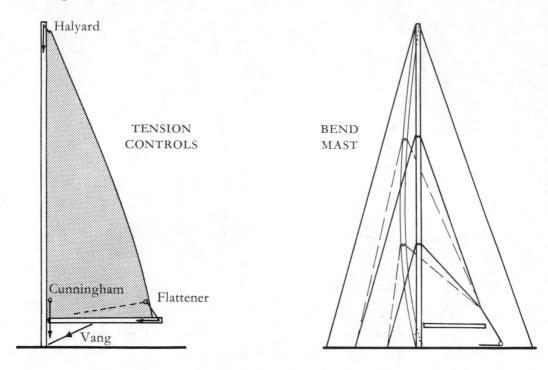

13. *Flattening the mainsail.*

halyard whilst sailing it is better to use the Cunningham; this is an eye in the sail luff, about 18 inches above the boom. A rope through this eye can be led to a winch and tension applied.

The foot is controlled by an outhaul tackle or by a flattening reef. The flattening reef is an innovation which provides an advantage under the I.O.R. handicapping rule (which does not concern us here), but it also helps to tension the foot of the sail by effectively reefing the bottom 12 inches. This results in a slightly shorter foot which tensions as it is pulled out to the end of the boom. The leech is tensioned by increasing the pressure on the mainsheet (if close-hauled) or on the vang (sometimes called the kicking-strap). See diagram 13.

Fullness 2 can be affected in only one way—by bending the mast: if bent forward in the centre it will take up the curve cut into the luff of the sail. This will remove all of fullness 2. Only recently has it been possible to bend the mast of a large yacht with any degree of safety; now it is common practice on inshore racers. Sailing across an ocean is a different matter, as reliability is a lot more important. However, bendy controllable rigs are already to be found on marathon race yachts. The actual bending of the spar is achieved as shown in diagram 13. If the masthead is held stationary, the inner-forestays taken up and the running-backstays eased, the mast will curve as desired. To be held straight for lighter weather the running-backstays can be taken up. See diagram 13.

A yachtsman who wishes to cruise across an ocean may rightly question the necessity for this degree of mainsail control. In fact, while cruising, if the main looks well set then it probably is. A cruising yacht will have a mast that is always straight and the mainsail should be cut accordingly. However to achieve a sail that *stays* in the correct shape fullness 1 must be reduced, as described above, as the wind rises. This is simply because the wind will stretch the centre of the sail and unless the edges are tensioned the mainsail will resemble a wrinkled bag, i.e. to keep the sail in the same shape more tension is required on all controls in more wind.

There is one more mainsail control that should be considered; the leech-line, a thin line led up inside the leech seam of the sail. This line is normally fixed at the head of the sail and adjustable to a small cleat at the clew. A good option is to lead the leech line either along the boom, or via a small block at the sail head and then down the luff, so that it arrives at the tack of the sail. This way it is within easy reach of adjustment when the boom is eased outside the guardrails. The purpose of the line is to stop the leech fluttering—a common occurrence, especially on an older sail. On no account must a leech-line be over tensioned as this will cause a hook to form at the aft end of the sail. This would do more harm to the airflow across the sail than would a flapping leech.

Mainsail Reefing

The aim is to reduce the size of the mainsail by progressively taking area from its foot. There are two methods of reefing commonly in use.

Roller reefing is achieved by rotating the boom as the main halyard is eased and thus rolling up the foot of the sail. This method has a number of disadvantages, and no advantages over the much better system of slab reefing. The major problem is the difficulty of getting a good set to the shortened sail. As the halyard is eased a handle— either on the side of the boom or on the forward side of the mast—is turned, causing the boom to rotate and the sail to roll up. To avoid the sail bunching forward on the boom a crewman has to hold the leech aft as the reef goes in. This is very difficult as the mainsheet has to be eased so the boom is flogging about dangerously. Once several rolls are in, the halyard, and then the mainsheet can be tightened. Another disadvantage now appears—there is no way of fixing a vang to the boom as it is completely cocooned in sail. Unreefing also has its problems. Whilst the boom is unrolled the halyard is taken up to hoist the sail again. But the slides on the luff of the sail have of course come out of the mast track and it is a fight to get them back in again. This last problem is slightly eased if the luff of the sail is a groove rather than a slide system. In all cases slab reefing is the better method.

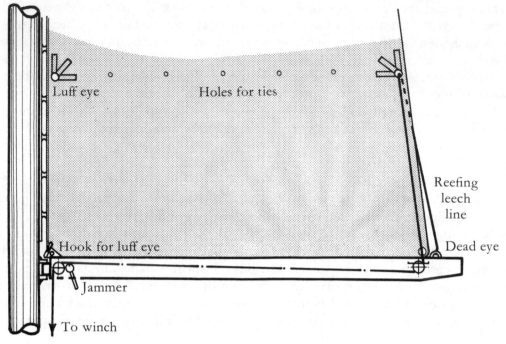

Luff eye   Holes for ties

Reefing
leech
line

Hook for luff eye   Dead eye

Jammer

To winch

14. *Slab reef set-up.*

Slab reefing is suitable for yachts of all sizes. The sail sets well, the reefs are easy to take in and out and very few crew are required. The system functions this way: one takes out the bottom few feet of the sail by pulling down the luff and leech and creating a new foot. The luff can be pulled down as the halyard is eased, but the leech cannot be reached, so it is necessary to sail with a line rove from the boom, up through an eye in the leech of the sail, and back down to the boom. This line is then led forward along the boom, either internally or externally, to a winch. See diagram 14.

To put in a reef, these are the steps to follow:

1. Ease the halyard and pull down the luff of the sail by hand.
2. Hook or tie the luff eye on the sail to the boom goose-neck. See diagram 15a.
3. Winch up the halyard to tension the shortened luff.
4. Ease the mainsheet and pull, first by hand and then by winch, the reefing leech-line until the new foot is stretched very tight. See diagram 15b and 15d. (Do not confuse the term leech-line).
5. Sheet in the mainsail completely.
6. Put ties round the loose sail along the boom. These ties should not take any weight but are simply to tidy up the flap of the sail. See diagram 15c. A mainsail may have ties permanently fitted to it in which case they can be done up with reef knots. Otherwise temporary lashing may be employed. See diagram 15c.

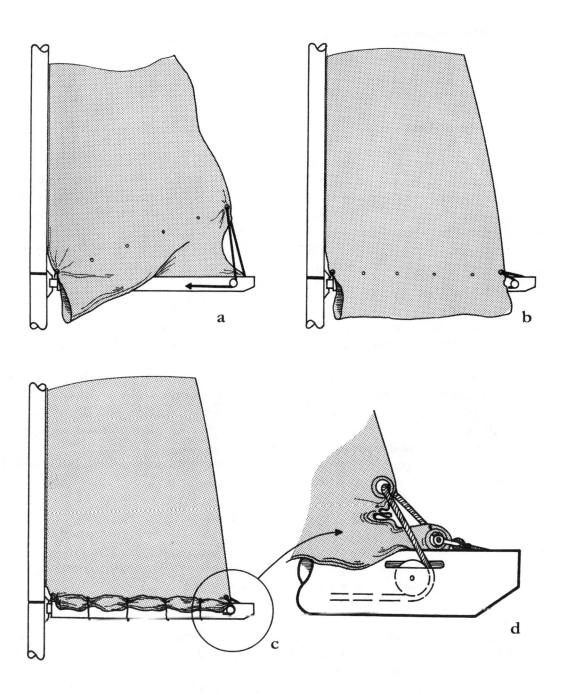

15. *Stages in slab reefing.*

To unreef the procedure is the same but in reverse:

1. Take off the ties.
2. Ease the reefing leech-line completely.
3. Ease the halyard a few inches, enough to release the luff eye.
4. Hoist the sail, easing the mainsheet as it goes up.
5. When the sail is hoisted, sheet in.

Two or more reefs may be put in using this method. It is usual to sail with the first two reefing leech-lines rove ready for use.

If the luff of the mainsail is a grooved system it will slide in and back easily as the sail is reefed and unreefed. Should the luff have slides it is important to ensure that they do not have to be removed from the track as a reef is taken in. The sail should be made with each luff-eye situated in the middle of a gap between slides; the length of the gap big enough to allow the eye to be pulled down to the boom over the top of the lower slides. It may be necessary to remove the slide nearest the luff-eye in order to achieve this. Taking a reef out is quicker and easier if the luff slides have remained in the mast.

Mainsail Setting

When sailing offshore the same rules apply to mainsail setting as at any other time. There are a number of points, especially those concerned with boom control, which are worth considering. The actual angle at which the mainsail is set depends of course on the set of the genoa or jib. Assuming the latter is set correctly, the proper set for the mainsail is found by easing the mainsheet as much as possible without the leading edge of the main flapping or lifting. This is an obvious statement but worth making as it is surprisingly easy accidentally to oversheet a sail. The more eased the sail the better the angle of its drive. At the same time the amount of twist in the sail has to be controlled.

A fairly common sight is a cruising yacht sailing with the boom sheeted well in and the top part of the sail twisted to leeward and flapping merrily. This is obviously wrong and should be cured by vang tension. See diagram 16. With less twist the sail will be more efficient, and consequently the yacht will sail faster and be more under control. Inshore racing yachts use very powerful hydraulic vangs; these are also used by some yachts offshore. As there is a potential reliability problem (a deck covered in hydraulic oil is no joke) a system using rope, blocks and winches to give maximum control for the least strain on boom and yacht is arguably a better choice.

Roving Vang. Instead of using a vang between the mast and the boom, a roving vang can be used between the boom and the toerail of the yacht. This vang is rigged from the aft end of the boom when close reaching; as the wind moves aft and the boom is eased, so the vang attachment point is moved in along the boom till the lead is vertically down to the toerail. See diagram 17. In this way the leverage applied is always the maximum

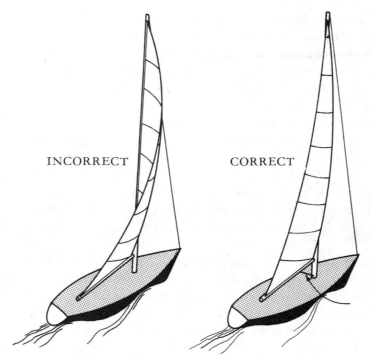

INCORRECT   CORRECT

16. *Removing twist.*

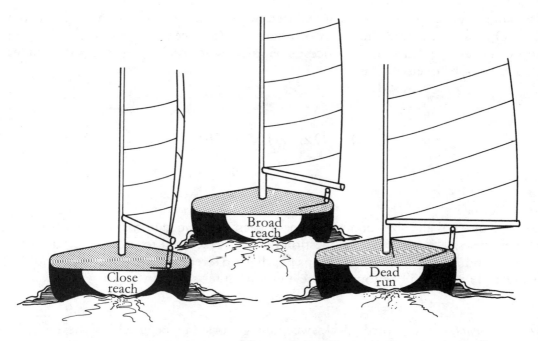

Broad
reach

Close
reach

Dead
run

17. *Vang and preventer.*

possible for the particular setting. The vang itself can be a simple block and tackle with a tail led to a winch. The attachment to the boom can be either a sliding eye or a canvas strop. Such a vang to the rail will also act as a preventer stopping the boom swinging in to the centre of the yacht in light, rolly conditions. It can also prevent an accidental gybe, but will have to be very strong to stand up to such treatment.

Preventer. An additional and better way of preventing a gybe is to take a line from the outboard end of the boom to the bow of the yacht. This type of preventer is simple to set up if two permanent wires are rigged on either side of the boom. These wires are shackled at the outboard end and tied off, when not in use, at the inboard end. When a preventer is needed (by which time the boom is already eased beyond reach) the inboard end of the leeward wire can be untied and attached to a rope that is in turn led to the bow. The rope can then be led to a winch or cleat and the boom is safely restrained.

Boom Control. Rather than use a preventer on *Great Britain II*, I always relied on a vang to the rail. When running square the vang was led slightly forward along the rail and shackled down to the main-mast rigging chainplates. This set-up was very strong—perhaps too strong as the boom eventually broke at the vang attachment point. Two other yachts in the race suffered the same fate when their booms hit the water on heavy weather reaches. A proper preventer might have saved the boom in the latter two cases. Of course a preventer cannot be used alone as it does not hold the boom down, only forward.

In 1979 there were several accidents caused by unintentional gybes on un-prevented yachts. One was fatal and one or two others would have been, had they occurred offshore and away from rescue services. The importance of keeping the boom under control cannot be over-emphasised.

GENOAS AND JIBS

Which Genoa?
The different types and sizes of headsails have been mentioned in chapter 1 with a view to choosing a sail wardrobe. The question now is, which sail to use when. Summary tables of recommended sail combinations for all wind strengths and directions, both for cruising and racing, will be found at the end of chapter 5.

Sailing close-hauled, low-footed, deck-sweeping genoas can be used, as they will be sheeted well inside the rail of the yacht and not out in the waves. Thus the No 1, No 2 and No 3 genoas are used, changing down as the wind rises to avoid being overpowered. A racing yacht will probably carry two or three No 1 genoas made from different weights of cloth, and of slightly different cuts. In this case care must be taken to use the right sail in the right conditions. If the light genoa is carried in too much wind it will stretch into an inefficient shape. Conversely the heavy genoa may be too flat for very light winds. The weight of its cloth will also prohibit its setting well in light airs.

With the wind free, yet not free enough to allow a spinnaker to be carried, it is advisable to set reachers. By doing so two advantages are gained. Firstly, a reacher can be cut a bit fuller than a genoa as it is not used close-hauled; so more drive is achieved. Secondly, the sail is made with a high clew so it can be set, when sheets are eased—with the foot outside the rail and yet up clear of the reach of destructive wave tops. This is a very important factor offshore where large seas can easily rip the foot of a genoa. As the wind rises, so the reachers are reduced in size; the No 2 or blast reacher corresponds to the No 2 genoa, and the No 3 reacher, or jib-top, corresponds to the No 3 genoa.

While cruising it is unlikely that such a comprehensive sail wardrobe will be carried. Rather than genoas and reachers the headsails, numbers one to three, should be cut like a genoa (i.e. not too full) but with a high clew like a reacher. They will then double up admirably for both purposes.

Once the wind is too high for either No 3 genoa or jib top it is necessary to change to the No 4 jib top and then the No 5 jib-top (usually the storm jib) whether close-hauled or close-reaching. It pays to set a staysail inside the jib tops thus forming the traditional cutter rig.

Genoa Trim

Regardless of which headsail is set, it is most important to set it properly. Four factors affect this (i) sheet lead position fore and aft, (ii) sheet lead position athwartships, (iii) halyard tension, and (iv) how much the sail is sheeted in.

Fore and aft position for the sheet lead for any jib can be found approximately ashore, either by studying the sail plan or laying out the sails. The angle of the sheet lead is found by bisecting the sail luff and taking a line from that point through the clew of the sail; a projection of this line is the direction the sheet should follow. If the sail is laid out ashore an arrow can be drawn on the clew to show the correct line. Once sailing, with the sail sheeted to the lead position calculated, and trimmed for close-hauled work, it can be inspected to see if any adjustment is required. As the yacht is gently luffed up into the wind observe where the luff of the sail lifts first. If it all lifts together the lead is correct; if the head lifts first the lead should go forward; and if the lower part of the luff lifts first the lead should go aft. The desired result is the leading edge of the sail lining up exactly with the apparent wind all the way up the luff.

Athwartships position of the sheet lead is a more complex problem and depends very much on the design of the yacht, its mast and sails. Traditionally the genoa sheets have always been led to the rail of the yacht. This is because vessels with narrow beams were looking for as wide a sheeting angle as their hulls allowed. As yachts were designed wider and wider, so the optimum sheeting angle moved, relatively, inside the rail. On ocean cruising yachts there is little to be gained from moving the sheet lead inboard. Actually the position of the chainplates, and hence the shrouds, on or near the rail will probably prohibit this anyway. Inshore racing yachts, designed for flat water, have progressively moved their sheet leads and their rigging inboard until now an angle of 7° between the centre line and a line connecting the tack and clew is common for a No 1 genoa. Marathon racers have been slow to follow suit as the necessity of sailing very, very close to the wind has not been considered important. However it is worth noting that *Condor*, the 23 metre-sloop, sheeted her genoas to the rail in the 1977 world race and has since improved her windward potential tremendously by moving the leads almost two feet inboard.

A sensible range of angles for optimum deep sea sailing would be: No 1 genoa 8°, No 2 genoa 9°, and No 3 genoa 10°. The No 3 would be sheeted inside the cap shroud when on the wind, assuming the mast and sails are designed to make these angles possible. If these angles cannot be achieved without fouling the cap shrouds, then the best is a sheeting angle with the foot of the sail touching the shrouds, when sheeted fairly hard in a medium wind. This means sheeting to the rail if the cap shrouds are also anchored there—as is often the case on a cruising yacht.

Halyard tension on the jib should be varied with the wind strength. The stronger the wind the more tension required. 'Scallops' between the hanks, or horizontal wrinkles from the luff are signs of not enough tension. Vertical creases, folds, or hard lines up the luff are signs of too much tension. What is happening is that the fullness of the sail is blown aft by the wind and pulled forward by halyard tension; it is essential to keep the balance correct so that the sail stays in its designed shape.

The amount of sheet required is most important. When sailing slightly free of the wind on a close reach the sail should be sheeted in until its leading edge just stops lifting. This much is obvious, however, there is a temptation to oversheet, so that the sail never lifts even with a bad helmsman weaving either side of the course. This is a particular problem when on a long trip where there is a likelihood of a sheet being cleated off and only adjusted every so often. It is a mistake to oversheet in this way as more drive is lost from an oversheeted sail than from one which lifts occasionally. As the wind frees, move the sheet lead outboard to the rail, so far as the wind angle allows, if it is not already there.

When sailing close-hauled the same rules apply, but by now the headsail is sheeted hard in. A good guide-line to follow is, regardless of the wind strength, to sheet a genoa in until it is almost touching the end of the spreaders on the mast. To achieve this the

Winching up a genoa.

sheet will require quite different amounts of tension as the wind varies. It is easy to forget to ease the sheet as the wind drops, and as well as loss of drive, there is a fair chance that the spreader will damage the sail. Once the trim is correct the yacht can be sailed as close to the wind as is efficient—i.e. until the apparent wind is meeting the yacht in the direction of the leading edge of the genoa; then the sail is nearly luffing—but not quite.

Luff Telltales. Whatever point of sailing the yacht is on it is obviously important to know when the leading edge of a sail is on the point of lifting. Genoas should be fitted with telltales to indicate when the airflow is correct. The telltale is best made by fixing two pieces of wool or strips of light material, each about 9″ long, on either side of the sail about 9″ aft of the luff. If possible the telltales should be fixed through a small window in the sail so that the leeward one may be easily seen. When the trim of the sail is correct the telltales on each side of the sail stream aft. If the leeward telltale starts to rise, fall, lift or generally twirl about, then either the sail should be eased or the yacht steered closer to the wind. If the windward telltale flutters the sail should be sheeted in or the yacht should be borne away from the wind. See diagram 18. A sail should have three or four sets of telltales up the luff as this will not only facilitate the trim, but will help give an indication of the correct fore and aft sheet lead as previously explained.

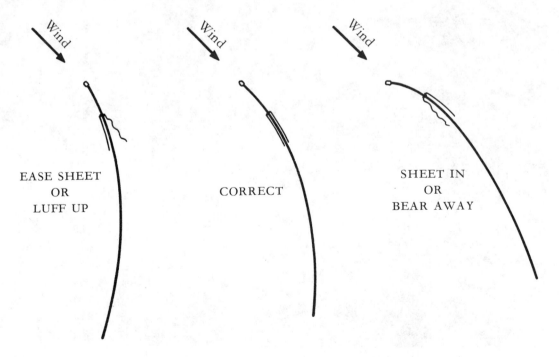

18. *Cross section of genoas showing tell tails.*

Jib Changing

There is a golden rule applicable to all sail changing, including jibs, reefs and spinnakers; it applies to cruising and racing. When changing sail up or changing sail down, the rule is: 'If you are thinking about it—do it!' If, for instance, a skipper or watch leader is wondering whether or not to put a reef in, then yes; it should go in. The theory is that he would not have thought of the possible need for it unless it was already necessary. The same applies the other way. If a skipper is thinking that maybe he could try a spinnaker, then yes, he probably should have it up. Sometimes the situation is a bit more complex: the problem may be whether to reef or, instead, to change jibs; the best solution may still be to follow the rule and do both.

Having decided that a headsail change is necessary the best way to set about it will depend on whether the headsail is fixed to the forestay by hanks or by a luff-groove. Hanks, and shackles before them, have always been used to fix a sail luff to a stay. By the mid 1970's nearly all coastal racing yachts had switched to a luff-groove system. However, even in 1977, hanks were employed on the headsails of all yachts in the round-the-world race. *Flyer*, the eventual winner, used a luff-groove system for the two 'calmer' legs of the race but switched to hanks for the two Roaring Forties legs. Never-the-less the general feeling at the end of the race was that, if racing, and with sufficient crew on board, then a luff-groove system should be used deep sea also. On the other hand cruising yachts, especially short-handed, are far better off with hanks; the reason is control, as when a hanked headsail is lowered to the deck it is basically under control, as the luff is well fixed to the forestay. With a groove system, where a bolt rope on the luff of the sail fits up a groove in the forestay (or up a groove in a plastic or alloy extrusion round the forestay) the sail, when lowered, is not attached to anything; this can cause sail handling problems in rough weather. The great advantage of a groove system is in achieving a sail change without ever going 'bare-headed', as will be seen shortly.

Changing a Jib with Hanks. To help follow the routine we will use a crew of six. Nos 1, 2 and 3 are on the foredeck, No 4 on the halyard and No 5 on the sheet.

    1. Crew 1, 2 and 3 get the new jib on deck and unbag it.

    2. They hank it on to the forestay underneath the bottom hank of the old jib (the one in use). If there is not enough room for all the hanks the bottom hank of the old jib can be removed. If this is impossible, due to wind strength, attach the remaining hanks above it and remember it is still there.

    3. Pull the clew of the new sail aft so that the whole sail is laid close to the lee rail. The clew itself is folded back, if necessary, so it is by the leeward shrouds.

    4. If the clew of the old sail is within reach (as it will be on the No 1, 2 and 3 genoas), untie the windward (lazy) sheet and tie it to the new sail. This saves a bit of time later.

    5. This step should be undertaken if changing to a larger jib—i.e. the old jib still setting is not overpressed. No 5 eases the sheet a few inches, No 4 eases the halyard a foot, and

No 1 pulls down the luff an inch or two, enough to release the old tack from the deck fitting and replace it with the new tack.

6. Finally we are ready for the change. No 5 eases the sheet (not too much as a bit of tension will help hold the falling jib inboard); No 4 lowers the halyard; No 1 pulls down the luff; Nos 2 and 3 pull the sail in, **over** and to windward of the new one.

7. As soon as the sail is down No 5 changes the sheets (or sheet) to the new jib, altering the lead position of the leeward sheet if required, whilst No 4 sits on the old jib. Simultaneously No 1 is unhanking the old jib from the top, passing it aft to No 2 with the halyard still attached; while No 2 continues to receive unhanked sail, No 3 can take the halyard off the old head and pass it back to No 1 when the unhanking is complete. The halyard is attached to the new head.

8. If the tacks have been changed (step 5) hoisting commences immediately with Nos 2 and 3 helping No 4. If the tacks have not been changed this should quickly be done first. During hoisting No 1 helps the sail over the rail and No 5 takes in the sheet enough to prevent the clew of the sail flogging, but no more. No 1 calls when the sail is up tight and No 5 sheets in with help from whoever reaches him first.

9. The old sail is stowed.

The whole process may take 30 minutes or more but nearly all of this is in the preparation stages. The vital time between letting the sheet fly and sheeting it completely home again—steps 6 to 8—should not take more than two minutes even in rough conditions. On *Great Britain II*, despite large headsails, we could manage 90 seconds in good weather. On smaller yachts it can be done a good deal quicker.

There are several things that can, and occasionally do, go wrong. Common among these is mixing up the clews and retying the sheets to the old jib; or forgetting to relead the sheet; or unhanking the new jib as well as the old one in the dark. Careful preparation and care can save the day. However, in bad weather, especially if in no hurry, it is wise to lower the old jib and get it below before bringing the new one on deck. Although the yacht will be bare-headed longer, the total time spent on the nasty foredeck will be less—with the yacht at a safer speed and angle of heel.

Changing a Luff-Groove Jib is a very different procedure. The system is facilitated by the forestay having two grooves in it. This means the new jib can be hoisted on a second halyard before the old one is lowered. There are three possible combinations of this change, depending on which groove (windward or leeward) the old jib is set in. They are:

(a) Hoist new jib to windward (inside); lower old one to leeward (outside).
(b) Hoist new jib to leeward; lower old one to windward.
(c) Hoist new jib to windward; lower old one to windward.

As both lowering and hoisting are best done to windward of (inside) the jib already set, system (c) is the favourite, and it is achieved by executing a tack during the change. This is how it works:

1. Ensure that the free groove is to windward by tacking if necessary.
2. Prepare the new jib by laying it out on the foredeck, inside the foot of the old jib, with the luff flacked out ready for hoisting.
3. Take the windward (lazy) sheet off the old jib, re-lead if necessary (but still on the windward side) and tie it to the new jib.
4. Hoist the new jib in the windward groove on the windward halyard.
5. As soon as the new jib is up tack the yacht, immediately lowering the old sail and sheeting the new one on the new leeward side.
6. Take the second sheet off the old jib and tie it to the new one.
7. Stow the old jib.

This system is fine on a beat but is unlikely to be used very often offshore as tacking about all over the ocean is not always required. Possibly a change of jib will be needed and yet the same tack has to be maintained. In this case we have to use system (a) or (b). Both are feasible and work like this:

1. Prepare the new jib on the foredeck, laid out by the foot of the old jib and with the luff flacked out ready for hoisting.
2. Remove the windward sheet (lazy) from the old jib, re-lead it and tie it to the new one.
3. On the leeward side attach a temporary sheet to the sail, lead it to a spare winch, and take up the weight of the sail.
4. Ease the leeward sheet (the temporary sheet is now doing its job), remove it from the old jib, re-lead it and tie it to the new one.
5. Hoist the new jib in the spare groove with the respective halyard. If this is to leeward the new sail has to be fed under the foot of the old one.
6. Sheet in the new jib.
7. Ease the temporary sheet and lower the old jib. If the new one was hoisted to windward the old one must be lowered to leeward, which means gathering it under the foot of the new.
8. Stow the old jib.

When a series of jib changes are done whilst on one tack they will alternate from windward hoist—leeward lower to leeward hoist—windward lower and so on. This was exactly our experience on *Condor of Bermuda* on the gale-swept reach from the Fastnet back to the Bishop Rock in 1979. Despite large sails (an I measurement or mast height of about 30 metres) and wet cloth which tends to cling, we had no great difficulty with the sail changes. The hardest operation was lowering a wet sail to leeward; this needed a fair amount of gorilla strength, but it always came down in the end.

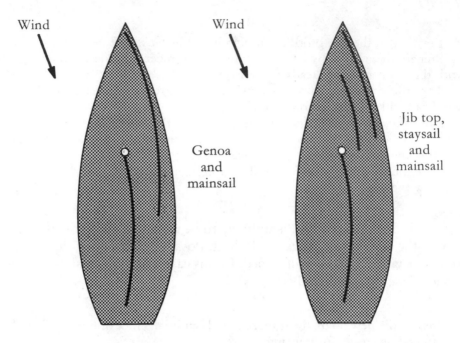

Wind

Wind

Genoa
and
mainsail

Jib top,
staysail
and
mainsail

19. *Genoa or jib top (yankee) and staysail.*

OTHER FORE AND AFT SAILS

The Mizzen

Ketches and yawls have mizzen masts and sails. The mizzen is smaller than the mainsail and is rigged near the stern of the yacht. Its use on the wind is fairly limited. In fact a number of crew who have raced round the world in ketches would describe it as 'a sail that the crew continually have to hoist and lower and which makes no difference anyway'. This is not strictly true but never-the-less is not far off the mark.

The same rules apply to setting and controlling the mizzen as described for the mainsail. However the boom will always set nearer the centre line than the main as the mizzen is trying to sail in headed wind.

Its greatest effect on the yacht is one of balance. As the wind rises, the yacht heels, the drive of the sails moves to leeward and weather-helm—the tendency to turn to windward—develops. By lowering the mizzen the helm can be improved a great deal; although very little drive has been taken away, the centre of effort of the remaining sails is further forward and hence reduces, or removes, weather-helm. The mizzen is therefore unlikely to be used in more than 20 knots of apparent wind; yet it can earn its keep when the wind reaches gale force, as will be seen in chapter 6.

Forestaysail

When on the wind or close reaching a staysail can be of great benefit. It will certainly be no help inside a genoa and should not be used, as the windflow between genoa and mainsail will be detrimentally affected. Inside a jib-top (yankee) the staysail definitely helps, because a small jib has little or no overlap of the mainsail and the staysail will improve the airflow between the two. It can be thought of as an extension forward of the mainsail. A jib-top and staysail form the traditional cutter rig, which is very effective in heavy airs to windward. See diagram 19.

Drifter

A very useful sail in calms—there are more calms in the middle of an ocean than one might imagine. This sail is made of the same cloth as a medium weight spinnaker; it is cut to the size of the No 3 genoa or slightly larger, its purpose being to try and catch the lightest airs. Consequently it is often set when there is not enough breeze to fill it. By cutting the drifter with an almost vertical leech it will hang, even in still air, in the correct shape ready to make use of the first hint of wind. If it were cut full size, like a No 1 genoa, it would collapse in on itself, with its leech in folds, whilst waiting for wind.

The drifter should be set on a spinnaker halyard, loose luffed. This is especially important if the yacht has hanked jibs, because as soon as there is any noticeable wind and the yacht starts moving, the drifter has done its work; the light No 1 genoa or the reacher should quickly be hoisted and sheeted in before the drifter is lowered.

Trysail

A storm trysail is designed to provide an alternative to a fully reefed mainsail in storm conditions. In fact as it is smaller than the fully reefed sail, and is set without a boom, it can safely be used in extreme conditions. The sail has never been very popular because of the difficulties encountered rigging it. By the time it is needed the weather is so bad that it becomes a bit tough for the crew to rig it, especially as they have probably never seen one before; with the majority of racing skippers I have always favoured using a reefed mainsail. If there is too much wind for that the yacht will go to windward, or anywhere else, with a storm jib alone. However, as a result of their experiences in the 1979 Fastnet storm a number of skippers now believe that a trysail is indispensable.

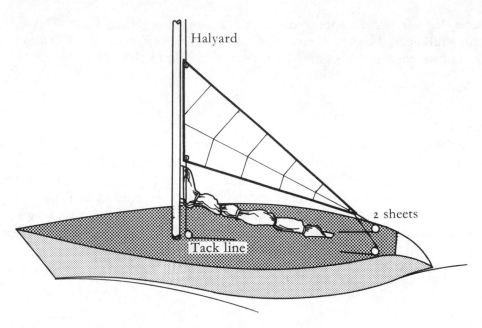

Halyard

2 sheets

Tack line

20. Set of a storm trisail.

Diagram 20 shows how the sail is set. Firstly it has to be fed into a track on the mast. This may mean having to remove the mainsail slides first; or there may be a second track on the mast reserved specifically for the trysail. It is difficult, anyway, fiddling with slides in a storm. Once the luff is organised the sail can be hoisted, using the main-halyard, with two sheets on the clew and a down haul on the tack at the bottom of the luff. When the clew is clear of the deck and a reasonable sheeting angle obtained, make the tack line fast and winch up the halyard. The two sheets are taken, one to each quarter, and both winched up until the clew is just to leeward of the centre-line for windward, or near windward, work.

This sail generally lives in a bag hidden at the bottom of the sail locker, only to be seen in a storm; it should be brought to the surface well before it is needed. The time to try it out is in a marina; anyone who saw a seamanlike skipper checking the sheet leads and tack position of a trysail in Cowes before the 1979 Fastnet race may have laughed. They won't anymore.

TACKING

There are no special secrets about tacking offshore. If it is rough the helmsman should try and find a slightly flatter piece of water for the manoeuvre in order to avoid hitting a wave bows-on while passing through the eye of the wind; this should be common practice in any waters.

It is very important to check the windward sheet carefully to make sure it is clear of all obstructions and is correctly led for the jib in use. Take up all the slack in the sheet before going about. In some yachts it is unnecessary to use full helm to complete a full tack, and in any case the helm should be put over fairly slowly. Backing the jib is not normally required and can be a mistake, as it slows the yacht at a critical moment. The jib should be released as it starts to back. The only possible exception to this is in light airs, when backing the jib may speed up the tack. It is a question of trial and error for the particular yacht.

It is a good idea to have a man on the foredeck helping the sail round the inner forestay or babystay. The correct way to do this is to face aft, standing on the new windward side, and pull forward on the foot of the sail, working from forward to aft, throwing the gathered sail forward and to the leeward of the stay. See diagram 21. Beware of the last few feet of sail, and of the clew and sheets, as they will go round in a dangerous rush as the sail fills on the new side. The big mistake here, often made by new hands, is to try and carry the clew forward before the middle of the sail is round the stay. This makes a balloon of the sail, not only stopping it tacking, but slowing the yacht down. See diagram 21.

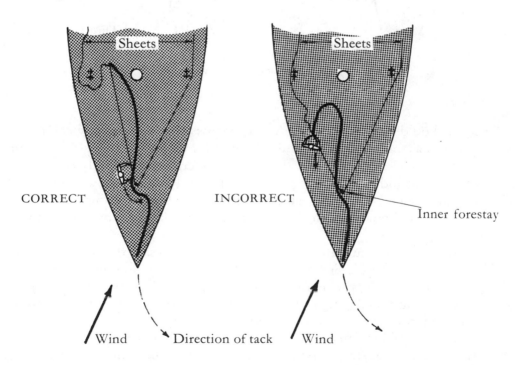

21. *Helping the genoa round when tacking.*

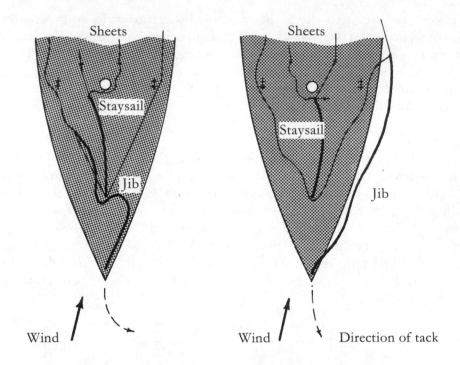

Sheets   *Sheets*

Staysail   Staysail

Jib   Jib

Wind   Wind   Direction of tack

22. *With a staysail set, tack the jib first.*

The sail should be sheeted in as quickly as possible. The sheet winch tailer should work very fast as the sail comes round, taking in as much slack as possible before the sail fills with wind. To help in this objective one or two crew should grab the new sheet once the jib has tacked and run down the deck carrying and pulling it towards the lead block. This will ease the tailers a great deal. The winchman (or men), using a lot of muscle, can now bring the sail home fast but slowing down for the last foot or so to allow the yacht to gather way.

When sailing with a cutter rig, that is jib-top and staysail, the staysail should be left aback while the jib-top is tacked. The backed staysail will allow the jib-top an easy passage around the stay, preventing it from blowing to leeward, aft of the stay, as the bow passes through head to wind. Once the jib-top is round, let the staysail go, and both can be sheeted in together on the new side. See diagram 22.

The question of how many turns of sheet to put on a winch is one of personal preference. This is illustrated by the story of a yachtsman in Auckland whose wife crewed for him, and to improve her skills he sent her on one of Penny Whiting's yachting courses. When the wife returned she was full of good ideas; her husband would say 'put three turns on the winch' and she would reply 'Penny says use four'. After several weekends of disagreement on this and other points of detail he gave up and changed the name of his yacht to 'Penny says'! My suggestion is that when the sheet winch is powered by a handle on top of the drum, use three turns initially for tailing in the slack; still with three turns, and with no time wasted, the sheet can be winched in to within a foot of right home; the handle is then taken out, another turn added to the drum, and the last foot winched in.

If the sheet winch has a remote drive—such as a coffee grinder—the tailer can start with two turns on the drum. As soon as he has all slack in, and the winches start work, he can add a third and fourth turn as the drum is turning.

5 Sail Handling and Setting Off the Wind

In this chapter systems are discussed for spinnaker handling, the use of staysails and bloopers (commonly called big boys or shooters), and techniques for poling-out jibs.

SPINNAKERS

As the quality of equipment improves and as the general knowledge of deep sea sailing increases, so the way yachts are handled offshore tends more and more towards the way they are handled by inshore racers. However, handling spinnakers has to be done a lot more carefully when deep sea than when sailing round the buoys. There are two main reasons for this: damage to the sails and damage to the crew. While certain risks are acceptable when sailing close to sailmakers and civilisation, they are not acceptable in the middle of an ocean. Therefore certain systems which aid the smooth running of spinnaker work, especially in heavy weather, are worth following.

Spinnaker Sizes and Weights

A modern racing yacht may carry five or more different designs of spinnaker; this may seem unnecessary, but if the object is to achieve that last half a percent of speed, then it is essential. Because a spinnaker has to lift into shape from the force of the wind alone it is no use always using a heavy cloth, which in light airs would be too heavy to set. Conversely a light cloth cannot be used all the time, as it may rip in stronger winds; as well as this, the lighter the cloth, the more porous it is to the wind. The ideal is to use as heavy a cloth as will set. Thus in a rising wind change up to a heavier weight spinnaker as soon as there is enough wind to set it. Do not wait until the one set is about to burst. In a falling wind change to a lighter sail as soon as the wind is too light to lift the sail set.

The author 'snaps' a spinnaker on Second Life.

Thus for a large yacht we could have the following spinnakers (as recommended in chapter 1):

Floater of	0.5	oz cloth
Light of	0.75	oz cloth
Medium of	1.5	oz cloth
Heavy of	2.2	oz cloth
Storm of	2.6	oz cloth and of smaller size.

The storm spinnaker should be about 80% the size of a full spinnaker. Some yachts may also carry special flat-cut reaching spinnakers, but it is my view that this is not required offshore, where it is usually possible to alter course to accommodate an all-purpose spinnaker, or a reaching jib, without affecting miles sailed. With several thousand miles to go an alteration of course of 10° or so for a relatively short period will make little difference.

When cruising deep sea, if a spinnaker is used at all, it will probably be one of medium weight and only used when the wind suits, as it is as tedious to carry a spinnaker in too little wind as in too much. Other than spinnaker changing, the systems described here still apply.

Spinnaker Hoisting

The secret of a successful hoist is careful preparation beforehand, and proper co-ordination between all the crew involved.

Because the spinnaker is set free it is difficult to control during hoisting. If it starts to set halfway up it will be difficult to hoist the rest of the way; on the other hand if it does not set, it will flog about frighteningly. The way round these problems is to 'stop' the spinnaker before hoisting. Fortunately the days when a spinnaker was laid out and tied up in wool or cotton are past. The modern use of elastic bands is very efficient. The saloon of the yacht, as the largest space available, is the best venue for the operation. First load a bucket with the bottom cut out (or washing up bowl on maxi yachts) with enough bands for the sail. Having roughly sorted out the sail, pass it through the bucket, head first, dropping bands off every two or three feet. Keep the luff tapes in hand to prevent them twisting; when at a distance from the bottom of the sail equal to half the width of the foot (mark the luff previously) drop off two or three bands together and remove the bucket; then stop the foot by working in from each clew in turn, thus forming two legs. See diagram 23.

The spinnaker, once stopped, can be stowed in a bag ready for use. Sailmakers may supply spinnakers in a full length spinnaker turtle. The purpose being to allow the sail to be hoisted in the turtle instead of stopped in bands. The disadvantage of the turtle is its lack of legs.

A light spinnaker need not be stopped, as it is always hoisted in light winds.

The routine for a spinnaker hoist is as follows:

1. *Prepare the spinnaker pole*. Place the inboard end of the pole in the heel fitting on the mast track. Attach three control lines to the outboard end, (a) the topping lift from the mast, (b) the fore guy led to the bow, and (c) the pole guy. The pole guy, a line not used inshore but very useful for pole control deep sea—especially in rough weather—is led aft. The inboard end of the pole is hoisted to the height required (see spinnaker trim), and the outboard end is hoisted to head height with a bit of weight on the pole guy to keep it off the forestay. In all pole adjustments move the inboard end first, otherwise compression loads on the heel will cause friction which will make it difficult to move.

2. *Prepare the sheets and guys*. On each side of the yacht there should be rigged a spinnaker guy and sheet. The pair on one side are joined to one snap shackle, and the same happens

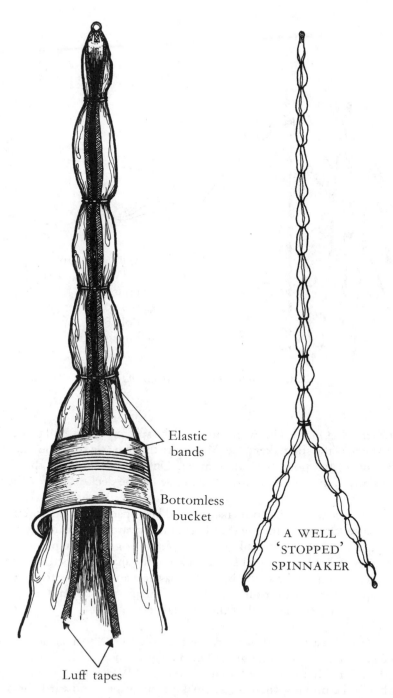

Elastic
bands

Bottomless
bucket

A WELL
'STOPPED'
SPINNAKER

Luff tapes

23. *Stopping a spinnaker using a bottomless bucket and elastic bands.*

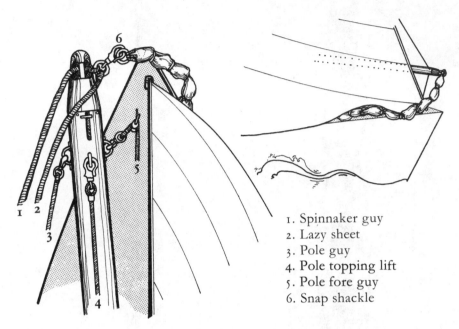

1. Spinnaker guy
2. Lazy sheet
3. Pole guy
4. Pole topping lift
5. Pole fore guy
6. Snap shackle

24. *Preparing to hoist a spinnaker.*

on the other side. On the windward side take the spinnaker guy and place it through the jaws at the end of the spinnaker pole. Make sure the sheet on that side (the lazy sheet) lies over the top of the pole. See diagram 24. On the leeward side the sheet, and lazy spinnaker guy, joined at their snap shackle, lie on the deck ready for the spinnaker.

3. *Prepare the spinnaker.* The spinnaker should be unpacked on the foredeck and one of the 'legs' passed under the foot of the jib, round forward of the forestay from leeward to windward, and the clew snapped onto the spinnaker guy at the pole end. See diagram 24. The other 'leg' is laid aft on the foredeck and the sheet snapped onto the clew; make sure the sheet is outside the shrouds, the genoa sheet and over the top of the guard-rails. Take the spinnaker halyard round the back of the jib, pull the end in under the foot of the jib and attach it to the head of the spinnaker.

4. *Set the pole.* Hoist the outboard end of the pole to the correct height and pull it aft several feet using the spinnaker guy. (The pole guy is not needed, but is left on the pole and kept slack ready for a gybe or an emergency). Winch the spinnaker guy and fore guy tight. While moving the pole aft make certain the windward leg of the stopped spinnaker feeds out freely with it.

5. *Hoist the spinnaker*. If conditions are at all hairy steer downwind with the breeze thirty or forty degrees off the stern. Make sure the sheet and lazy spinnaker guy are slack and then hoist away. The head should reach the top of the mast before the sail breaks out. But watch it carefully and if it starts to go early, immediately put several turns of halyard on the winch, otherwise the hoisters will be hoisted! Should the sail break out completely before being fully hoisted it may still be winched up if the sheet is kept slack to prevent the spinnaker setting. If all goes well it will still be stopped when fully hoisted.

6. *Break out the spinnaker*. Take in the spinnaker sheet on a winch; the bands will start to break and the spinnaker will rapidly set. Beware: in order to get the sail to break out it is necessary to oversheet. Immediately it sets the sheet must be quickly eased until the set is correct.

7. *Lower the genoa*. In light airs the spinnaker may not set at all until the jib is out of the way.

8. *Adjust* the pole height, spinnaker guy and sheet until the spinnaker trim is correct. See next section.

A spinnaker is like a bad habit—it is easy to start and difficult to change or give up. Hoisting a spinnaker is easier than gybing it or taking it down.

Spinnaker Trim

The spinnaker is setting but is it providing maximum drive? Reference to diagram 25 will help clarify this section.

Pole. Begin by checking the pole height; the outboard end of the pole should hold the windward clew of the spinnaker at the same height that the leeward clew takes up of its own accord. The foot of the spinnaker should be level. The pole itself should be horizontal, so the inboard end must be at the same height as the outboard end; but remember the inboard end must be altered first. Should the windward clew of the spinnaker appear to be set too low, move the inboard end of the pole up a bit, then the outboard end until it is level, check the clew height again, and so on. In general a higher pole is needed in strong and medium winds and a lower pole in light winds.

The pole should be pulled as far aft as the wind direction allows; with the wind on the beam, or forward of the beam, it should be an inch off the forestay; with the wind right aft it should be squared up nearly back to the main mast shrouds. A good rule to begin with is to keep the pole at right angles to the apparent wind. When the pole is set there should be weight on the topping lift, pole fore guy and spinnaker guy only. These three lines are used to alter the pole position; meanwhile the lazy sheet and pole guy must be kept slack, otherwise the spinnaker guy will chafe in the pole end. So to square the pole, ease the fore guy and take in the spinnaker guy; the lazy sheet and pole guy should be taken in a bit to prevent too much slack flapping about. To move the pole forward ease plenty of slack into the pole guy and lazy sheet, then ease the spinnaker guy and take up on the fore guy.

Sheet. On the leeward side the weight is taken on the sheet, and the lazy guy is always kept slack. Assuming the pole is at the correct angle, the sheet should be taken in until the spinnaker sets, and then eased slowly until the luff of the sail just starts to curl. Ideally the spinnaker should be continually trimmed so that the luff is always on this fine edge. On a long ocean crossing it may be impractical to keep the spinnaker sheet in hand. The sail may be up for days on end, such as in the Cape Town to Rio (now to Buenos Aires) race, when in 1976 we sailed for 21 days with a spinnaker set and the occasional gybe or change to a different spinnaker were the only activities. Rather than oversheet the sail to ensure it stays set over a long period, trim correctly and make it up on a cleat. The helmsman then steers to the sail. The trim can be checked every five minutes or so and adjusted to suit the correct course if necessary. Even at night this is possible, the spinnaker can easily be seen as a dark shadow against the sky.

Barber-hauler. The spinnaker sheet lead is normally taken right aft to the stern of the yacht. This is a mistake offshore on long passages; it will continually chafe under the boom or on the leech of the mainsail. It is far better to lead the sheet nearer amidships, where it will be clear under the boom. This is best achieved with the use of a barber-hauler (a line from a floating block around the sheet, led down to the rail abeam of the mast, through a block and to a winch. See diagram 25). As the boom is eased for a square run the barber-hauler can be taken in to keep the sheet just clear of the boom. The trim of the spinnaker is not adversely affected.

In Heavy Weather it is useful to pin the storm spinnaker down fairly tightly to avoid it swinging about and causing a death roll to develop. It is wrong to ease the pole forward for 'safety', as this will in fact unbalance the yacht. There may be no danger of the luff collapsing but there is a greater danger of a broach resulting from this imbalance. Oversheeting makes it worse. The better course of action is to set the pole slightly lower than normal and to take in the barber-hauler. This will hold the foot of the spinnaker down, which has the effect of flattening the sail and improving control. If the yacht is still rolling and threatening to broach it is time to take the spinnaker off and boom out the blast reacher (see later). Remember that the highest average speed over days or weeks is what we are after. It is not a question of hanging on to a kite at all costs until the leeward mark is reached. It is more a question of comparing the miles sailed over a day.

1. Topping lift
2. Pole fore guy
3. Pole guy
4. Spinnaker guy
5. Lazy guy
6. Lazy sheet
7. Barber-hauler
8. Spinnaker sheet

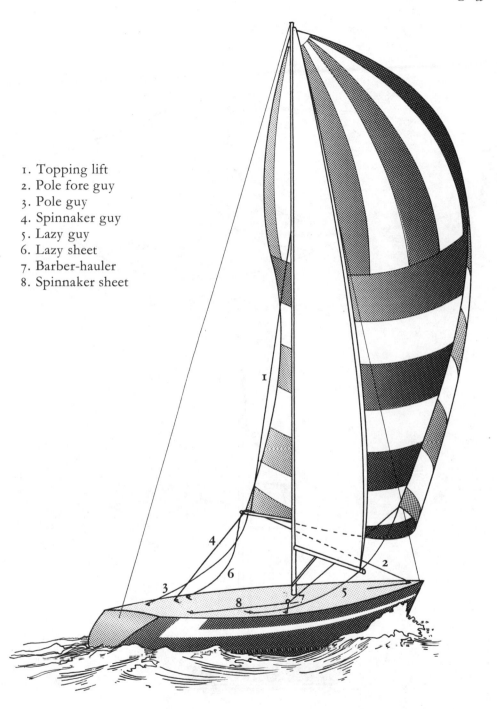

25. *Spinnaker controls.*

Wind

Reaching strut

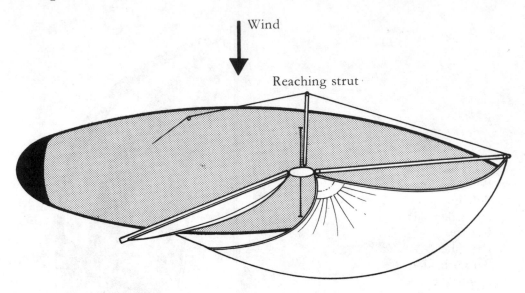

26. *Use of a reaching strut or jockey pole.*

Snap shackles

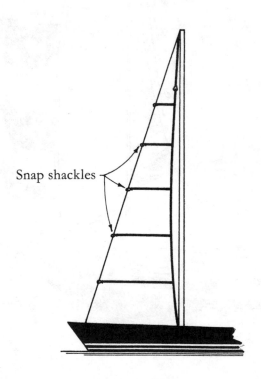

27. *Spinnaker net.*

For instance six hours of fast spinnaker sailing, surfing and broaching followed by half an hour stationary sorting out the bits of sail and a broken pole, may not achieve the same distance as six and a half hours of running with a boomed-out jib. Another consideration is the accuracy of the course steered, which may be better with less sail.

Very Light Airs require that the spinnaker be trimmed with the sheet in hand—regardless of the size of the yacht—in order to keep the sail flying. Fighting a light spinnaker in virtually no wind is the most tiring part of any sail handling. On a run the sheet trimmer can easily see the luff and can 'tweak' the sheet if it starts to collapse. Pull in as much as possible by hand, from forward of the winch, and the luff will open and the sail set again. As soon as it sets let the sheet go back to its base point on the winch. When on a reach the sheet tail can be taken to windward so that the luff can still be seen; alternatively a crewman can relay instructions back from the foredeck to the trimmer. It is advisable in these conditions to pull the leeward clew in and tie on a light sheet (with a long bowline or light snapshackle) and remove the sheet and lazy spinnaker guy.

Spinnaker Reaching brings the spinnaker pole near to the forestay and hence the spinnaker guy bears on the windward shrouds. To prevent chafe at this point a reaching strut (or jockey pole) is used to hold the guy clear; it also acts as a spreader and gives the guy a better angle to work on. See diagram 26. The inboard end of the strut fits on an eye, or in a special fitting, on the side of the mast. The outboard end must be well secured, either by the use of two guys (in large yachts) or by tying it to the forward side of the mast cap shrouds (in smaller yachts).

Wraps. In almost any condition there is a danger of the spinnaker collapsing and wrapping itself round the forestay. A well wrapped spinnaker can take hours to unravel and for this reason a spinnaker net should always be used offshore. See diagram 27. The routine should be (a) spinnaker up, (b) jib down, (c) net up (using jib halyard). The net should only be taken down when a spinnaker shift is imminent. If the net is made of a reasonably heavy line, 10 mm say, it is much easier to handle and keep tangle-free when not in use. Should the net for some reason not be used, and the spinnaker wraps itself, this is what can be done: (a) run dead down wind, or slightly by the lee, to reduce the wind in the wrap; (b) send a man up the mast in a bosun's chair, then lower him down the forestay; (c) while he hangs on with his hands he unwraps the sail with his feet.

I have tried unclipping the halyard off a wrapped sail and bringing its head to the deck—it did not help. On one occasion we achieved a wrap in a fair breeze and it was impossible to unwind because of the amount of wind. The remedy was to hoist another spinnaker outside the wrap; when the new sail set the old was suddenly in still air and slid down the forestay to the deck! Since that nerve-racking occasion I have always used a net and have had no more trouble.

Spinnaker Gybing

If done incorrectly this can be a rather frightening operation. Some yachtsmen will avoid a spinnaker gybe at all costs—even to the extreme of lowering the sail, gybing, and rehoisting it. Actually a gybe done correctly is much safer and easier than a lower, and if the conditions allow a spinnaker to be carried at all, they will allow it to be gybed.

There are two gybing systems in common use. (a) The dip-pole, which uses only one pole, and (b) the slower and more cautious two-pole.

The two-pole gybe is used more frequently deep sea; better sail control is maintained, especially if a sea is running. The dip-pole is faster and this gives it its big advantage inshore, as it allows a tighter alteration of course. It is worth discussing both systems even though the two-pole system is preferred; the dip-pole may have to be used if one of the poles becomes damaged.

Two-pole gybe. This example describes the manoeuvre from port (the wind on the port quarter, the port pole in use) to starboard (the wind on the starboard quarter, starboard pole in use):

1. Check that the port (lazy) spinnaker sheet is over the pole end; if it has fallen off try to flick it back over. If this fails continue anyway.
2. Take the starboard pole and place the inboard end on the mast track.
3. Fix the starboard topping lift, pole guy and fore guy to the pole's outboard end. Hoist to shoulder height.
4. Take a bight of the starboard (lazy) spinnaker guy and loop it through the pole end. Make sure it is the correct way through; it should come from the leeward clew, forward to the bow, over the top of the pole, and back through the jaws from forward to aft. See diagram 28a.
5. Hoist the starboard pole inboard end until it is level with the port one; if the mast has only one heel track, with both fittings on the same car, the starboard pole will have been lifted to the correct height by step 2.
6. Hoist the outboard end of the starboard pole and pull it aft, taking in the starboard (lazy) spinnaker guy so that the pole end fetches up at the starboard clew. A useful tip here is to ease the starboard spinnaker sheet slightly as the pole is coming up and aft, which lets the clew move forward to meet the pole end. The spinnaker is now symmetrical with two poles set and weight in both spinnaker guys.
7. Alter course to starboard, moving the apparent wind from 30° off the stern to port to 30° off the stern to starboard. The main gybes under the control of the mainsheet and vang; the sheet should be taken in as the vang and/or preventer are eased. Once the main is nearly central the yacht is gybed and the vang and/or preventer eased under control to allow the main across the centre line. Once the weight is on the sheet again the vang/preventer can be let go, the sheet eased and the vang/preventer rigged immediately on the new leeward (port) side. See diagram 28b.
8. To clear away the port pole take the weight of the spinnaker on the port sheet.
9. Pull the release wire at the inboard end of the port pole which will open the jaws of

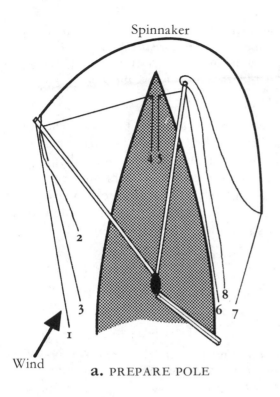

Spinnaker

Wind

a. PREPARE POLE

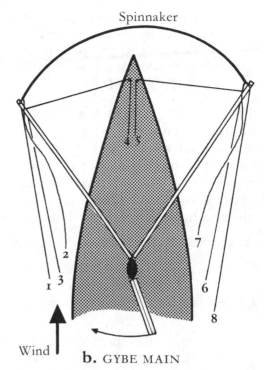

Spinnaker

Wind

b. GYBE MAIN

1. Port spinnaker guy
2. Port spinnaker sheet
3. Port pole guy
4. Port fore guy
5. Stb. fore guy
6. Stb. pole guy
7. Stb. spinnaker sheet
8. Stb. spinnaker guy

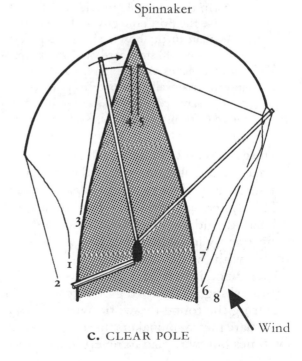

Spinnaker

c. CLEAR POLE

Wind

28. *Two-pole gybing.*

the outboard end. The pole should be lowered immediately away from the port spinnaker guy which is now free of the pole end. Trim the sheet as required.

10. Ease the port pole guy and port topping lift and take in the port fore guy; the pole swings in and down to the foredeck under perfect control. See diagram 28c.

11. Stow the port pole.

There can be a complication if the port sheet is under the port pole at the start of a gybe. This will make moves 8 and 9 more difficult. When the pole jaws are opened the pole cannot fall away from the guy; instead the guy must be cleared by skilfully juggling the weight of the sail from guy to sheet. Once it is clear take the weight on the guy. The port sheet—still under the pole—is slackened completely to allow the pole to be lowered clear to the foredeck. Once there, a crewman can lift the port sheet over the pole and free it; the weight is then taken back on the port sheet and all is well.

As can be seen the spinnaker is under tight control at all times.

Single-pole gybe for the same manoeuvre would be performed as follows:

1. Remove the inner forestay, babystay and spinnaker net. The foredeck is now clear.
2. Take a bight of the lazy spinnaker guy forward to the forestay and standby.
3. On the port side take the weight on the port (lazy) sheet.
4. Snap the port pole to release it from the port spinnaker guy. See 8 above.
5. Ease the port pole guy and topping lift and pull in the port fore guy.
6. A man in the bow swings the pole inside the forestay, quickly changes the pole guys—port off, starboard on—and snaps the starboard spinnaker guy through the pole end. He leaves the topping lift and fore guy alone. Simultaneously the helmsman gybes and the mainsail goes over to port, controlled as above.
7. The same pole is then swung out to starboard and hauled to the starboard clew. See move 6 from the previous system.

The gybe is now complete. This manoeuvre is even quicker if pole guys are not used; this may be possible on small and medium yachts, but I prefer the security and control that a pole guy gives to a heavy spar in a seaway.

This system is quick. The only disadvantage is that it requires excellent crew co-ordination, and good helming, to keep down to a minimum the time the spinnaker is flying free. A less experienced crew can two-pole gybe with ease, but they may have trouble with the dip-pole.

If the wind is light, and the pole set low, it will be necessary to hoist its inboard end before gybing, in order to give it room to dip inside the forestay.

During the round-the-world race on *Great Britain II* we used two poles to gybe our 470 square metre spinnakers, until a pole became damaged; we successfully dip-poled a few times but were glad to revert to the old system as soon as the other pole was fixed.

Spinnaker Lowering

The surest way to get a spinnaker down is to leave it up until the wind takes it down for you. One occasionally hears of skippers who have done just that—they obviously suffer from too much money and too little sense. One also hears of yachtsmen sailing at the limit of control with a flare, or Very pistol in hand, ready to blow the spinnaker out of the sky just as it starts to take over the yacht. Again, this system is a bit extreme and a slightly more scientific approach should save a few nerves—and money.

In recent years several spinnaker lowering systems have been developed for use inshore where speed of sail handling is vital. These systems basically involve bringing the sail down to the foredeck—probably with the help of a recovery line fixed to the dead centre of the sail—with the guy and lazy sheet still attached. The advantages of this system are: (a) the sail can be lowered without the need to winch down the pole into reach, and (b) the sail is gathered to the foredeck clear of the genoa trimmers and helmsmen. The system is unsuitable for rough weather and difficult to use in any weather on large yachts. The problem is that while the sail comes down perfectly well, it becomes difficult to control on the flat foredeck; there is no convenient cockpit to shove the sail into—a danger in bad weather. We also found on *Great Britain II* that if the crew lose control of the sail during lowering, the fact that it is still attached to its guy compounds the problem. A nasty incident in the Roaring Forties taught me this fact; it is told as a cautionary tale in the chapter on health. The result of this and other experimentation brings me to recommend lowering a spinnaker in the conventional way under the boom. As there is no leeward mark to round in mid-ocean the speed of the manoeuvre is not critical.

This is how the spinnaker should be lowered:

1. Hoist and set the jib.
2. Ensure that the lazy sheet and the pole guy are slack on the windward side.
3. Take the lazy guy forward on the leeward side so that it comes from the clew of the sail into the yacht underneath the boom but aft of the shrouds. Standby to recover the sail using this lazy guy, which can be made fast well inboard—within reach of several hands.
4. Ease the spinnaker guy forward, ease the topping lift and winch in the pole fore guy (it needs a lot of winching in a breeze); this brings the pole forward and down until it is within reach of a man on the foredeck.
5. When the pole end is within reach snap the shackle (see diagram 24) which releases the spinnaker from its combined guy and lazy sheet. Be careful: the pole will jump when the weight comes off it. It should be noted here that 'snapping the spinnaker' and 'snapping the pole' are two different operations: the former leaves the guy in the pole end but releases the sail, the latter opens the jaws to release the guy but with the spinnaker still attached. It has been known for enthusiastic amateurs to snap the pole instead of the spinnaker, in an attempt to lower the sail. It does not work!
6. The spinnaker is now flying like a flag behind the mainsail. The halyard should be eased and the sail gathered in. Make sure the foot is brought in clear of the water as the

sail starts to come down. The crew gathering the sail should sit well inboard to give themselves plenty of room; this is also safer, as the spinnaker has some deck to land on.
7. Stow the pole and clear away all guys, sheets and the halyard.

The problem with this method is that it takes a while to winch the pole down to a position where the spinnaker can be released.

Caught in a Squall with the sail required to come down in a hurry, the following emergency routine could be followed:

1. Tighten the pole guy.
2. Let go the lazy sheet—make sure there is no knot in its end.
3. Check there is no knot in the end of the spinnaker guy and then let it go.
4. The spinnaker guy and sheet run out through their leads and clear of the pole, which is still held safely by its own guy.
5. Lower the sail under the boom in the normal way, recovering the lazy sheet and spinnaker guy out of the water as soon as the clew is in hand.

A refinement to this system was used by two yachts in the 1977 round-the-world race; this was to fly the spinnaker with a standing line from the spinnaker pole outboard end to the snapshackle (see diagram 29). For a quick lower the pole guy is kept tight and the spinnaker guy eased; weight comes on the standing line, which automatically snaps the spinnaker, which can then be lowered conventionally. Personally I would not use the system; I would worry about the possibility of the sail snapping accidentally, wasting a lot of time.

Spinnaker Changing

The simplest system, and the one in common use deep sea, is to hoist a genoa, lower one spinnaker, hoist the other, and lower the genoa again. Unless sailing with an experienced crew this is probably the best bet in all conditions. However, if it is not too rough and the crew are up to it, time and speed can be saved by peeling spinnakers. This is how it is done:

1. Prepare the new spinnaker on deck; attach the second halyard to the head and a spare sheet to the leeward clew; take the windward leg round forward of the forestay in readiness for step 3.
2. Ease the pole forward and down so that it is within reach of a man on the foredeck. Steer on a reach to keep the sail full.
3. Attach the windward clew of the new spinnaker to the eye on the end of the spinnaker guy using a second snap shackle alongside the old one which at that time holds the spinnaker. See diagram 30.

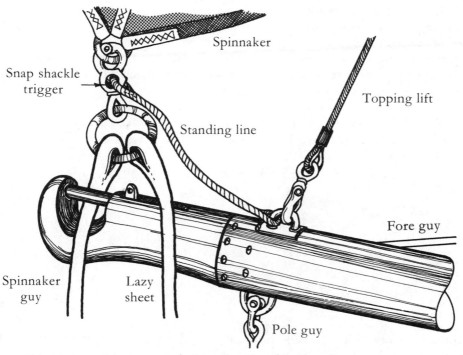

Spinnaker

Snap shackle
trigger

Standing line

Topping lift

Fore guy

Spinnaker
guy

Lazy
sheet

Pole guy

29. *Automatic spinnaker snapping.*

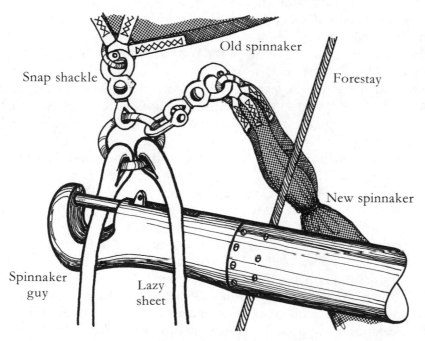

Old spinnaker

Snap shackle

Forestay

New spinnaker

Spinnaker
guy

Lazy
sheet

30. *Spinnaker peel arrangement.*

4. Hoist the new spinnaker—it must be in stops.

5. Sheet in the new spinnaker, and as it breaks out snap the old one which peels off the back of the new one.

6. Lower the old sail and trim the new one correctly.

7. If a gybe is anticipated pull in the leeward clew and attach the proper sheet and lazy spinnaker guy, then take off the spare sheet.

A peel from the leeward to the windward halyard does not cross halyards. A peel from the windward to the leeward does. After two peels it is necessary to go aloft and untangle the halyards.

A successful spinnaker peel is one of the most satisfying sail operations.

BLOOPERS AND STAYSAILS

Bloopers

No-one seems to know what to call these sails. In England they were, and still are occasionally, called Big Boys. Elsewhere the term was Blooper, and now some sailmakers want to call them Shooters.

A blooper is a sail that is unlikely to be used by a cruising yacht. It is not an easy sail to set well, especially in the rolling conditions so often encountered in deep sea. However, they were used to advantage by all yachts in the 1977 world race—even in the Southern Ocean—so we must look at the beast closely.

Bloopers evolved in the endless search for more sail area down wind. A spinnaker is limited in size by the International Offshore Rule, and two spinnakers may not be set at the same time. But to set a genoa with a spinnaker *is* allowed. In the early 1970's it was found that a genoa, set loose-luffed to leeward of the spinnaker on a long halyard, which let it fly to leeward of the mainsail, would catch some wind. Very careful trimming of the halyard and the sheet, which leads to the stern, was required. It was not long before sails were custom made for this job and hence the blooper was born. The sail has to measure legally as a jib but can be constructed similarly to a spinnaker, and out of spinnaker material.

The correct trim of a blooper is fairly hard to achieve. The halyard must be slack enough to allow the sail to blow well to leeward; it sets with the foot near the water— O.K. as long as it does not collapse. The tack is fixed to the forepeak by a 75 cm strop (the maximum allowed by the rules); the sheet is kept well eased so that the sail pulls forward and not sideways. See diagram 31. In any amount of sea, or in variable wind, a great deal of 'tweaking' is required. Once set the blooper will help the control of the yacht in medium off wind work, as it balances the large area of the spinnaker. The

31. *Spinnaker and blooper.*

combination of these two sails keeps the centre of effort of the sail plan nearer the yacht's centre line. The blooper can be used to advantage in wind directions from 20°–45° off the stern, and in winds from 2–15 knots apparent. Below two knots it will be impossible to set and above 15 knots the risk is not worth taking with a long way to go.

The blooper is hoisted using the spare spinnaker halyard, with the sheet completely free, so that it does not fill until right up; once it sets the halyard can probably be eased back a few feet to get better trim. Although it can be stopped, this is not necessary before hoisting. Getting it down can be done in two ways. In normal conditions let the sheet fly and recover the sail from the tack to the foredeck. This is tricky in strong winds, as only one or two pairs of hands can reach the sail over the bow. Therefore it is better, in a breeze, to release the tack and take the sail in, sheet first, like a spinnaker.

Spinnaker Staysail

When the wind is near the beam and a blooper cannot be set is the time for a spinnaker staysail. Several shapes and sizes have been tried—tall and thin or short and fat—but now the general favourite is a full hoist sail with a high clew and some mainsail overlap. The staysail should be tacked down forward of the mast, at a distance from it equal to 70% of the foredeck length, and on the centre line if the wind is on the beam. As the wind moves aft, and the spinnaker pole moves round, the staysail tack can be moved out to windward. But if it interferes in any way with the spinnaker's air it should be taken down.

Mizzen Staysails

The mizzen mast can be used to carry staysails when off the wind. This is the time the ketch or yawl rig comes into its own. The most common staysail is one which is, in effect, a large jib in front of the mizzen mast. The staysail tacks down on the deck at a point between the main and mizzen masts, level with the mid-point of the main boom and slightly to windward of the centre line. See diagram 32. The sail is hoisted loose-luffed on a halyard to the head of the mizzen mast, and sets to leeward of the main mast backstay; the luff should be as tight as possible, but watch for chafe on the backstay itself. Lead the sheet to a block at the end of the mizzen boom. This sail can be used effectively in a wind range from 20° forward of the beam to 45° aft of the beam.

Mizzen Spinnaker

A small spinnaker can be set instead of the mizzen staysail when the wind is nearer the stern. Again it is set to leeward of the main backstay with a guy from the windward clew

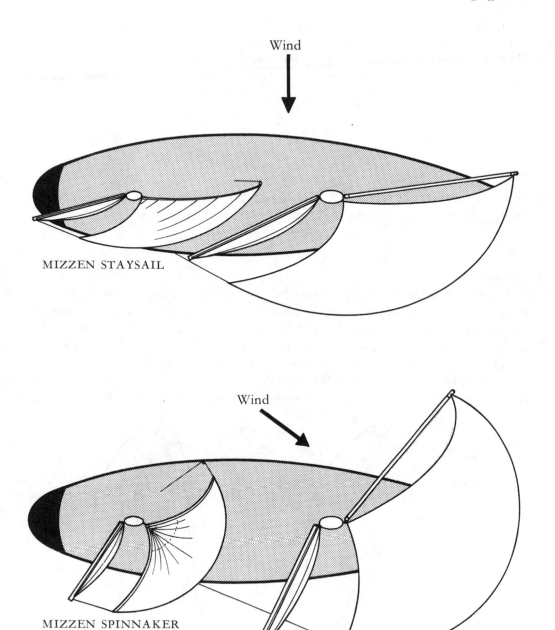

Wind

MIZZEN STAYSAIL

Wind

MIZZEN SPINNAKER

32. *Mizzen staysail and spinnaker.*

across to the windward rail, and a sheet to the end of the mizzen boom. See diagram 32. It is possible to set this mizzen spinnaker with the wind practically astern, but in this case it will pay to lower the mizzen sail in order to get clearer air. In light winds it is often best to forget the mizzen altogether and concentrate on a main spinnaker and blooper.

DOWNWIND WITHOUT A SPINNAKER

This section applies to the cruising yacht that does not wish to set a spinnaker and also to the racing yacht which, because of extreme conditions, dare not.

Reaching

When reaching in a rising wind the time when it becomes necessary to reduce sail will be obvious. As well as simply being overpowered there is no future in broaching around the ocean. The agony may be prolonged by carrying a smaller spinnaker and by reefing the main. Eventually an alternative will be needed and for this the best sail is the blast reacher. It has a high clew, clear of the waves, and as it is set on the forestay not only is it under control, but all its drive is in the right direction. This allows for very fast and safe reaching. Under these circumstances it would be a mistake to carry the larger number

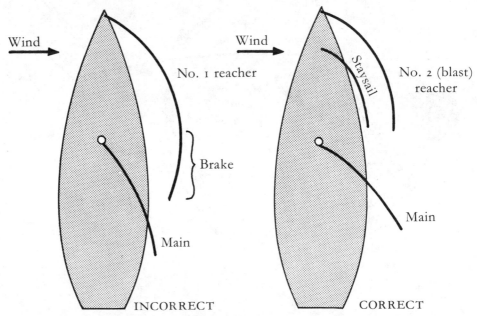

33. *Beam reaching in strong wind.*

one reacher because with an eased sheet, the aft part of the sail would curve back into the yacht and act as a brake. The blast reacher, set with a staysail inside it, is a much better bet. See diagram 33. A cruising yacht should set its No 3 jib and staysail.

Running

When running with a storm spinnaker the time to take it down, as mentioned earlier, is when the helmsman starts to lose control. This loss of control will appear as a roll which gets worse and worse; the roll starts as the spinnaker swings slightly to leeward; the drive from the sail is then slightly to leeward as well as forward and this tugs the mast over to that side. The spinnaker then oscillates to windward, pulling the mast after it. The rolls get larger and larger and the yacht becomes impossible to steer for two reasons. Firstly the effort of the sails as they swing to one side causes a turning moment, and secondly, as the vessel heels, the underwater shape also causes it to turn. Both these factors take the yacht away from the direction of roll.

The result is a boat chasing its sails first one way, then the other. The helmsman can try and help by steering into the roll, i.e. in a starboard roll he steers to starboard to try and keep the yacht under the sails. Eventually the rolls will develop to such an extent that a broach results. The yacht will spin round, beam onto the wind, and waves either to windward or leeward. In the former case the boom goes in the water, spinnaker pole in the air and the spinnaker collapses and probably blows out. The latter case is still worse as the boom is in the air, the mainsail backed, the spinnaker pole in the water and something, possibly the mast, will break. All these antics are common practice when racing inshore, but are best avoided deep sea.

As soon as the yacht is near the edge of control, take down the spinnaker and boom out a jib. The best sails to boom out are the blast reacher on a racing yacht, and either the No 2 or No 3 genoa/jib on a cruising yacht. Whichever sail is used must have a high clew to keep the pole clear of the waves; it is also important for the sail not to be too long for the pole—as the No 1 reacher would be. A boomed-out sail will set provided the wind is within 40° of the stern.

Setting a Boomed out Jib. For example, assume that the wind is on the port quarter and booming out a sail is desired. This is the routine:

1. Hoist the blast reacher (or No 2 or 3 jib if a cruising yacht) and lower the spinnaker as described previously.
2. The blast reacher is set to starboard with the wind 40° off the stern to port.
3. Rig the port spinnaker pole with a topping lift, fore guy and pole guy; the outboard end should be at shoulder height and held off the forestay by the pole guy.
4. Place the port (lazy) reacher sheet through the pole jaws.
5. Hoist the pole's inboard end to the top of the track.

6. Hoist the outboard end and take in the pole guy, until the pole is horizontal and squared up (as for a spinnaker run); secure all pole controls. See diagram 34a.

7. Ease the starboard sheet and take in the port; do not let the starboard sheet go completely, as this will allow the clew to blow right forward to starboard of the forestay. Keep the clew under control and tight in to the inner forestay. See diagram 34b.

8. As the clew passes the centre line the starboard sheet can be let go and the port one winched further until the clew reaches the pole end. It is imperative that the clew comes hard against the jaws, and the pole guy must be kept slack. See diagram 34c. If the jib is small, ease the pole forward, so that the clew can reach it. If this is not done the sheet will work through the jaws at the pole end and chafe through in an hour or less. As soon as the reacher is across the centre of the yacht the helmsman should steer with the wind 20° off the stern to port.

9. When the manoeuvre is completed the yacht can be sailed with the wind from dead astern to 40° off the stern to port. This still allows a safety margin of 10° or so.

Gybing with a boomed out jib is very simple. Rig the second pole behind the mainsail with the starboard (lazy) jib sheet through its outboard end. As the yacht and mainsail are gybed the clew of the jib is winched across from one pole end to the other. The old pole is then stowed.

To unrig the boom the reverse of the boom out procedure can be followed. It is quicker, however, to do it like this:

1. The jib is boomed out to port; make sure the port sheet is free to run.

2. Alter course to port until the wind is about 50° to 60° off the stern to port. This will be enough to back the boomed-out jib.

3. As it backs let the port sheet run free and the sail will fly fast and clearly to the starboard side, where it can be sheeted home.

4. Lower and stow the pole.

Should the angle of the wind alter when broad reaching, thereby putting the jib in the lee of the mainsail, booming out the sail will suit the new wind direction. Similarly, if the wind angle goes to the quarter when boomed out and threatens to back the jib, the sail will set nicely if back on the same side as the mainsail.

Incidentally, an important point that is brought up in booming out the jib is the length of the jib sheets. The ability to boom out requires longer jib sheets than normal and it is this requirement that should determine the length of the sheet. It has to go from the clew of the sail, round the inner forestay, out to the pole end, back to the lead block and to a winch. See diagram 34a. An approximate guide is twice the length of the yacht, but it might be wise to rig the pole in harbour and measure the length correctly.

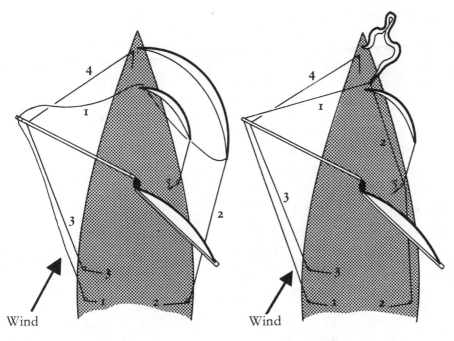

a. PREPARE POLE   **b.** WINCH JIB OVER

1. Port blast reacher sheet
2. Stb. blast reacher sheet
3. Pole guy
4. Pole fore guy
5. Staysail sheet

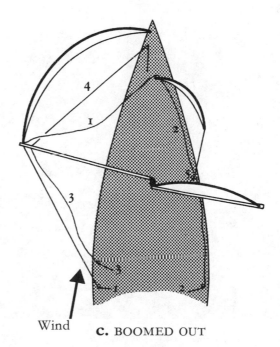

c. BOOMED OUT

34. *Routine for 'booming out' a reacher or jib.*

SUMMARY OF WHICH SAILS AND WHEN

Accepting the fact that all yachts are different, that crew experience varies, and that the nature of the voyage affects sail carrying decisions, I am still going to make some suggestions which effectively summarise the previous two chapters.

In diagram 35 the recommendations are for the average trans-ocean racing yacht. The sail wardrobe, and the code letters, are as suggested in chapter 1, and are repeated here for reference purposes. The wind strengths are apparent, so where, for instance, a reef is suggested at 22 knots on all points of sailing, this means when beating in 17 knots true, or running in 30 knots true—both of which are 22 knots apparent. The wind directions are also apparent, i.e. as read by instruments on board.

Code for diagram 35, for racing yachts:

M	Full Main	2	No 2 Genoa	Sp.St	Spinnaker Staysail
M1	Main—1 reef	3	No 3 Genoa	B	Blooper
M2	Main—2 reefs	J3	No 3 Jib Top	F.Sp	Floater Spinnaker
M3	Main—3 reefs	J4	No 4 Jib Top	L.Sp	Light Spinnaker
T	Trysail	SJ	Storm Jib	M.Sp	Medium Spinnaker
D	Drifter	R	Reacher	H.Sp	Heavy Spinnaker
1L	Light No 1 Genoa	BR	Blast Reacher	S.Sp	Storm Spinnaker
1H	Heavy No 1 Genoa	St	Working Staysail		

Running with an incorrectly boomed out No. 4 jib top. The pole end should be up against the clew of the sail.

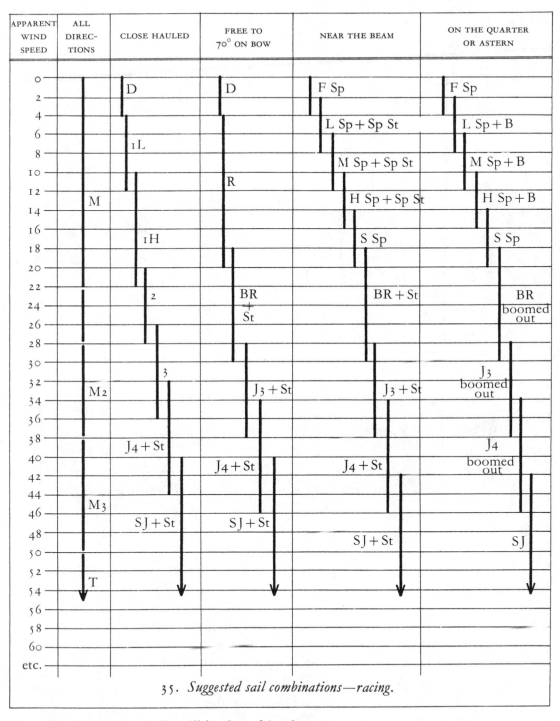

35. *Suggested sail combinations—racing.*

More details of these sails will be found in chapter 1.

APPARENT WIND SPEED	ALL DIRECTIONS	CLOSE HAULED TO WELL AFT OF ABEAM	NEAR THE STERN
0			
2			
4			
6		1	1
8			
10			
12	M		
14			2 Boomed out
16			
18		2	
20			
22	M1		
24		3 + St	3 Boomed out
26			
28	M2		
30		4 + St	
32			
34	M3		4
36			
38			
40			
42		SJ	SJ only
44	T		
46			
48			
50		NO SAIL—LIE A-HULL OR RUN OFF	
52			
54			
56			
58			
60			
etc.			

36. *Suggested sail combinations—cruising.*

In diagram 36 are the recommendations for the much simpler cruising yacht sail wardrobe, as described in chapter 1. The codes are repeated here for ease of reference.

Code for diagram 36, for cruising yachts:

M	Mainsail	1	No 1 Genoa high clew
M1	Mainsail—1 reef	2	No 2 Genoa high clew
M2	Mainsail—2 reefs	3	No 3 Jib high clew
M3	Mainsail—3 reefs	4	No 4 Jib high clew
T	Trysail	SJ	Storm Jib
St	Staysail		

6 Crew Safety and Yacht Survival

A yacht and its crew can expect no outside help, should they run into trouble in the middle of an ocean. Although there are a lot of ships at sea, an ocean is a big place and the chances of one being near when needed, are very remote. Therefore it is essential for a yacht sailing deep sea to be as independent as possible; careful preparation and correct heavy weather procedures will reduce the chances of an emergency.

CREW SAFETY

Clothes

Cold and damp can dangerously reduce a crew's efficiency. A cold, wet man is far more likely to make a dangerous mistake than someone who is warm and dry. Fortunately, modern yachting clothes are very good indeed. Warmth is best taken care of, not by several sweaters, but by thermal underwear and a man-made, fibre-pile warm wear suit. The combination of the two is the best way to fight cold. A waterproof sailing suit (which used to be called oilskins and is now called foul weather gear) and boots complete the rig. This may seem to require a fortune, but it is worth paying for the best gear. Standing in the warmth of a boat show or a chandler's shop it is easy to convince oneself that cheap foul weather gear 'might be O.K', but halfway across the North Atlantic one might well change one's mind.

I learnt my lesson in the first round-the-world race in 1973. Before the start of the second leg—from Cape Town to Sydney—I was completely broke and unable to buy any warm wear or to replace the doubtful foul weather gear I had. As a result watches in the Roaring Forties, Fifties and Sixties were pretty miserable. Finally, in Australia, I decided to buy some new boots. Unfortunately the prices were high, and we were in the middle of a heat wave, so it was easy to spend the money on beer instead. Of course I paid for my folly; by the time we reached Cape Horn my boots leaked badly and my feet were permanently like ice. Be warned!

Safety Harness

There is much controversy over the value of safety harnesses. One view is that a person who falls overboard while securely hooked on to a fast moving yacht will be towed under and drowned before recovery is possible. This argument loses sight of the fact that the primary object of a harness, if properly used, is to stop the crewman going over the edge in the first place; a harness clipped to the centre of the yacht or to windward will pull tight before the wearer reaches the lee rail.

The big disadvantage of a harness is that it causes a crewman to lose manoeuvrability when hooked on. Also it is very often impractical to remain hooked on while moving around the deck—preparing for a sail change, for instance—as several harness hooks get jammed up on the same safety line; in fact when moving around the deck holding on there is less risk than when stationary and performing a job with both hands. In bad weather, harnesses should be used by the helmsman and watch sitting in the cockpit. There is more danger of going overboard in a broach while inactive, than when alert during a sail change.

A skipper should formulate his own rules about when and where a harness should be used. There are several danger points he should identify, such as the helmsman, the foredeck man hanking or unhanking a jib, and the crew recovering sail—see diagram 37. If the order is given to hook on, then hook on to a strong point inboard or to windward. Do not hook on to the guard rails, as they are often not strong enough and are also too near the edge of the boat. Do not hook on to the shrouds or stays (imagine where a person might end up if the yacht was knocked flat or worse). Special eyes should be fitted in the cockpit and two strong life lines rigged down either side deck. It is worth reminding yourself always to hold on rather than to rely solely on your harness.

A harness integral with a foul weather gear jacket is very convenient to put on and a lot quicker than struggling with the conventional type. The latter, however, with proper shoulder straps and worn good and tight, is stronger and more reliable.

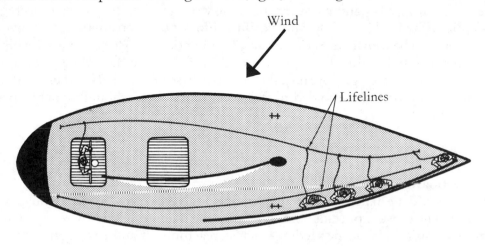

34. *Hook on to windward while helming and lowering a jib.*

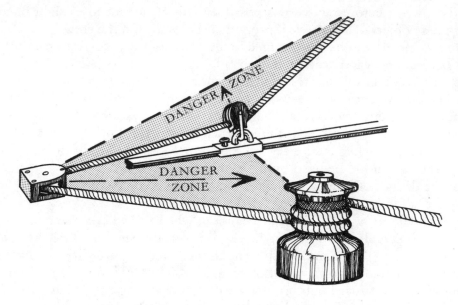

38. Beware of blocks breaking.

Gear Failure
Some accidents can be avoided if the crew are continually aware of what equipment could break and what would happen if it did. The failure of some equipment can be dangerous if anyone is standing or sitting in the wrong place. Beware of a sheet, guy or running backstay held in a V by a block. If the block fails then anything, or anyone, in the V is going to be damaged. See diagram 38. Other points to look out for are bights in a rope (they can pull tight), lazy spinnaker guys (if the sheet fails the guy will jump), spinnaker poles (in case a guy breaks), the boom (in case of accidental gybes), and several others which are basically avoided by common sense. Eyes should be kept open and heads down.

Man Overboard
All crew should be familiar with the routine for recovering a man who has gone overboard. The most important point is to keep the man in sight. Any recovery routine that means losing sight of the victim—such as reaching off and back again—is wrong. This is especially true when a sea is running, as even the smallest waves will hide a head in the water. The following method is suggested as having the best chance of success, assuming that a helmsman and two crew are on deck when a crewman goes overboard.

1. The helmsman shouts: 'Man overboard!' and starts a procedure to stop the yacht—see later.
2. The other crewman keeps his eye on the man, and if he can, throws overboard the lifebuoy, danbuoy (a float with pole and flag) and anything else that will float. He must keep his eye on the man, and if this precludes him throwing the lifebuoy etc., then this must be done by the first extra crew on deck.
3. The yacht is stopped and the man is in sight not far away. All the crew are now on deck. Lower the sails and motor back to the man. If the motor is out of action sail back.
4. Recover the man. If he is conscious, throw him a line. If he is unconscious, someone will have to get into the water to put a line on him. The hero who goes in should be well tied to the yacht. Hauling a man up the high side of a vessel is not easy in a seaway, but providing there is enough manpower it can be done. Even if he gets knocked about a bit he will not mind.

Stopping the Yacht. The helmsman stops the yacht as follows:

If the boat is close-hauled he throws the wheel over to windward and tacks; the sails are left alone so that they back. Once round, the wheel is put amidships and the yacht stops.

If reaching, the same rule applies; tack, but this time let the mainsail go over. The yacht stops.

If running without a spinnaker react as if reaching.

If running with a spinnaker the problem is greater. If a spinnaker is up it is to be hoped that more crew are available on deck to get rid of the sail. This is best done by letting go the sheets, guys *and* halyard. As soon as the spinnaker blows clear turn the yacht into the wind and it will stop. If the wind is light turn head to wind with the spinnaker up.

In the emergency take care that, when the motor is used, no ropes are over the edge near the propeller. There is a good chance of some sheet or other falling into the water in the rush to lower sail.

At night the man will most likely be found by sound rather than sight, so everyone should carry a whistle in their foul weather gear. In the dark the crewman whose job it is to keep his eye on the victim should throw over an automatic light (kept handy on the stern) and then keep that in sight, and also listen for the whistle. Needless to say everyone on deck should keep quiet.

Life-rafts

The last resort. Do not use a life-raft until the yacht is actually, finally sinking. If the yacht appears to be sinking, then by all means prepare the raft, but do not get into it until absolutely essential. In the 1979 Fastnet race storm 24 yachts were abandoned—nearly every one of which was believed to be sinking—and yet only five actually went under; the others were recovered. The proximity of rescue helicopters and a bad weather forecast encouraged people to leave their craft, but this does not alter the fact that yachts believed to be sinking, were in fact still floating. One of the reasons for this is that a capsizing yacht fills with water, appearing to be holed, when it rights itself. As the hull is pumped out the water level initially refuses to go down because water is running into the bilges from lockers and from the ends of the vessel.

In extremis the life-raft has to be used and all boats should be prepared for this eventuality. The raft should be stowed where it can be reached easily, and yet *not* where it can be trodden on. While running sailing charter-holidays I had the life-raft on one yacht stowed where it could be trodden on, despite instructions to the contrary. When it was sent off for servicing it was found to be useless. A tin of water had been squashed, had split open, and cut the raft material. Whether a raft is in a valise or in a glass fibre container, the best place for it is in a locker, or under a cockpit seat, specifically designed for the purpose.

When launching an automatically inflatable life-raft care must be taken with the trip line. This line is very long—about 18 metres—and very thin. It will be impossible to hold if a lot of wind and a large sea are pulling the raft away. Having launched the container the line is taken in by hand, in order to trip the automatic inflating mechanism. As the line comes in it should be made fast on board, so that the raft will be alongside the yacht when it inflates. Make sure a knife is handy to cut this line once the crew are aboard the raft. When the yacht *British Steel* foundered the skipper launched the raft; a breaking wave tore it away and it was impossible to hold the line. The end of its scope was reached, the line broke and the raft was gone. Fortunately, as it happened, the raft was not needed, but the lesson is clear—keep the line on a cleat or winch as the slack is taken up.

'Abandon Ship' Kit

If a yacht has to be abandoned it is likely to be done in a hurry, if not in a panic. For this reason it is a good idea to keep in one container, near the main hatch, the major items that one would wish to take into the raft. As an example, this is the system used by Naomi James during her solo circumnavigation. The 'abandon ship' pack was in a bin by the hatch. As well as this she had a priority list of other equipment taped by the exit; this list was in order of priority and indicated where the items were to be found. The theory was that she could read down the list as time allowed, calmly collecting gear without wasting precious seconds thinking 'Do I need this?' or 'Where is that stowed?' The list is reproduced in table 5.

TABLE 5—'ABANDON SHIP' PRIORITY LIST.

1. *Water*—By main hatch.
2. *Abandon Ship Kit*—In emergency bin.

3. *Emergency Radio*—Under companion way steps.
4. *Flares Container*—By main hatch.
5. *Medical Kit*—In emergency bin.
6. *Navigation Equipment*—Drawer under chart table.
7. *Radio Receiver*—Chart table.

The *Abandon Ship Kit* contained:

Life Jacket.	Tin opener.
Harness.	Solar still.
Spare foul weather gear.	Heliograph.
Spare clothes in sealed bag.	Pencils and paper.
Some tinned food, chocolate and raisins.	Life-raft survival book.
Torches and batteries.	

The other vital piece of equipment, a knife, was also kept by the main hatch, ready to cut the life-raft trip line.

Life-rafts are very small and only by carrying greater raft capacity than total crew could all this gear be loaded. However the point is—be prepared.

An important note is that water containers should have an inch or two of air in them; they will then float with their tops visible above the water should they have to be thrown into the sea.

Flares

Flares may be needed at times other than when abandoning ship. Make sure that the flares are in date and that sufficient are carried. White flares are for attracting attention— if in danger of being run down by a ship for instance. Red parachute flares are essential for indicating distress at a distance. Red hand flares are useful to help a rescue boat home-in to the distressed vessel. As manufacturers fit their own striking mechanism (there is no standardisation) make sure all the crew are familiar with the flares carried.

YACHT SURVIVAL

The only way to find out how to survive extreme weather conditions is actually to experience them. Different boats may require handling in different ways and trial and error is unfortunately the only way to find out which system suits a vessel best.

There are some universal principles which are worth studying.

Gales

When the wind is strong the biggest enemy is the waves that accompany it. It is possible to evade the wind (by reducing sail area), but impossible to evade the sea.

Going to windward in force 8 (40 knots of wind) is just possible with proper storm sails. A storm jib alone, or maybe a storm jib and trysail, would work best. The big danger is caused by pounding into the waves; even so it is surprising how much slamming a yacht will take before damage occurs. The helmsman can help a lot by good steering; he should luff up slightly as a wave approaches and, most importantly, bear away quickly at least 20° as the bows reach the peak of their rise. Thus the yacht, instead of going bows first into space and then crashing into the trough, will slide down the back of the wave sideways. The routine is repeated for the next wave. See diagram 39.

At night, when nothing can be seen, the helmsman should simply bear away quickly and momentarily as he feels the bows rise. Because of the speed of the wave and the reaction time of the helmsman and yacht, any bear-away action initiated as the bows rise, will just be in time for the fall into the trough. This action will not stop pounding altogether, but it will certainly help.

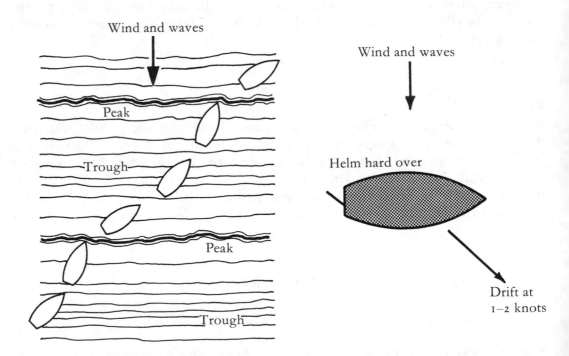

39. *Steering to windward through waves.* 40. *Drift while lying a-hull.*

The alteration of course as described above also suits the varying apparent wind. As the yacht rises up the face of the wave, it slows down; the bows rise and hence the rig kicks aft, which also slows the sails down relative to the wind. As the boat slows the apparent wind moves aft and is thus accommodated by the luff. As the yacht falls down the back of the wave it speeds up, the rig accelerates forward, and the apparent wind moves ahead. This time it is accommodated by the bear-away.

Off the wind, a yacht can keep sailing with only a storm jib, even in very severe conditions.

The biggest difficulty faced in a rising wind is lowering the mainsail; it will be blown into the mast and shrouds, to which it sticks like glue. There is no question of coming head to wind, as it will already be too rough for such action. The remedy, when cruising, is to get the main off in plenty of time. When racing, it is unlikely that the main will ever have to be taken right down. However, the same difficulties will be encountered while trying to reef. A useful idea here is to reeve lines through the reefing eyes on the luff of the sail; these lines can be led to a winch or hauled on by several crew and the sail will come down easily.

We had this problem on *Great Britain II*, as there is no easy way of gripping a mainsail to pull it down; on one occasion we rigged lines through all three luff eyes and this enabled six or more crew to get a good pull and the problem was solved.

The time may come when, even with only a storm jib, it is not possible to sail. A yacht going to windward will find it is making no progress; a yacht off the wind may start to surf and broach uncontrollably. So what is to be done? If the aim is to get to windward, and the seas are not overwhelming, then lying a-hull is the best practice; if the waves are dangerously large, it will be safer to run off. Running off is obviously the better course if the desired direction of progress is to leeward anyway.

Lie A-Hull

Take down, and lash, all sails. Secure the helm hard over in the direction that will hold the bows up towards the wind. The yacht will lie beam on to the wind and seas and will drift at about 1 to 1½ knots in the direction shown in diagram 40. There will be a considerable rolling motion and this is the danger if the waves are too steep and large. A breaking wave could roll the yacht over with subsequent loss of mast and maybe hull damage.

The point at which the waves become dangerous depends on the size and the shape of the vessel: Chay Blyth found that *British Steel*, an 18-metre Robert Clark design, would lie a-hull happily in heavy weather. Naomi James, on the other hand, was knocked almost upside down on the only occasion she tried lying a-hull in her Van de Stadt designed 16-metre yacht. In general I favour lying a-hull when beating in Force 7, say, and a rest is required. The big advantage is that no-one is needed on the helm—or on deck at all. In Force 8 or more I favour running off.

Run Off

Take down and lash all sails; steer downwind with the windage of the hull and rigging providing the driving force. The yacht should be steered dead downwind and will probably make about 5 knots in winds over Force 8. Provided there is sea room to leeward, running off is reasonably safe and comfortable. There are, of course, dangers: a wave over the stern is one, but this is fairly rare provided the yacht has a buoyant counter. The accommodation hatch should be kept closed, so that if a wave does come aboard, no water goes below.

If the wind reaches storm force the yacht may start to surf even under bare poles. A surf could result in a broach or a pitch-pole (the bows dig under and the stern cartwheels over the top). By steering 20° or so off dead downwind the danger of pitch-poling is reduced and that of broaching increased. As broaching is the lesser evil, this is a good plan in a smaller yacht. A large vessel—over 15-metres—is unlikely to pitch-pole and should be kept dead downwind.

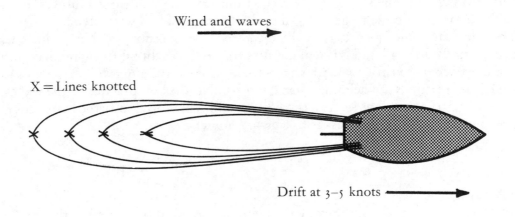

41. *Towing warps.*

Stream Warps

A better way to handle the dangers of surfing is to stream warps which slow the yacht down, back to 5 knots or so. Several long ropes will be required to have the necessary effect: put out the jib sheets, knotted together so that they form a bight; put out the anchor warp, spinnaker sheets and mooring warps. Four long loops should be enough to slow down a 16-metre craft. The slower speed will increase the danger of a wave over the stern, but that is a small price to pay for the greatly increased control. See diagram 41.

There can be no hard and fast rule, and no system is going to give 100% protection from a storm. It is interesting to note the experience gained from the 1979 Fastnet race. During the storm over 150 yachts tried lying a-hull, running off, and streaming warps. An analysis of the results of these tactics show that there was equal danger of capsize regardless of which was adopted. I believe this was due to the very mixed up nature of the seas, with waves coming from all directions. A yacht running off downwind was in as much danger of receiving a breaking beam sea as a yacht lying a-hull. In the middle of an ocean, and in a more ordered sea, I believe running off is safer than lying a-hull. In a storm in the Bay of Biscay in January 1977 we lay a-hull in a 15-metre cruising yacht. We were knocked flat and the engine broke free of its mounting. We then ran off and the world became safe and comfortable again.

Steering Failure

The yacht is sailing well, there is a lot of weight on the wheel, and suddenly it goes completely slack—a horrible feeling. Hopefully the breakage is in the steering linkage and the rudder is still there. The first thing to do is to fit the emergency tiller to the rudder stock head and steer with that. If this has no effect the rudder is probably broken and it will be necessary to lower sail and investigate. If the emergency tiller is fitted quickly, and it works, then sail can probably be left up. In some cases the tiller is short and not as powerful as a geared wheel; this, combined with heavy steering conditions, may mean sail has to be reduced. In either case, once the yacht is sailing under control, the breakage can be investigated. If the linkage is a wire and quadrant system it will be easy to inspect and a broken wire can be quickly replaced; if the linkage is a bevel box, rod, gearbox system, it will probably be impossible to fix at sea. In fact a more likely problem with a gearbox is that it can become stiff or seize up.

A steering failure on Naomi James's *Express Crusader* nearly caused a serious problem during her circumnavigation. The steering gear box seized up and for the last 3,000 miles of the voyage the yacht was controlled by the self-steering alone. In order to navigate up the river Dart at the end of the journey the gear box had to be hack-sawed free of the rudder stock, so that the emergency tiller could be used.

A steering failure on *Great Britain II* in the Roaring Forties was easier to fix. While running fast under spinnaker we occasionally needed the weight of two crew on the wheel to prevent a broach. On one of these occasions the steering broke. We lowered the spinnaker and then fitted the emergency tiller. The fault was a break in a steering wire, but we had several spares, and the only difficulty encountered during fitting one of these, was in the removal of one of the sheeves through which it had to be led. Even so we were back to top speed in less than 20 minutes.

A more serious case occurred on board a Castle 15-metre cruising ketch while on charter in the English Channel. The wheel rudder linkage failed in mid-Channel, and the emergency tiller was fitted; this also failed, as the mild steel was soon worn away by the

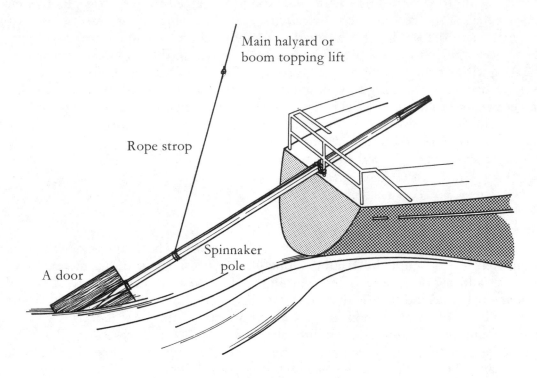

Main halyard or
boom topping lift

Rope strop

Spinnaker
pole

A door

42. *An emergency steering system.*

stainless steel rudder stock. Fortunately the crew were able to get the yacht sailing to windward under the balance of the rig. Tacking was just possible if the mizzen was hauled way to windward and then let go as the bow went through the wind. Eventually the home port was safely reached.

Complete loss of the rudder is another matter. If this happens in mid-ocean, some way of controlling direction must be found. Balancing the yacht by sails alone will probably only be possible while sailing to windward.

A Jury rudder can be made using a spinnaker pole with a piece of wood, aluminium, door or locker top lashed to the end. See diagram 42. It would be a mistake to expect too much from such a jury system. Lines from the inboard end led to winches, and a halyard to the mid point of the pole may help to rig and control it. The 24-metre *Kriter II* sailed several hundred miles back to Sydney using this rig, after losing her rudder in the Clipper ship race of 1976. Because of that success, and because there is no alternative, this course of action could be recommended.

Dismasting

Unlike the redoubtable Olivier de Kersauson ('I have broken over 100 metres of mast') I have only been dismasted in a dinghy. I have, however, received a lot of advice from those unfortunate enough to lose their rigs. Some of it is recorded here.

Perhaps the mast has broken and has gone over the side: it will still be attached to the yacht by the shrouds, halyards and sails. The traditional approach is to cut everything free before any damage is done. The problem is, that after the resultant mess has been cleared, a jury rig has to be made, and to achieve this some part of what has already hastily been cut clear may be needed. If the hull is in imminent danger of damage from the wreckage in the water, then obviously it should be cut away. Bolt croppers are usually carried for the purpose of cutting rigging; however, they are difficult to use as they require both hands and will make little impression on stainless wire, and even less on rod rigging. A hack-saw can be used but several blades will be needed. The best plan is to clear any rigging with no weight on it by undoing a split-pin and removing a clevis-pin. Note that the split-pin should be splayed 30° or so, not bent back through 180°. Once all slack rigging is released the remaining wire or wires under tension will have to be attacked with hacksaw or cutters.

Should the mast be in a position where it is not damaging the hull, it is worth seeing what can be saved; any sheets, halyards or the boom may come in handy. Maybe the bottom few feet of the mast itself can be salvaged; this would give a good base for the jury rig.

A jury rig can be made from spinnaker poles, the boom, part of the mast, or any combination of these. It is surprisingly difficult to get a spar, or spars, vertical on a flush deck. Their weight, plus that of the jury shrouds, blocks and halyards makes raising them very hard. When the 16-metre trimaran *Great Britain IV* was dismasted in mid-Atlantic, Chay Blyth cut everything free and was left with only the boom and a lightweight spinnaker pole. He and his single crew were unable to get the boom to the vertical. They now think that if they had saved a stump of mast, they would have had less trouble. As it was, they had to use the flimsy spinnaker pole, which soon bent.

Once a jury mast is rigged sail can be set. Even the smallest sails may have to be set on their sides; alternatively a knot tied in the head of a sail is a good way to make it smaller.

7 Navigational Day's Work

All the navigational activities to be performed each day at sea are discussed in this chapter. Starting at noon one day with a position and a planned destination, we can work through all the activities required to find a yacht's position the next day. The actual computation of a sunsight, which is a sub-section of the day's work, will be found in the next chapter. Navigation for speed, as well as safety, is important. For that reason I have included in this chapter a discussion of V.M.G. (velocity made good) for the various points of sailing.

Daily Routine

Laying off a Course. One of the first decisions of the day must be which way to steer. As a result of some planning (see chapter 2) there is now a line on the chart representing the ideal route. It is a simple matter to measure that course on the compass rose. As we are steering a magnetic course, it will be necessary to allow for the difference between the true and magnetic directions.

Magnetic Variation and Deviation. It is quite possible for the coastal navigator never to have had to think about the magnetic variation of the world, or the deviation of his yacht. Assuming the compass is fairly well adjusted, he may simply have used the magnetic compass rose on the chart for all purposes. This is quite acceptable. Unfortunately, however, the difference between the direction of true and magnetic north (and hence between true and magnetic bearings or courses) varies in different parts of the world. For this reason, on charts covering more than a few hundred miles, overall compass roses cannot be used, and indeed are not printed. Hence an understanding of variation is required for an ocean crossing.

The magnetic compass is affected by two factors—variation and deviation. Deviation is caused by the local effect of the yacht and is usually only a degree or two. It is corrected when the compass is swung. Unfortunately, deviation can change without one knowing, and this will cause compass error.

Variation is the difference in direction between true and magnetic north. It can be found from the chart of the ocean or from a special world chart. Either of these charts will have lines of equal variation. To establish the variation take the value of the line nearest to the position of the yacht. See diagram 43.

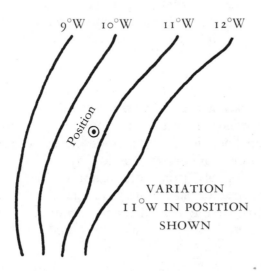

43. *Variation as shown on a chart.*

The combination of variation and deviation is the total compass difference. In practice, once the compass has been swung, ignore deviation. To set your course for the first few days simply measure it on the true compass rose and apply the variation, as read from the chart, to find the magnetic course. For example:

True course required	Variation	Compass course to steer
240°	15° west (add)	= 255°
240°	10° west	= 250°
240°	0°	= 240°
240°	10° east (subtract)	= 230°

Having arrived at the course for the day it should be rounded off to the nearest 5°, so that the helmsman can steer it comfortably.

After a few days it will be good practice to check the compass and to establish whether or not the deviation is still negligible. This is done by taking a sun's amplitude. The procedure is explained later in this chapter.

Keeping a Log. Throughout the 24 hour day the helmsman is attempting to steer the course set by the navigator. He will rarely succeed, as the influences of the wind direction are often against him. It is therefore important that as accurate a record as possible is kept of what has actually been steered. At the end of each hour the watch leader should record the course averaged in the period, as well as the log reading.

At the end of the watch the wind speed, direction, and the barometric pressure should be recorded, as these facts will help the navigator analyse the weather and hopefully to forecast what is to come.

Plotting a D.R. A dead reckoning (D.R.) position is one arrived at by taking into account the course and distance sailed since the last position fix. It is traditionally indicated by + on the chart. An estimated position (E.P.) includes the same factors as a D.R., but it also takes into account an estimate of tide, current, leeway and any other factor that may have influenced the yacht's progress; it is the best approximation to the yacht's position without taking a fix. It is traditionally indicated by a △. In yachting circles an estimated position is commonly referred to as a D.R. and in practice any reckoned or estimated position, regardless of how accurately it was computed, tends to be called a D.R.

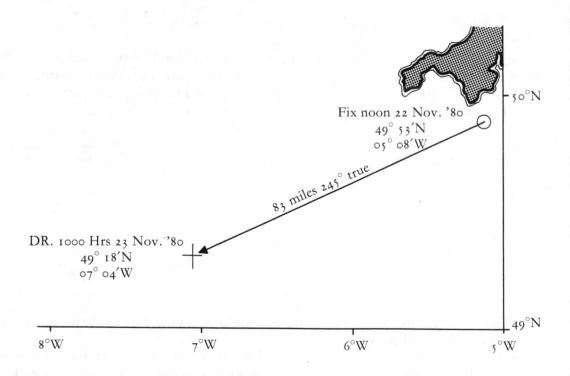

44. *Plot a D.R.*

In the day's work a D.R. position will be needed to assist with the calculation of the exact position obtained by sextant observation of the sun. Following the imaginary voyage planned in chapter 2, let us consider the first day of the trip as land is left behind.

Assume that on 22nd November 1980 the noon position was 49°53′N, 05°08′W, just off the Lizard Point. During the next 22 hours the yacht sails W.S.W. At 10.00 hours the next day—the 23rd November—a D.R. is required. From the logbook it can be seen that 83 miles have been sailed on an average course of 255° compass. By applying the magnetic variation of 10° West we see that a course of 245° true should have been achieved. A simple plot gives a D.R. for 10.00 hours on 23rd November of 49°18′N, 07°04′W. Remember that the 83 miles is measured as 83 minutes of latitude on the side of the chart, and level with the plot. See diagram 44.

Getting a Fix. Using the D.R. as measured above, and two observations of the sun, a position fix can be obtained for noon on the 23rd November. This process of getting a fix is described in full in the next chapter. Let us assume the answer is 49°16′N, 07°15′W.

If the day is completely cloudy the noon position must be worked out by D.R. alone and a try made for a sun sight the next day. As the time of taking sights is not critical, the observer can afford to wait for just a momentary glimpse of the sun. There are very few days when it is impossible to shoot a sight. In the 134 days of sailing in the 1977 round-the-world race there were only five when the sun was not seen at all.

Measuring Course and Distance Sailed. Having found the noon position, the day's run can be measured and recorded in the log, along with the average speed achieved. The measurement can be done on the side of the chart, or alternatively by using a pocket calculator, as follows:

Take the difference between the latitudes of yesterday's and today's position, express it in minutes of arc, and call it d.lat.; do the same for longitude and call it d.long; take the average of the two latitudes to the nearest degree, and call it mid-lat. Then:

$$\text{Day's run} = \sqrt{\text{d.lat}^2 + (\text{d.long} \times \text{cos.mid-lat})^2}$$

In the example:

Noon 22nd	49°53′N	05°08′W
Noon 23rd	49°16′N	07°15′W
d.lat.	37′	d.long. 127′

Mid-lat is 50°N

$$\text{Day's run} = \sqrt{37^2 + (127 \times \cos 50)^2}$$
$$= 89.6 \text{ miles.}$$

As well as the details of the day's run the navigator should calculate and record the total miles sailed and the average speed made good on the trip so far.

Course and Distance to Go. From the noon position the course and distance to the destination can be measured on the chart. This can be done as explained in Route Planning (see chapter 2). It is more accurate, though not necessary, to calculate them. The distance along the rhumb line can be found by using the above formula, but due to the complexities of the earth's shape, this is only accurate if the distance is of the order of 500 miles or less. A better method is to calculate the shortest, or great circle, distance. This is done accurately by using the formula:

$$\text{Cos}\left(\frac{\text{distance}}{60}\right) = \text{Sin(Lat.1)} \times \text{Sin(Lat.2)} + \text{Cos(Lat.1)} \times \text{Cos(Lat.2)} \times \text{Cos(d.long.)},$$

where the present position is Lat.1, Long.1, the destination is Lat.2, Long.2, and the d.long. is the difference between Long.1 and Long.2. All factors are expressed in degrees and decimals of a degree.

In the example:

Noon position	49°16′N	07°15′W
Destination Barbados	13°10′N	59°45′W
	d.long. 52°30′	

$$\text{Cos}\left(\frac{\text{distance}}{60}\right) = \text{Sin } 49.267° \times \text{Sin } 13.167° + \text{Cos } 49.267° \times \text{Cos } 13.167° \times \text{Cos } 52.50°$$
$$= .1726 + .38677$$
$$\therefore \text{ Distance} = 55.9878 \times 60$$
$$= 3359 \text{ miles.}$$

A similar formula can be used to calculate the initial great circle course. If it has been decided to follow the great circle route, the courses to steer may have been arrived at by the use of a gnomic chart, as explained in Route Planning. An alternative is to calculate the initial course and steer that for the day until a new fix is obtained. Repeat the procedure each day.

The formula is:

$$\text{Sin(initial course)} = \frac{\text{Sin(d.long)} \times \text{Cos(Lat.2)}}{\text{Sin(distance/60)}}$$

The distance is that just calculated. It is divided by 60 in order to turn it back to degrees and fractions of a degree.

In the example:

$$\text{Sin(initial course)} = \frac{\text{Sin } 52.50° \times \text{Cos } 13.167°}{\text{Sin } 55.9878°}$$
$$= \frac{.7934 \times .9737}{.8289}$$
$$= .9320$$
$$= \text{S } 69°\text{W} = 249°$$

The answer is called S.W by inspection.

Having established the course and distance to go, the facts should be recorded in the log, as these are the details the crew want to know.

Special Problems

Compass Error Check. Because magnetic variation is recorded on the chart, it can be carefully monitored and allowed for. On the other hand the deviation could vary. The best way to check total compass difference, true to magnetic, is by sun's amplitude.

Using the compass to be checked, take a bearing of the sun as it rises or sets. The correct time to take the reading is when the sun is about half its diameter clear of the horizon.

Look up the declination of the sun, to the nearest degree, in the nautical almanac; record the D.R. latitude of the yacht to the nearest degree. Use these two figures to enter the sun's amplitude table. The figure found is the true bearing of the sun at point of rising or setting: now apply the rule found at the bottom of the amplitude table, i.e. 'Name the bearing the same as the declination, N or S, and E if rising, W if setting', in order to turn the bearing into the 000–360 notation always used.

As an example of this naming, assume the amplitude was 67°. Then:

Sun rising and declination N, amplitude is $N67°E = 067°$
Sun setting and declination N, amplitude is $N67°W = 360 - 67° = 293°$
Sun rising and declination S, amplitude is $S67°E = 180° - 67° = 113°$
Sun setting and declination S, amplitude is $S67°W = 180° + 67° = 247°$

The true bearing, as calculated, is now compared with the compass bearing taken initially. The difference between the two is a combination of variation and deviation (error). It is this total difference that should now be allowed, to all courses or bearings, *instead of* the variation. In practical terms this is as far as the navigator need go. If, for instance, he has established that the compass bearing was 12° higher than the true, then he must steer a compass course 12° higher than the true course required.

If one desires to know how much of this total difference is compass error, then the calculation must go a bit further. Let us assume that on 24th November 1980, the yacht on the imaginary voyage is at 48°North. The navigator measures sunrise as 134° on the compass. The variation on the chart is 10°W. The questions are:

1. What is the total difference true—magnetic?
2. Is there any deviation (error)?
3. If the desired course is 240° true, what should the helmsman steer?

So now we set about finding the answers to these questions step by step

Look up declination. It is 21°S.
The latitude is   48°N.
Look up amplitude table and get 58°. As the declination is south and the sun is rising, this is S58°E.
This, by using the rule, becomes 180°−58° = 122° true.
Compare this with the magnetic bearing 134° compass.

The compass is therefore 12° high. This answers question 1. This also tells us that, to achieve 240° true, we must steer 252°, which answers question 3.

When the compass bearing is higher than the true bearing, the difference is called West. Thus the total difference is 12°W. We know the variation is 10°W (from the chart), thus the deviation (error) is 2°W. Regardless of how the 12°W (high) is made up, it is only this 12° that now has to be allowed for. See diagram 45.

A good way to remember that a compass bearing higher than a true bearing gives a westerly difference, is to use the mnemonic 'CADET': 'to Compass ADd East to obtain True'.

The Complication of Local Time. To keep daylight at sensible hours it is necessary to alter clocks as the yacht moves round the world. The chronometer should of course be left on G.M.T.

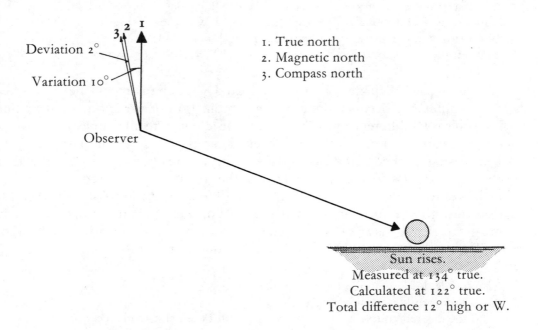

1. True north
2. Magnetic north
3. Compass north

Deviation 2°
Variation 10°
Observer

Sun rises.
Measured at 134° true.
Calculated at 122° true.
Total difference 12° high or W.

45. *Sun amplitude for total compass error.*

Ship's time can be adjusted on a zonal basis: keep it on G.M.T. when between 0° and 15°W, on G.M.T.—1 hour if between 15° and 30°W, on G.M.T.—2 hours if between 30° and 45°W, and so on. Going the other way, the time should be G.M.T.+1 hour if between 0° and 15°E, G.M.T.+2 hours if between 15° and 30°E, and so on. This system of zone time is a good base to start with. However, it does mean that midday is between 1200 and 1300 hours. By always keeping the clocks one hour ahead of zone time, midday will be pushed to between 1300 and 1400. This tends to make a better balance of daylight (a form of Daylight Saving time). Whatever time is used is fairly academic. But for simplicity, adjust clocks one hour at a time. The difference from G.M.T. (G.M.T.+2, G.M.T.—5, for example) must be recorded at the top of the log book page for the day, otherwise the navigator will get lost.

The Date Line. A problem rarely encountered, but included here as a bit of light relief amongst all this heavy navigation.

During the 1977 round-the-world race we naturally had to cross the date line. I didn't think about the implications until we actually got there, and it took a few minutes of brain power to work out how it affected the navigation. Because of this I thought I would send an explanatory telegram to Naomi James, who was sailing a month or so behind on our track. It read:— 'At the date line 180° longitude put clocks back 24 hours from G.M.T.+12 stop. This means you have two days same day and same date stop. From then on continue advancing clocks as you sail east from G.M.T.—12 towards G.M.T. stop After 180° you will be in westerly longitude so for a morning sight you must add 360° to G.H.A. before subtracting longitude for L.H.A. stop G.M.T. continues unaffected by crossing date line stop'.

As it happened she had worked this out for herself and was justifiably insulted by my telegram. The date line does not follow 180° longitude exactly everywhere as it weaves round islands; but that is immaterial to a ship at sea.

I was worried that my transmission might be heard by one of the other competitors in the world race. It would have been a trifle embarrassing. In fact I need not have worried; at the end of that leg of the race, at Rio de Janeiro, the skipper of the swiss entry *Disque d'Or* thanked me—he had heard the telegram and it had answered all his queries!

Speed Made Good

This section discusses the ability of a yacht to go faster on some points of sailing than on others. That is, navigation considerations aside, will it pay to sail a few degrees away from the planned course, if the yacht obtains a greater speed as a result. This is often the case when the required course is dead downwind, but also to a lesser extent on windward and reaching passages.

V.M.G. To Windward. Velocity made good (v.m.g.) is a term used to describe a yacht's speed made good towards its objective. When sailing to windward v.m.g. indicates how quickly the vessel is making ground into the eye of the wind. The age old beating dilemma—sail free and fast or close and slowly—is simple to analyse. The object is to maximise v.m.g.: diagram 46 shows an example of two yachts racing from A to B; one sails at 45° to the true wind direction and makes a speed of 5 knots, arriving at B after tacking through 90°. The second yacht sails at 60° to the true wind and makes 7 knots, believing that the greater speed will pay off. Either by calculation or geometry it can be seen that the first yacht wins, arriving slightly before the second. Their v.m.g.s are respectively 3.53 knots and 3.50 knots.

A table can be produced, by using the formula:

$$\text{v.m.g.} = \text{yacht's speed} \times \cos (\text{angle sailed to the true wind})$$

For a given v.m.g., this gives the possible combinations of speed and angle to the true wind that are required to achieve it.

TABLE 6—V.M.G. TO WINDWARD

Angle sailed to true wind (half the tacking angle)	V.M.G. Achieved										
	2	2.5	3	3.5	4	4.5	5	5.5	6	6.5	7
	. . . by Yacht Speeds										
35°	2.4	3.1	3.7	4.3	4.9	5.5	6.1	6.7	7.3	7.9	8.5
40°	2.6	3.3	3.9	4.6	5.2	5.9	6.5	7.1	7.8	8.5	9.1
45°	2.8	3.5	4.2	4.9	5.7	6.4	7.1	7.8	8.5	9.2	9.9
50°	3.1	3.9	4.7	5.4	6.2	7.0	7.8	8.6	9.3	10.1	10.9
55°	3.5	4.3	5.2	6.1	7.0	7.8	8.7	9.6	10.5	11.3	12.2
60°	4.0	5.0	6.0	7.0	8.0	9.0	10.0	11.0	12.0	13.0	14.0

For example, this table shows that it is better to sail 6 knots at 45 degrees to the true wind than to sail 7 knots at 55 degrees to the true wind. (5.7 knots at 45 degrees and 7 knots at 55 degrees are equivalent, both achieving 4 knots v.m.g.).

A quick glance at the table may convince one that sailing free and fast is always going to pay. One may think that, if only 5.7 knots can be achieved at 45° to the wind, then at least 8 will be achieved at 60° to the wind. The reason why this argument is wrong is that the wind angles in the table are to the true wind. The apparent wind direction—which the instruments on board register and in which the sails have to work—is quite different.

Bearing away by 15° (from 45° to 60°) true will only alter the apparent wind angle by 7 degrees or so. This is not enough to give the increase in speed required to make it pay.

The relation of apparent wind direction and strength to true wind direction and strength depends on the speed of the yacht. Her forward motion creates a vector that combines with that of the true wind to form the apparent wind. See diagram 47. Using

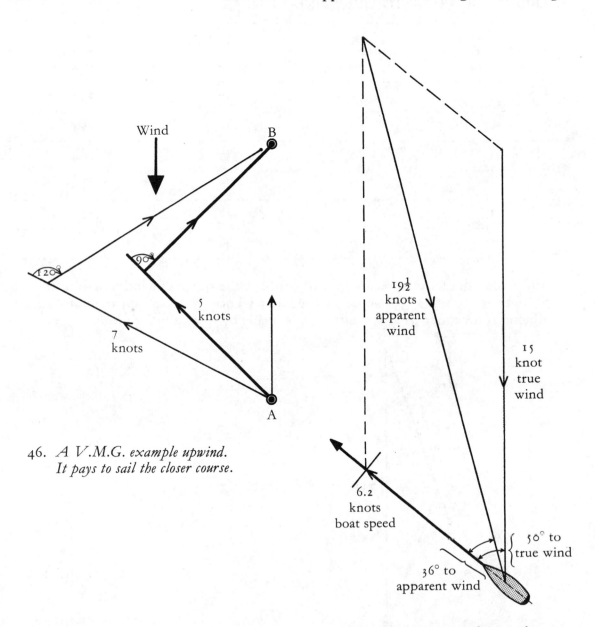

46. *A V.M.G. example upwind.*
It pays to sail the closer course.

47. *An apparent/true wind example.*

geometry, or the apparent wind formula (appendix 1), it is possible to make some comparisons. For instance, to achieve a v.m.g. of 4 knots in 15 knots of true wind, these are the possible combinations of yacht speed and angle:

TABLE 7—APPARENT TO TRUE WIND

Angle to true wind	at Boat speed in knots	would mean Angle to apparent wind	and Apparent wind strength in knots
35°	4.9	27°	19.2
40°	5.2	30°	19.3
45°	5.7	33°	19.4
50°	6.2	36°	19.6
55°	7.0	38°	19.9
60°	8.0	40°	20.2

From this table it can be seen, for example, that if the apparent wind is 19 to 20 knots it will be better to sail at 30° apparent wind at 5.5 knots than 40° apparent at 8 knots. Deductions for other wind strengths can be made by using the formulae.

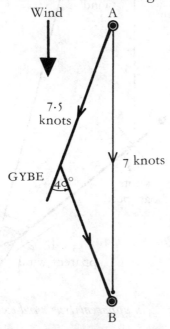

Wind

A

7.5 knots

7 knots

GYBE 40°

B

48. *A V.M.G. example downwind. It pays to gybe in this case.*

This detailed study of v.m.g. is not, of course, essential, but it is interesting to note how much it pays to sail as close to the wind as possible, even though speed is reduced.

V.M.G. Running Downwind. Off the wind one is nearly always better off making a series of very broad reaches instead of sailing with the wind dead astern. Diagram 48 shows two yachts racing from A to B; the course is to leeward. One keeps the wind right aft and makes 7 knots along the shortest route. The other decides to reach 20° off course, gybe, and broad reach back. Her speed is 7½ knots. Will she win?

The answer is yes, as the extra distance covered is made up for by the extra half a knot. One factor helping the reaching vessel is that, by steering 20° off dead down wind, he has brought the apparent wind direction to about 30° off the stern; this will have improved the efficiency of his rig enormously.

The formula:

$$\text{v.m.g.} = \text{yacht speed} \times \cos (\text{angle off course})$$

gives a table which will tell at a glance what speed will be needed at varying angles off course, to improve on a certain speed obtainable on course.

TABLE 8—V.M.G. DOWNWIND

Angle steered off course	Speed obtainable on course								
	2	3	4	5	6	7	8	9	10
	Speed required								
10°	2.0	3.0	4.1	5.1	6.1	7.1	8.1	9.1	10.2
15°	2.1	3.1	4.1	5.2	6.2	7.2	8.3	9.3	10.4
20°	2.1	3.2	4.3	5.3	6.4	7.4	8.5	9.6	10.6
25°	2.2	3.3	4.4	5.5	6.6	7.7	8.8	9.9	11.0
30°	2.3	3.5	4.6	5.8	6.9	8.1	9.2	10.4	11.5
35°	2.4	3.7	4.9	6.1	7.3	8.5	9.8	11.0	12.2
40°	2.6	3.9	5.2	6.5	7.8	9.1	10.4	11.7	13.0
45°	2.8	4.2	5.7	7.1	8.5	9.9	11.3	12.7	14.1

It is interesting to note that a deviation off course of up to 20° will always be a better bet if there is any noticeable increase in speed as a result.

During any race or cruising passage involving a downward slide in the trade winds it is a good idea to have this table taped to a bulkhead, where it can continually be referred to by the watch leader or helmsman. It should be possible to see at a glance whether or not a course alteration is advisable.

V.M.G. Reaching. This final v.m.g. case is fairly complex. When beating or running, any variation relative to the wind can be followed by an equal and opposite variation (after tacking or gybing) to arrive at the destination. When reaching, this is not the case; for instance, while sailing with the wind abeam in a blow, it may seem a good idea to free off 20 degrees, increase speed, and hence improve v.m.g. However, it will eventually be necessary to come close-hauled to make the finish. The resulting loss of v.m.g. will probably wipe out the early advantage gained. See diagram 49, top example.

A good rule to follow when reaching is to stay on course if one anticipates the wind conditions and direction staying more or less the same until the destination is reached. On the other hand, if a change is expected, by all means reach off to maximise v.m.g. Then, when the change comes, the yacht will be nearer to the objective than it would have been if the direct course had been held. See diagram 49, lower example. Thus in mid-Atlantic, when sailing in a reaching wind, v.m.g. should be maximised by steering down (or up in light winds). In this case the v.m.g. table 8 should be used.

When to Tack? Sailing to windward the navigator has already decided which angle to the wind gives optimum performance; the question now is, which tack to sail on? As the wind direction is never steady, it would be a mistake to sail a beat—however short or long—in just two legs, staying on one tack until the objective can be laid on the other.

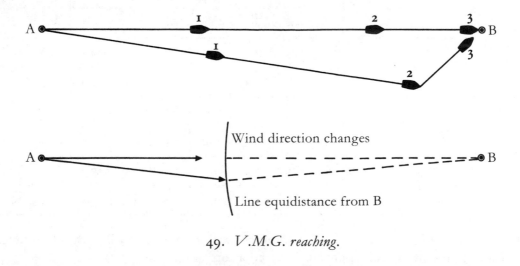

49. *V.M.G. reaching.*

The reasons for this are fairly obvious: in an extremely bad case, imagine a yacht trying to beat to a point 1,000 miles due west of its starting point; if she sailed for 750 miles S.W. in the westerly wind, and then tacked, all would be well if the wind stayed westerly, but if it went N.W. she would face a further 750 miles of dead beating! Alternatively, if the wind went S.W., although it would be possible to lay the finish, a lot of the ground gained to windward on the first tack would be wasted.

The correct approach is to stay on the tack that gives a course nearest to the course required. This ensures that the yacht stays on the longest leg. For example, assume the required course is 100°; on port tack the helmsman finds he can steer 140°. The yacht is known to tack through 90°, so obviously this is the favoured tack. If the wind shifts, so that the helmsman can only make 150°, it will pay to tack and steer 060°. On an ocean crossing it is incorrect to tack every few minutes. In a very shifty wind, try to estimate the average course achieved over an hour or so, before making the decision to go about. If the wind is completely steady and the destination is dead upwind, the favoured tack would change every few yards or so. Obviously common sense is needed here.

A typical instruction from the navigator to the helmsman might be 'Course required is 100° and we can now make 130°. If the average course heads to worse than 150°, we should tack, and if it lifts to 090°, we can ease sheets'.

Modern Aids to Navigation

While it would be a mistake to ignore this chapter and the next, there is no doubt that some modern aids take all the skill, worry and possibly interest, out of navigation. Anyone who has undertaken a long ocean voyage will know that it is foolish to rely 100% on anything electrical—there are too many weak links in the chain, the electronic device itself, the batteries, the generator, or the fuel system, all have been known to fail. Because of this a wise navigator always carries a sextant and knows how to use it. Even so, it is worth considering three modern systems of interest.

Satellite Navigation. Now that SAT-NAV receivers can be bought for less than half the cost of a H.F. transmitter-receiver, they are within the range of many ocean sailors. There is certainly a lot to be said for a system that gives, at the push of a few buttons, a position, expressed in latitude and longitude, to an accuracy of within a quarter of a mile. Not only is it accurate, but it works in all weathers, day and night.

The system uses five satellites in polar orbit, any one of which can provide a fix: the onboard receiver picks up a signal from the satellite, and by comparing the received frequency with the known transmission frequency, it can calculate the speed of approach or recession of the satellite by measuring the doppler shift. Taking a series of readings during the pass, the receiver can calculate the position relative to the satellite. The satellite itself is tracked by ground stations which, once every 12 hours, give it the details of its orbits. From this information it can calculate its position relative to the earth, and transmit it in turn every few minutes to any yacht or ship receiver within range. Thus the onboard computer has the satellite's position, a series of doppler shift measurements, and the course and speed of the yacht. From these it can compute an accurate position. The time between satellite passes, and hence between fixes, is 90 minutes or less, depending on latitude. As the computer is reading the yacht's course and speed it continues to update and display a D.R. position between satellites.Magic!

The satellites in use today are the U.S. Navy's Navigation Satellite System. In 1987 a new series of satellites will come into operation; they will be called Navstar Global Positioning System, and will be more sophisticated in that a receiver will be able to pick up several satellites simultaneously. This will provide an accuracy of 10 metres both vertically and horizontally. As well as your position, the receiver will tell the navigator whether the tide is high or low!

Loran—C. Very popular in America, as the coverage there is good; unfortunately the system does not cover the Mediterranean, the south coast of England to Gibraltar, or anywhere south of latitude 20°N.

The onboard receiver measures the time difference between transmissions from a pair of stations, from which it produces a hyperbolic position line. Reception from a second pair (one station is common to both pairs) gives a second position line. Charts are required with the Loran-C position lines printed thereon.

Omega. Better than Loran-C, as the coverage is global. The greater range is achieved by using the very low frequency of 14 Khz (Loran-C uses 100 Khz). Eight stations cover the whole world. The trade-off comes in reduced accuracy, which can be as bad as 2 miles or more; however, this is not too bad for a yacht in mid-ocean.

Of these three devices the Satellite Navigation is the best choice for a yachtsman. The accuracy is good and getting better. The price is not prohibitive and is coming down.

8   Sun Sights

To understand the theory of celestial navigation much study is required. For that reason my advice is just to ignore the theory—at least until the relatively easy practical side has been mastered.

This chapter explains how to fix the yacht's position by observations of the sun. The first day of the voyage (planned in chapters 2 and 7) will be used as an example. The two forms found at the end of this section will help the reader follow the working.

Greenwich Mean Time (G.M.T.) is used for navigation and the chronometer should be set accordingly. In the case of our example, ship's time is also G.M.T. Later on the effects of ship's time and G.M.T. differing will be discussed.

The exercise is to find the position of the yacht, at noon or thereabouts, on 23rd November. To do this two observations of the sun, approximately two hours apart, are taken. Each observation provides, after simple calculations, a position line. By running one line to the other a fix is obtained. This is how it is done:

Step 1—Plot a D.R.

The best time to take the first sun sight is around 10.00 hours. We need a D.R. for this time and it is obtained as explained in the last chapter—Day's Work. The D.R. for 10.00 on 23rd November 1980 was measured as 49°18′N, 07°04′W. This position should be recorded on the sight form—see page 142.

Step 2—Take a Sight

The morning sight can now be taken. If it is cloudy at 10.00, the observation has to be taken at a later time and the D.R. adjusted accordingly.

The quickest way to learn how to use a sextant is to be shown by someone who knows. However, if no-one is available, this is the routine to follow:

Select the shades. If the sky is clear use the darkest shade on the sun-mirror; the sun should be visible but not too bright—it must have clear edges. Use a light shade on the horizon-mirror only if the sun is reflecting on the sea, otherwise leave it clear. See diagram 50.

Bring the sun down. The object is to adjust the angle of the sun-mirror so that the image of the sun appears, after reflection in the sun- and horizon-mirrors, to sit on the horizon, which can be seen in the clear part of the horizon glass. To do this, set the arc to zero—it is moved large amounts by releasing the arc from the scale thread, and small amounts by turning the micrometer (minutes of arc) knob. Having found a comfortable spot on deck—preferably sitting down—hold the sextant in the right hand and point it at the sun. See diagram 51. Now smoothly bring the sextant down to horizontal while moving the arc slide away from you down the arc, with the left hand; in this way the image of the sun stays in the sun-mirror until it meets the horizon. This is not easy to master and should be practised several times. A useful tip is to put a heavy shade on the horizon glass while looking directly at the sun, in order not to blind yourself.

Take the altitude. It is necessary to get the image of the sun directly on the horizon; fine adjustment can be made with the micrometer knob to achieve this. As the sun is rising, so its image will rise, and continual adjustment is needed to hold it down. When you are happy that it is right—see diagram 52—shout 'Now', or more traditionally 'Stop'. This is the signal for the time-keeper to record the chronometer time.

There are two complications: it is possible to measure too large an angle in error. See diagram 53. To avoid this, the sextant must be swung side to side, rocking about a

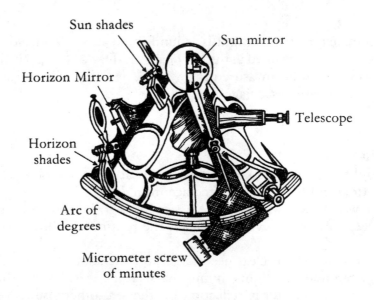

50. *A sextant.*

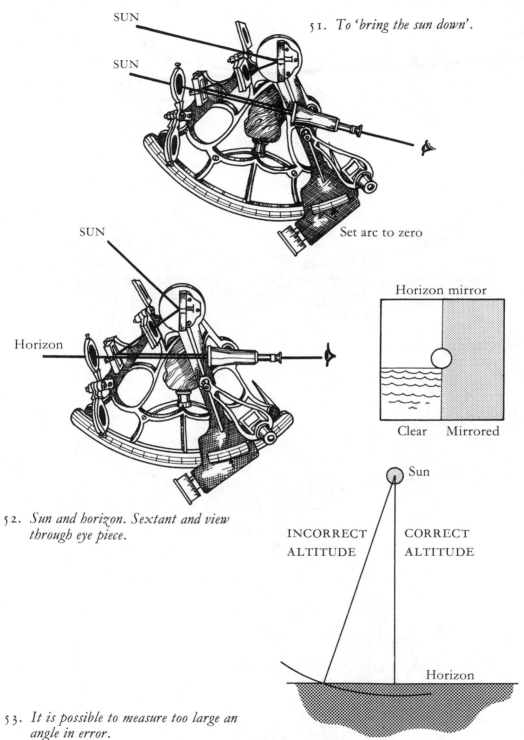

SUN

SUN

51. *To 'bring the sun down'.*

Set arc to zero

SUN

Horizon

Horizon mirror

Clear   Mirrored

52. *Sun and horizon. Sextant and view through eye piece.*

Sun

INCORRECT
ALTITUDE

CORRECT
ALTITUDE

Horizon

53. *It is possible to measure too large an angle in error.*

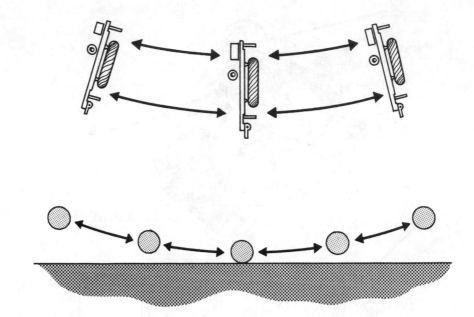

54. *Swinging the sextant side to side, tilting the axis simultaneously. The apparent motion of the sun is shown.*

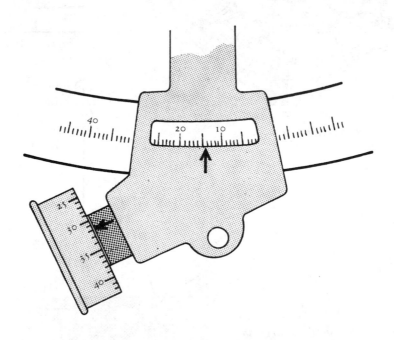

55. *Reading the sextant*

vertical axis at the same time; this has the effect of moving the image of the sun so that it swings in an arc. This arc should just kiss the horizon. See diagram 54. The other problem is rough weather, where it is difficult to identify the true horizon; the secret here is to take the sight when you are on top of the highest wave. This is bound to be correct, as the horizon itself has to be a wave top.

Returning to the example, 'Stop' has been called, the time was 10 hours 04 minutes 31 seconds and this is recorded on the sight form as CHRON. Read the sextant and record the degrees and minutes on the form as SEXT.ALT. In our case it is 14°32'. See diagram 55.

Step 3—Work out the Sight

Initially I will explain the use of sight reduction tables, as they are reliable. Later on the alternative of using a calculator is considered.

At this stage three items are on the sight form:

A D.R. position with the date and ship's time
The sextant altitude
The chronometer time of that altitude

Several calculations must now be undertaken. As well as the explanation here, there are notes on the sight form itself, which should be enough to keep you on track by the time a few sights have been completed.

Correct the sextant altitude. It must be corrected to allow for Dip (height of eye of the observer) and Total Correction. Tables for these can be found in the Nautical Almanac. Much simpler is to assume that one's height of eye is three metres and then the following table can be used.

Sextant Altitude between 12° and 18°	add 10 minutes
between 18° and 27°	add 11 minutes
between 27° and 50°	add 12 minutes
greater than 50°	add 13 minutes

In our example add 10' and the true altitude is found to be 14°42'. This true altitude is needed at a later stage, to compare with the result of the calculations.

Correct the chronometer. Apply any chronometer error to give the G.M.T.; an error 'fast' is subtracted. In our example G.M.T. is 10 hr 04m 26s, as the chronometer is 5 seconds fast. See sight form.

Look up G.H.A. and declination. These are the equivalent to the sun's latitude and longitude. Take the Nautical Almanac and turn to the page for the day's date—23rd November 1980. From the column headed 'sun' take the G.H.A. for the whole number of hours of G.M.T.—it is 333°22′6. Alongside the G.H.A. is the declination; record it on the sight form along with its name N or S. In the example it is 20°25′S. See appendix 2 for the relevant page of the almanac.

Look up the increment. This is the extra bit of G.H.A. corresponding to the minutes and seconds of G.M.T. It is found in the yellow pages of the Nautical Almanac. Look under the column headed by the minutes, and alongside the seconds. In our example it is 01°06′5. See appendix 3 for the relevant page.

Get the total G.H.A. Add the increment to the G.H.A. on the form, to get the total G.H.A. Remember that there are 60 minutes of arc in a degree (not 100), so watch the addition. The total G.H.A. can be rounded to the nearest minute (i.e. 29′1 becomes 29′).

Choose an assumed position. The D.R. is adjusted to give an assumed position which will facilitate the calculations.

The assumed latitude is taken as the whole number of degrees nearest to the D.R. latitude: therefore a D.R. latitude of 50°31′ becomes an assumed one of 51°00′. In our example the D.R. of 49°18′N becomes 49°00′N.

The assumed longitude is a bit more complicated. The next step will be to apply the assumed longitude (subtract if W, add if E) to the total G.H.A. to obtain the L.H.A. The L.H.A. must be a whole number of degrees, so the assumed longitude must be chosen accordingly. Thus for a westerly D.R. longitude, choose an assumed longitude in which the minutes of arc equal those of the total G.H.A., so when the assumed longitude is subtracted from it, the answer (L.H.A.) will be 00′. Conversely, for an easterly D.R. choose an assumed longitude where the minutes, added to the minutes of total G.H.A., will equal 60 (i.e. 60′ = 1°00′). While conducting this apparent fiddle remember that the assumed longitude must be as close as possible to the D.R. longitude. Here are some examples

    1. D.R. long. 5° 27′W and total G.H.A.   326°34′
        choose assumed long.   5°34′
                        gives L.H.A.   321°00′

    2. D.R. long. 5°01′W and total G.H.A.   326°34′
        choose assumed long.   4°34′
                        gives L.H.A.   322°00′

3. D.R. long. 7°16′E and total G.H.A.   326°34′
   choose assumed long.   7°26′
                  gives L.H.A.   334°00′

4. D.R. long. 7°58′E and total G.H.A.   326°34′
   choose assumed long.   8°26′
                  gives L.H.A.   335°00′

In our example the assumed longitude should be taken as 07°29′W: this fiddle is justified, as the original D.R. was only an approximate estimate anyway. We have simply re-estimated it to suit our purpose. This is in order, provided we use the assumed position for the calculations *and* the subsequent plot. The D.R. is no longer needed and should be lightly crossed out to avoid possible mistakes.

Apply assumed longitude. This is done as explained above. If the total G.H.A. works out at less than a westerly assumed longitude, add 360° to the G.H.A. in order to make the subtraction possible. If the L.H.A. becomes more than 360°, subtract 360° from it.

We now have on the sight form:

L.H.A.	327°00′
Assumed Lat.	49°00′ N
Decl.	20°25′ S

These three factors are now used to enter the Sight Reduction Tables.

Enter reduction tables. Use volume IV of NP401. This table is arranged in two halves—the first covers latitudes 45° to 52° (north or south) and the second latitudes 53° to 60°. In our example the assumed latitude is 49°, so obviously we refer to the first part of the book. Look for the pages which cover the L.H.A. of 327° (page 68 and half of 69). Page 68 is titled LATITUDE SAME NAME AS DECLINATION and page 69 (top half) is titled LATITUDE CONTRARY NAME TO DECLINATION. In our example the assumed latitude is North and the declination is South (contrary names), so page 69 must be used.

Look up the column for the assumed latitude (49°) and the row for the degrees of declination (20°) and take out the readings (see appendix 4):

Hc	15°00′.3
d	− 55′.7 (do not forget the + or − sign)
z	148°.0

From the same pages (68 or 69) note the rule for changing z to zn. As we are in a northerly latitude and the L.H.A. is greater than 180°, the rule is zn = z; apply the rule to give a zn or azimuth of 148°.

The degrees of declination have been allowed for, and it is now necessary to look up a correction for the minutes. If the minutes of declination are less than 30, turn to the interpolation table at the front of the reduction tables; if over 30, turn to the back. The correction is in two parts: firstly, look down the column headed Dec.Inc. and find the minutes of declination (25'.0) to be allowed for. Move along that row until you are under the column headed by the 'tens' of d (i.e. d is 55°.7, so the 'tens' is 50'). Take out the correction found (− 20'.8). Secondly, for the units of d (5'.7) pick the column headed 5' and the row for '.7 in the block of figures level with the Dec.Inc. (25'.0), when a correction of − 2'.4 is found. See appendix 5. These two corrections are negative because d is negative. Both should be recorded on the form and applied to Hc to give the Calculated Altitude. In the example it is 14°37'. This is the altitude that would have been observed with the sextant if the yacht had been at the assumed position at sight time.

Find the intercept. Compare the true and calculated altitudes; their difference, in minutes of arc, is the intercept in miles. If the true is greater the intercept is named 'towards'. If the calculated is greater it is named 'away'. In our example the intercept is 5 miles towards. This broadly means that we are 5 miles nearer the sun than the assumed position is. We can now plot a position line.

Step 4—Plot the Sight
Plot the assumed position (not the D.R.) directly on the chart in use. Draw a line through this position in the direction of the azimuth—148° true; mark off on this line

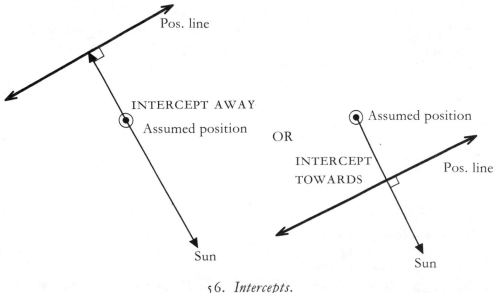

56. *Intercepts.*

the intercept in miles, towards or away, as found above. If the intercept is away, draw the azimuth line away, i.e. 328° instead of 148°. Now draw a line through the end of the intercept at right angles to the azimuth. This last line is a position line. That is, at the time of the sight (10.04 hours) the yacht was somewhere on this line. Examples of intercepts plotted towards and away are given in diagram 56.

In order to get a fix a second position line is required. The direction of the line depends on the azimuth of the sun, and this changes as the sun moves through the sky. By taking a second sight a few hours after the first, a second position line can be obtained at an angle to the first. The second sight can be taken in exactly the same way as the first; alternatively a meridian altitude (see later) can be used. Once two position lines are drawn, a position can be achieved by plotting a running fix.

Step 5—Running Fix

As a result of taking two sights (at 10.00 and 12.00 say) two position lines are drawn. Take any point on the 10.00 position line and from this point plot the course and speed of the yacht between 10.00 and 12.00 Draw a line parallel to the 10.00 position line through the point at the end of the course and distance. The point at which this transferred line crosses the 12.00 position line, is the yacht's exact position at 12.00 hours. See diagram 57.

The above is all that one needs to know to fix a position by the sun. However, it is worth learning the special case of the Meridian Altitude, as this is an easy, quick way of getting one of the two position lines required.

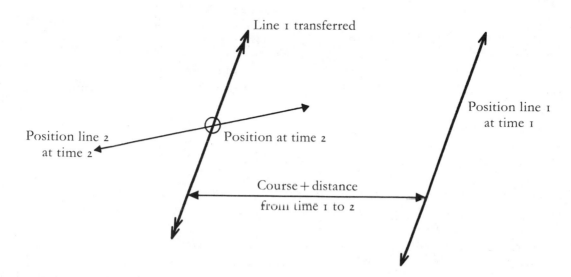

Line 1 transferred

Position line 1
at time 1

Position line 2
at time 2

Position at time 2

Course + distance
from time 1 to 2

57. *A running fix.*

Step 6—Meridian Altitude

Use of the meridian altitude form will help the reader follow this example.

The objective is to measure the altitude of the sun when it is at its highest at or near noon. At this time the azimuth (the bearing) of the sun will be exactly north or south.

To find the approximate ship's time of the meridian altitude, first look up the Time of Meridian Passage in the Nautical Almanac for the day. In our example, for 23rd November 1980, it is found to be 11.47 hours. This is the time (G.M.T.) the sun crosses 0° longitude. Record it on the form. This time must now be adjusted to allow for the yacht's longitude—if the observer is West, the sun will pass overhead later than at 0° (Greenwich) and if East, earlier. To find out by how much, look up the time equivalent of the noon D.R. longitude. This is done by using the yellow pages in the Nautical Almanac in a reverse sense. The time is required to the nearest minute only. Here are some examples:

Noon D.R. longitude	Time correction for this longitude
1°W	plus 4 minutes
2°W	plus 8 minutes
3°30′W	plus 14 minutes
16°W	plus 1 hour 4 minutes
15°E	minus 1 hour
10°E	minus 40 minutes
110°W	plus 7 hours 20 minutes

(As can be seen, 15° of longitude = 1 hour in time).

By applying the correction, the G.M.T. of merdian passage at the yacht is found. In our example it is 12.16 hours.

A few minutes before this time take the sextant on deck and bring the sun down to the horizon; it should still be rising very slowly. Keep checking every few seconds and eventually the sun will stop rising, steady, and then start falling. Do not adjust the sextant when it starts to fall. It is unlikely that any movement of the sun will be detected for a minute either side of the meridian altitude. Provided the time of the latter was calculated correctly, and the sun is not moving, simply take its altitude. The exact time need not be recorded.

Correct the sextant altitude measured. In our example the sextant altitude was 20°07′ and so the true altitude is 20°18′. Now look up the declination of the sun for the time of meridian altitude and record it, to the nearest minute of arc, on the form. In this case it is 20°26′S.

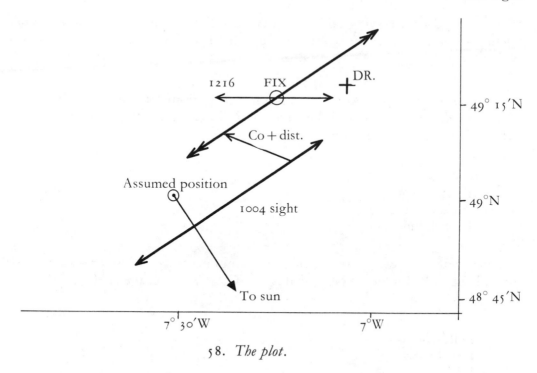

58. The plot.

A simple rule is now followed to turn the declination and true altitude into the latitude of the observer:

1. If the D.R. latitude and the declination are contrary names (one N, one S), then:
   True latitude = 90° − altitude − declination.
2. If the D.R. latitude and the declination are same names (both N or both S), *and* latitude is bigger than declination, then:
   True latitude = 90° − altitude + declination.
3. If the D.R. latitude and the declination are same names (both N or both S), *and* declination is bigger than latitude, then:
   True latitude = declination + altitude − 90°.

In our example rule 1 applies, and the latitude is found to be 49°16′N.

This latitude is simply a position line which can be drawn on the chart. It is a good way of obtaining the second position line required for the fix. Diagram 58 shows the 10.04 sight combined with this meridian altitude, giving a position of 49°16′N, 07°15′W.

Calculators

Calculators are useful navigation tools, and every yacht should carry one. However, as I have said before, it is common sense for a navigator to be able to use tables—they can never break down. Having said that, there is still no doubt that modern navigational calculators take much of the work out of a sight. There are three levels of sophistication available:

1. *The simple, non-programmable calculator*, with trigonometric functions. In this case the sight procedure described before must be followed until the point where the total G.H.A. is found. At this stage we have:

> D.R. latitude and longitude
> Total G.H.A.
> Declination
> True altitude.

Because of the power of the calculator it is not necessary to use an assumed position. Instead the D.R. longitude is applied to the G.H.A. to get the L.H.A. This now gives us:

> D.R. latitude
> Declination
> L.H.A.

These three factors, expressed in degrees and decimals of a degree, can be entered in the formulae, which can then be punched out on the calculator:

$$\text{Sin (calculated alt)} = \text{Cos(L.H.A.)} \times \text{Cos(Lat)} \times \text{Sin(Dec)} \pm \text{Sin(Lat)} \times \text{Sin(Dec)}$$

Use + if Lat and Dec are same name, otherwise use −.

$$\text{Sin(azimuth)} = (\text{Sin(L.H.A.)} \times \text{Cos(Dec)})/\text{Cos(alt)}$$

These two formulae require a fair bit of calculator work. The actual punching sequence of the various instructions will depend on the type of calculator and the number of memories it has. Using the instruction manual, the two formulae can be broken down into a series of easy to follow stages.

The calculated altitude and azimuth thus found can now be combined with the true altitude to give an intercept which can be plotted in the normal way.

2. *A programmable calculator*. This makes much more sense, because once the program has been worked out for the above formulae, it can be stored on a magnetic card. Then

for each sight it is only necessary to feed in the card, the L.H.A., the D.R. latitude and the declination. The same answers as above are found.

3. *Special navigation calculators.* For slightly less than the cost of a sextant it is possible to buy a calculator with several navigation problems pre-programmed into it. As well as the sight program they may have all the details of the Nautical Almanac, from now up to the year 2000 or more. In this case it is only the G.M.T., D.R. latitude and longitude, and the sextant altitude that need be entered into the unit. The intercept and azimuth are produced.

A further sophistication along these lines is available—at a price. It is a calculator, which not only contains the data above, but a chronometer as well. First the navigator punches in the height of his eye (used for correcting sextant altitude and usually about 3 metres), the identification number of the sun (the calculator also handles planets and stars), and the D.R. position. When you take the sight, hit the time button and then enter the sextant altitude—the intercept and azimuth appear. If two star sights are taken and entered as above, the calculator will give back your exact position in latitude and longitude. Of course it had already told you which stars to take!

Accuracy

Provided the navigator carefully checks his arithmetic (only addition and subtraction after all), or his key punching, the only error that can creep into a sight is in the physical use of the sextant. Here practice makes perfect—even if the navigator is a bit shaky at the start of a voyage, he will get plenty of practice on the way and his accuracy on arriving is sure to be good. In mid-ocean, with 2,000 miles to go till landfall, an error of 4 miles only affects the course to steer by 0.1 of a degree; as the helmsman is steering to the nearest 5 degrees, this is acceptable.

Even 50 miles from harbour an error of 2 miles makes a course difference of only just over 2 degrees. Do not worry too much about accuracy to begin with; remember a bad sight is still likely to be better than a good radio D.F. bearing.

The limitation of using only the sun is that, in general, a position is obtained only once a day. In fact sun sights can be taken at any time during daylight, and any two run together will give a fix. I believe this to be quite sufficient for the middle of an ocean, but stars and planets can be used to provide a position at dawn or dusk. The advantage of using the stars is that several can be taken simultaneously, which gives an immediate position. The disadvantage is that the sights have to be taken over the period of five minutes or so when both stars and horizon are visible, and hence any cloud at that time will upset the procedure. There is no real need for a cruising yachtsman to take star sights; even while racing they are only of special value when a landfall is to be made between sunset one day and noon the next. Because we do not need them they are outside the scope of this book.

This chapter ends with the sight forms which follow here.

SIGHT FORM

SHIP TIME	....hr....m	DATE	....
D.R.POS.	.... ..	....	....
CHRON.	....hr....m....s	SEXT.ALT.	....
CHRON.ER.	....s	TOT.COR.	..... 1.2.
G.M.T.	....hr....m....s	TRUE ALT.	....
G.H.A.	....		3.
INCR.	....		4.
TOT.G.H.A.	....	DECLIN.	....
ASS.LONG.	....	ASS.LAT.	.... 5.
L.H.A.	....		

INTO SIGHT REDUCTION TABLES

	Hc	d	z	
	....	.....	....	
Correction 1	....		↓	6.
Correction 2	....		apply rule in reduction tables	
CALC.ALT.	....			
TRUE ALT.	....			
INTERCEPT	.... miles	Zn or Azimuth ↓		
			......	7.8.

NOTES

1. If chron. error is fast, subtract it.

2. For value of TOT.COR. see page 133.

3. G.H.A. and DECLIN. from Nautical Almanac.

4. INCR. from Nautical Almanac yellow pages.

5. To decide ASS.LAT. and LONG. see page 134. A West long. is subtracted, East long. is added.

6. Corrections 1 and 2 found from Reduction tables, see page 136.

7. The difference between CALC. and TRUE ALT. in minutes is the intercept in miles.

8. If the TRUE ALT. is greater the INTERCEPT is TOWARDS, otherwise it is AWAY.

MERIDIAN ALTITUDE FORM

DATE   . . . .   D.R.LONG.   . . . .   1.

TIME(G.M.T.) OF MER.PASS. at o LONG.   . . . .hr . . . .m   4.
Correction for D.R. LONG.(+ for W, − for E)   . . . .hr . . . .m   2.
TIME(G.M.T.) of MER.PASS. at yacht   . . . .hr . . . .m

SEXT.ALT.   . . . .
TOT.CORR.   . . . .
TRUE ALT.   . . . .   DECLIN.   . . . .   3.

                        RULES . . .

                        LATITUDE . . . .

RULES

1. If LAT. and DEC. are CONTRARY names:—
$$LAT. = 90 - ALT. - DEC.$$
2. If LAT. and DEC. are SAME names, and LAT. is BIGGER than DEC.:—
$$LAT. = 90 - ALT. + DEC.$$
3. If LAT. and DEC. are SAME names, and DEC. is bigger than LAT.:—
$$LAT. = DEC. + ALT. - 90$$

NOTES

1. *D.R. LONG. is for noon and to the nearest ¼ degree (15′).*
2. *Correction for D.R. LONG. from yellow pages of Nautical Almanac backwards or by mental calculation (15° = 1 hour).*
3. *DECLIN. is from NAUTICAL ALMANAC for TIME (G.M.T.) of MER. PASS. at the yacht.*
4. *TIME from Nautical Almanac.*

---

9   Domestics

Buying food, storing it on board, cooking it and clearing up after it, are very unpopular jobs. Unfortunately it is a very important task; all those crew who shy away from domestic involvement would be the first to admit that—especially if it stopped happening and their food did not turn up. On *Great Britain II* in the round-the-world race any chore connected with the galley became known as 'domestic duty' and those performing it were referred to as mere 'domestics'. Watch systems allowing for full-time, or rotation of, domestics, have already been discussed. This chapter deals with every aspect of the unfortunate domestics' duties.

Food

The choice of food suitable for long voyages is extensive. The world has progressed a long way since the days of 'Salt Horse', whatever that was.

Tinned Food. In most cases tins are the ideal packaging method for food on a yacht. The quality of tinned food is very good and of course it lasts when kept sealed. Tinned meat, vegetables (for when the fresh run out) and fruit are all useful basics. One of the disadvantages of tins is their bulk and weight, but this is counteracted by their great advantage: tinned food contains all the fluid needed to cook it, and hence produces over half the daily fluid intake a person requires. This means that less water needs to be carried and, should any problem occur with the fresh water system at sea, there will be an alternative supply of liquid. Ten days before Cape Town, during the 1973 round-the-world race, Chay Blyth and his crew of paratroopers ran out of water. The second tank on the yacht *Great Britain II* was found to be empty when brought into use—a fitting had broken and the fresh water had done no more than wash the bilges. As all their food was dehydrated, it could not be eaten and there was no liquid—except what could be somewhat crudely distilled. Had they carried tinned food the problem would not have been so bad.

Stowing tinned food is not difficult. Provided the journey is not more than two months long no tin preparation is needed. The tins may rust slightly, and a few labels come off, but nothing serious will happen. For any longer voyage the tins should be varnished and paint-coded, with the labels thrown away before they clog up the bilge pumps. The tins should be stowed on board according to their contents: i.e. meat in one compartment, vegetables in another, etc., and a record made of the stowage plan. We got into a terrible mess on *Second Life* in 1973, when we tried to stow by meals rather than by contents. The reasoning was that if all the boxes of tins were broken up and stowed (by taking 4 tins of meat, 4 of vegetables, 4 of fruit, and then repeating the cycle), it would be easy to find the ingredients for one meal at a time. It did not work too well and all we achieved was a terrible confusion of loose tins. Not only that, it took all day to organise beforehand. In addition, one of the food bins was under the centre of the saloon floor, where it collected the water dripping off our foul weather gear. When we reached the tins near the bottom, we found 6 inches of water there as well. The tins above and below the 'water line' were intact, but those on it were badly rusted—elementary physics.

The tinned food store on *Great Britain II* was a vast area underneath the main cockpit—see accommodation plan in chapter I. Access was by a small door down below, and inside the tins were stowed up to three feet deep. A common sight was a domestic disappearing into this tin mine, and after a certain amount of tinny clattering, re-appearing triumphantly with our dinner. The access door had a securing bolt on the outside and one day, seeing it flapping open, I bolted it shut. It was a rough, noisy day, so much so that we heard nothing unusual and it was not till over an hour later that we noticed one of our domestics was missing!

Frozen Food. Steaks and roasts are more appetising than tinned stew; the disadvantage of frozen food, though, is the need for a deep freeze. A deep freeze needs a power source; fine if nothing goes wrong, but it would be foolhardy to rely on frozen food entirely. Two of the ten yachts carrying deep freezes in the 1977 world race had either freezer or electrical breakdowns and were forced to eat six steaks a day for a few days and then go hungry; so frozen food should only really be considered as an addition to tins or dehydrated food, not as an alternative. If a life relatively free of hassles is your aim, leave ashore as many of the electrical devices as can be done without; if good food is your priority, then take a deep freeze—and some tins just in case.

Dehydrated Food. An alternative to tins, dehydrated food takes up less space, saves weight, but needs extra water. If all the food carried is dehydrated, about twice as much fresh water is needed as would be required for drinking only. See later. Dehydrated food must be stowed in a dry part of the yacht.

Fresh Food
Beyond than during the first few days at sea, one is limited to the types of food which

keep longest. Fruit and vegetables are particularly good and have lasted on board for the lengths of time shown in table 9.

TABLE 9—KEEPING TIME OF FRESH FOOD

Grapefruit	4 months
Oranges	3 months
Potatoes	3 months
Onions	2 months
Apples	1 month
Cabbages	1 month
Carrots	1 month
Green tomatoes	1 month
Eggs (untreated)	4 months
Margarine in tubs	2 months or more
Vacuum packed bacon	2 months or more

The longevity of any fresh produce pre-supposes the best quality and complete freshness when delivered on board. The life of an egg is extraordinary: when Naomi James sailed from Cape town she spent four months at sea, sailing non-stop past Australia, New Zealand and Cape Horn, until she reached the Falkland Islands; throughout this period the eggs were edible—in this particular case they were refrigerated by the southern oceans. However, even in the tropics they should last two months.

Margarine will melt in hot weather, but this does not matter so long as the tubs are upright.

Bread can be made to last. A french firm markets bread specifically for long ocean voyages. It has been known to last for seven months. If bread is not carried it can be made, or biscuits used as a substitute.

All fresh food will last longer if kept in a dry, airy environment; this fact was illustrated by the cabbages we carried from England on *Great Britain II*. As all the lockers, cupboards, bunks and other spaces were full when the cabbages arrived, they were stowed in a net slung down aft with the steering gear; after a few days a strange smell found its way from aft up through the yacht—the cabbages were rotting. However, after removal of the outside leaves they were as good as new. Every week the cabbage ritual was repeated until, by Cape Town, the few remaining resembled Brussels sprouts.

How much Food. Anyone stocking a yacht for the first time will invariably take too much of everything; this may be better than running out but, as stowage is limited, it is good to be as accurate with the quantities as possible.

Start by considering the menus for each meal for a week. This would make a reasonable cycle—i.e. seven different main meals. Alongside each meal estimate the total quantity of all ingredients to feed the whole crew for that meal. By adding up each ingredient, the total requirements for a week are found. It is then an easy matter to multiply this master list by the number of weeks of the voyage. As an example, here is the way we arrived at the food requirements of a crew of 17 for 6 weeks.

TABLE 10—PROPOSED MENUS

Breakfast		Lunch		Dinner	
Day 1		Soup	9 lbs	Tuna Fish	4 lbs
Bread	1 loaf	Onions	1 lb	Milk	1 pint
Margarine	1 tub	Cabbage	1	Flour	a bit
Marmalade	1 jar	Potato Salad	2 lbs	Onions	1 lb
Cereal	1 pkt	Pickles	1 jar	Potatoes	10 lbs
Milk	3 pts	Bread	2 lvs	Carrots	5 lbs
Eggs	3 doz	Margarine	1 tub	Pears tinned	6 lbs
Bacon	2 lbs	Sardines	4 tins		
		Ham	2 lbs		
Day 2		Corned Beef	2 lbs	Spaghetti	3 pkts
Bread		Tinned Fruit Juice	4 pts	Onions	1 lb
Margarine		Jam	1 jar	Minced Beef	7 lbs
Marmalade		Marmite	1 jar	Tinned Tomatoes	3 lbs
Grapefruit	9	Oil	a bit	Tinned Peaches	6 lbs
Eggs	3 doz	Vinegar	a bit	Ideal Milk	1 lb
Sausages	3 lbs	Condiments	a bit		
Tinned Tomatoes	3 lbs	Fresh Fruit			
Day 3				Stewed Steak	7 lbs
Bread				Oxo Cubes	2
Margarine				Cabbages	2
Marmalade				Potatoes	10 lbs
Cereal	1 pkt	*This lunch*		Mushrooms	1 lb
Milk	3 pts	*repeated daily*		Onions	2 lb
Sausages	3 lbs				
Bacon	2 lbs				
Baked Beans	4 lbs				

continued over page

Table 10 continued

Breakfast		Lunch	Dinner	
Day 4		as before		
Bread			Steak and Kidney Pie	9 tins
Margarine				
Marmalade			Potatoes	10 lbs
Cereal	1 pkt		Tinned Peas	5 lbs
Milk	3 pts		Tinned Peaches	6 lbs
Bacon	2 lbs		Ideal Milk	1 lb
Eggs	3 doz			
Day 5				
Bread			Curry Powder	1 jar
Margarine			Stewed Steak	7 lbs
Marmalade			Onions	2 lbs
Grapefruit	9		Rice	2 lbs
Eggs	3 doz		Pickles	1 jar
Ham	4 lbs			
Baked Beans	4 lbs			
Day 6				
Bread			Sausages	4 lbs
Margarine			Onions	2 lbs
Marmalade			Carrots	5 lbs
Cereal	1 pkt		Potatoes	10 lbs
Milk	3 pts		Fruit Salad	6 lbs
Eggs	3 doz			
Bacon	2 lbs			
Day 7				
Bread			Beef Brisket	4 lbs
Margarine			Onions	2 lbs
Marmalade			Tinned Peas	6 lbs
Cereal	1 pkt		Potatoes	10 lbs
Milk	3 pts		Mushrooms	2 lbs
Eggs	3 doz		Instant Pudding	4 pkts
Bacon	2 lbs		Milk	4 pts
Tomatoes	3 lbs			
plus cooking oil each day				

By addition from the menus a list is obtained.

TABLE 11—TOTAL FOOD LIST

Item	1 week's requirement	6 weeks' requirement
Grapefruit	18	108
Cereal	5 pkts	30
Milk	38 pts	228
Bread	21 loaves	126
Margarine	14 tubs	84
Marmalade	7 jars	42
Eggs	18 doz	108
Bacon	10 lbs (vacuum)	60
Sausages	10 lbs tinned	60
Baked Beans	8 lbs tinned	48
Tomatoes	9 lbs tinned	54
Ham	18 lbs tinned	108
Onions	17 lbs fresh	102
Cabbages	9 fresh	54
Potato Salad	14 lbs tinned	84
Pickles	8 jars	48
Sardines	28 tins	168
Corned Beef	14 lbs tinned	84
Fruit Juice	28 pts tinned	168
Jam	7 jars	42
Marmite	7 jars	42
Tuna Fish	4 lbs tinned	24
Minced Beef	7 lbs tinned	42
Stewed Steak	14 lbs tinned	84
Steak and Kidney Pies	9 pies	54
Beef Brisket	4 lbs	24
Flour	$\frac{1}{2}$ lb	3
Potatoes	50 lbs	150 fresh; 150 tinned
Carrots	10 lbs fresh	60
Peas	12 lbs tinned	72
Pears	6 lbs tinned	36
Peaches	12 lbs tinned	72
Fruit salad	6 lbs tinned	36
Ideal Milk	2 lbs tinned	12
Oxo	$\frac{1}{6}$ pkt	1
Mushrooms	3 lbs	18

continued over page

Table 11 continued

Rice	2 lbs	12
Spaghetti	3 pkts	18
Curry Powder	1 jar	6
Instant pudding	4 pkts	24
Soup	63 lbs	378
Cooking Oil	1 litre	6
Salad Dressing	1 jar	6
Salt	1 lb	6
Pepper	1 pot	6
Mustard	2 pots	12
And in addition for drinking		
Coffee	¾ large tin	5
Tea	400 bags	2,400
Sugar	7 lbs	42
Milk	included above	
Cocoa	2 lbs	12
Orange Juice (Squash)	2 pts	12
Lemon Juice (Squash)	2 pts	12

This food list is very basic and contains few of the small luxuries that make a voyage more interesting. However, I hope it gives the reader food for thought.

It is very important, once the final food lists have been decided, to make sure the domestics use only their correct allowances of ingredients for the day; what they do with these ingredients is left to their skill and imagination.

Rough Weather Food. As a cook becomes more experienced his (or her) ability to produce food in rough weather will increase; by experience I imply expertise in the galley, not Cordon Bleu skills. Hot food is needed in a storm more than at any other time, and anyone who can produce it is elevated to hero level. The secret is to keep things simple: use one saucepan and put everything—within reason—into it. Tins of meat, potatoes and vegetables all go together to make a storm stew. The saucepan should be really large, so that it is only half full, or less. Serve in high-sided plates with spoons and the increase in morale will make the effort worth while.

Water

How much should be carried? A person normally needs 4 pints of water a day; of course no-one drinks that amount regularly (at least not at sea), as most of it is provided by the food one eats. So if all the food carried is dehydrated, 4 pints per person per day will be required to re-hydrate the food and to drink. (Any food re-hydrated in sea water only will be far too salty). A yacht with a crew of 6 on a 6 week voyage would need 126 gallons minimum; to allow for some wastage a more realistic figure would be 150 gallons. If, however, all the food were tinned, only 2 pints (5 or 6 drinks) per person per day would be required; the same 6 men would need only 60 gallons. If a small amount is allowed for some cooking (rice and spaghetti use 50/50 salt and fresh water, fresh vegetables use all sea water), and a little for wastage, a figure of 80 is realistic. During the first leg of the 1977 world race our crew of 17 used only 220 gallons in a leg of 41 days— an equivalent of $2\frac{1}{2}$ pints each per day—for drinking, some cooking, teeth cleaning, and possibly some wastage. As well as this amount we also had a beer and a glass of fruit juice each and every day.

The water should be stowed in two or more tanks, to guard against total loss in case of pipe or valve failure. Some extra, in plastic containers, is also seamanlike, doubling as abandon-ship security. Water in clean ship's tanks seems to last very well without developing a taste; use of a carbon filter on the tap may help ensure this.

Cleaning

A job even less popular with domestics than cooking. It is never-the-less important to keep a yacht clean; if the job is ignored for a long period nothing short of a complete refit inside will put the matter right. With a watch system working on rotation of domestics there is an advantage: one team will not take over the job from another unless the yacht is clean.

Washing dishes is an unpopular chore. There are ways of making it easier, and ways of making it harder. One of my lasting memories of the first round-the-world race is of standing in *Second Life's* galley, one foot on the bulkhead against the heel of the yacht, struggling with the debris left behind by the cook, and with half a basinful of tepid, greasy washing up water spilling each time we rolled. Two lessons were learnt from this; firstly, whoever cooks should wash up; secondly, a lot of washing up water should be used. If the sea water is to be heated there is a limit to how much time and gas can be spared for this purpose. A better idea is to use cold, pumped straight out of the sea in endless quantities, with Tepol as the washing up agent; this works very well.

Clothes are bound to come under attack at some stage of the trip. It is surprising actually, how long a piece of clothing can be worn in the very clean air found at sea: admittedly standards do tend to deteriorate when out of sight of land, but even so clothes stay fairly clean. They can be washed quite satisfactorily in cold salt water—I use a 'supermarket' shampoo instead of detergent. If the items are thoroughly wrung out after rinsing, most of the water—and hence of the salt—is removed, and they won't feel damp and sticky. If, for example, a pair of trousers have been caught in the spray three or four times, they will have a build-up of three or four loads of salt and will never dry; but rinsed again in salt water and wrung out, they will retain only half a load of salt and they will dry quite normally.

Exactly the same arguments apply to personal washing; salt water soap is of doubtful value—it is better to use shampoo. Even hair, washed in salt water from a bucket over the stern, will feel good if thoroughly dried.

10 Health

To Carry a Doctor or not

In the 1977/78 round-the-world race some of the entries carried doctors, some did not. Were some skippers over cautious, or were the others foolish? Of course, carrying a doctor is not going to keep all the crew fit and accident free, and a yacht is hardly the ideal place for surgery, should problems arise; the value of carrying a doctor lies in the peace of mind his analysis of a potential problem can provide.

For deep sea racing I believe a doctor is an essential member of the crew. This is so for the simple reason that a skipper, worried about the health of someone on board, may abandon a race unnecessarily. A doctor may recognise the pains as seasickness and say 'race on', while a cautious skipper, fearing appendicitis or some other well-publicised but unlikely ailment, may head for the nearest port.

We were caught out in this way on *Great Britain II* during the second leg, Cape Town to Auckland, of the 1977 world race. We had no doctor on board, and indeed had not needed one until 13th November. This is what happened:

We were sailing in the Southern Ocean, 1,000 miles from Tasmania—the nearest land. *G.B. II* had been running fast in strong westerly winds for several days. On the afternoon of the 13th November the wind started to rise and I decided to take down the storm spinnaker; it was getting very rough. The Noon-1600 watch were on deck and I called up the 16–2000 watch, who were on standby below. We prepared everything carefully, with crew allocated to each control. There were six of us on the foredeck, ready for a forward lower. The lazy guy was brought in to the base of the mast and winched in tight until we could get our hands on the leeward corner of the sail. Next I called for the lazy sheet and spinnaker guy to be let go from the windward side. The sail collapsed and flapped forward, partly in the lee of the mainsail. The halyard was eased and the sail fought to the deck. All was safe, and this caused a moment of relaxation at the wrong time, which was nearly fatal. At just that moment we were caught by a wave and knocked beam on to the sea, causing enough heel for our balance to be lost. Part of the spinnaker, or one of its sheets or guys, fell off the foredeck into the water. We were still moving very fast and the sea, rushing past, started to drag the sail out of our grasp and into the water.

In a case like this the best hope of stopping the sail going completely is not simply to pull it back, thus fighting the force of the water, but to get to the rail and pull the sail vertically clear of the sea, which will then hopefully lose its grip. Nick Dunlop and I rushed to the lee rail just forward of the main shrouds, got our hands on the sail and started to pull. Nick was kneeling and I was standing by his right shoulder. Unfortunately we lost our grip on the cloth and the rest of the sail rushed past us and disappeared astern. It was still attached by five ropes (2 sheets, 2 guys, 1 halyard) and one or more of these had formed a loop on the deck at exactly the point where Nick and I found ourselves. The loop snatched tight as the sail set in the water astern. It was around Nick's waist and my knees, and I think I had a hand caught as well. It pulled tighter and tighter, sinking into Nick's foul weather gear. My left knee was being forced into Nick's right side as my knee was squeezed by the rope.

I yelled for a knife. Nick was sick and then immediately lost consciousness, his torso hanging back limply from the rope loop. We had been dragged down the deck, breaking a stanchion, and were coming up against the rigging. I was still screaming for help when seconds later Ian Worley arrived on the scene and cut every rope in sight—there was so much weight on them, they parted like paper. The relief that I was free and could still stand was immense; the adrenalin was doing its job.

The situation was nasty. Nick was unconscious on the deck; the freed spinnaker was now flying from the masthead on a 100 ft halyard, way out of reach. I have no idea how the sail got there from the water, where it had been trailing aft a few seconds earlier. We were in quite a mess and it was cold and wet. Then, for the first time, I regretted not shipping a doctor for the race.

I left Ian in charge of Nick and gave him as many crew as he needed, while I organised the safety of the yacht. The standard routine for recovering a spinnaker from the masthead is to send a man aloft to tie a line on the halyard and hence get control to the deck; but that was out of the question in these rough seas. Luffing up did not help, as the sail streamed way above the mizzen, the main flogged badly, and spray covered the decks and also Nick, who had now regained consciousness. Running off again we had a lucky break: the sail touched the water ahead and we sailed virtually straight into it. It was recovered without hesitation by the crew; a jib was boomed out and we were under control.

Meanwhile Ian had his team well organised: the saloon table top had been brought on deck and using it as a stretcher, we managed to get Nick down below. This operation was not easy, as he was in a lot of pain, but eventually we had him wedged between the seat and table on the saloon floor. All attempts to move him further were halted by his agonised cries. I cut away his clothes and could see no visible damage. We covered him with sleeping bags and filled two empty Teachers whisky bottles with hot water to try and warm him up. A few minutes after this it was time for the daily inter-yacht radio schedule; I spoke to the doctor on *Condor*, who told us to get Nick on his back in his bunk and to give him morphine if necessary. I arranged a two-hourly radio schedule and signed off. Giving morphine is not as easy as the diagrams on the ampoules make out; no doubt the system is right, but it is surprising how tough human skin is. Eventually we got him to his bunk, moving him along the cabin floor by using a sleeping bag as a sled.

Through the next few days the doctor radioed instructions for Nick's nursing.

Meanwhile I had altered course to a point near Hobart, as there was a possibility that he would have to be put ashore. The yacht was being run by Ian, as I soon found myself unable to walk. This lasted for three days. Nick could not move or eat for several days and his eyes went bright red from the blood pressure build-up caused by the constriction round the waist. Eventually, on the fourth day, he felt better; the doctor radioed re-assurances, and so I altered course again and we resumed racing.

A doctor on board would have saved us a lot of worry and several miles lost.

Of course, if a doctor is carried, then his advice as to medical preparation can be taken and he will provide the medical kit. However, the majority of yachts go deep sea without a doctor and for that reason I have asked Dr. Robin Leach, a Cape Horner, to give us the following medical advice.

THE DOCTOR'S ADVICE

Preparations. If the crew of a yacht does not include a doctor, a regular member of the crew should be designated 'medical officer'. This will often be the skipper but in some instances the task is better given to someone with a special interest in First Aid or who is the holder of a Nursing, Red Cross or St John's Ambulance qualification. Two points are paramount: (i) there should be a continuity of medical facilities by the same person who (ii) should have the responsibility of maintaining the contents of the medical chest from voyage to voyage.

The problems of racing and cruising are similar but the task of deciding to stop a race to land a sick crew-member may be a particularly onerous one for the non-medically qualified.

The conscientious medical officer will know the particular problems of each crew-member and should check that any special drugs needed by an individual are supplied by that person well in excess of the projected time at sea. Chronic illness such as asthma, diabetes or specific allergies need not be a bar to long sea voyages, but the skipper and medical officer must be made aware of the problem prior to sailing. Indeed all crew members should have a full medical check performed by their general practitioners before a long voyage. Women may prefer to avoid menstruation at sea by taking the contraceptive pill continuously. This decision should be made by the individual and her GP; if the pill is used continuously there may be a slight increase in the incidence of vaginal thrush and Nystatin pessaries should be added to the medical chest for its treatment.

Immunisations. The following is a broad guide to which protection is required, but it is worth checking the regulations of specific countries well before sailing. It may take three months to complete a course of some injections.

Tetanus—whole World.

Smallpox—East African countries (Check).

Polio—warm countries especially North Africa, also some Arctic areas.

Infectious Hepatitis—areas with warm climates and poor sanitation. This disease spreads rapidly through small enclosed communities and it may be worthwhile for the whole crew to be immunised before a long voyage.

Typhoid and Paratyphoid—anywhere outside Northern Europe.

Cholera—Africa and Asia including the Middle East.

Typhus—South America and Africa.

Malaria—Africa, Asia and South America. There is no immunisation for malaria but one week prior to arriving in an infected area anti-malarial tablets should be started. In Africa Chloroquine (2 tablets per week), Asia and South America Pyrimethamine and Sulphadoxone (1 tablet per week) are recommended.

It is worth remembering that the planned stops on a voyage may be altered by circumstances beyond the crew's control and therefore the countries passed during a voyage should also be considered as far as immunisation is concerned.

The Medical Chest. The content of the medical chest is described in Appendix 6A. There is always a tendency to take too much in the way of drugs and medical equipment. The amounts suggested in the Appendix are for a crew of 8. Most yachts on long ocean voyages are prepared for the ultimate disaster of sinking and as such have an emergency bag placed near a hatch to be taken into a life raft. This bag should contain a supplementary medical box with essential drugs and dressings, see Appendix 6B.

Each medical chest should contain a pencil and notebook. All treatments, dosages and dates should be recorded as this may prove a valuable source of information at a later date.

The medical officer should be concerned with the viability of the radio communication system of the yacht, as this may mean the difference between life and death when a difficult decision has to be made. He should also be aware of nearby vessels who may carry medical help. In some instances medical advice is available by prior arrangement in the yacht's country of origin and this is the medical officer's responsibility to organise.

Dental Care. All crew members should have a scrupulous dental check before embarkation—and the necessary treatment. This is never a popular chore but serious complications from dental infections can occur and of course the miserable days of pain often reduce a much needed crew-member to his bunk.

Insurance. The National Health Service provides emergency treatment to any foreigner who falls ill in the United Kingdom, but not those who arrive specifically for treatment.

Unfortunately such a 'mercy' clause does not exist in the majority of other countries and the cost of medical treatment may run into many thousands of pounds. Adequate insurance, including the cost of repatriation, should be taken before sailing. This may be available at a reduced rate if the whole crew takes up the policy.

There is a reciprocal arrangement for medical treatment within the EEC and by simply completing a form from a local social services department, medical costs can be reimbursed. This must be done before leaving the United Kingdom.

Treatment

The Unconscious Patient. A patient may be rendered unconscious by a blow to the head, severe blood loss or asphyxiation. The events leading to the loss of consciousness will help determine which of these factors is involved.

If a blow to the head has been sustained the period of unconsciousness may be only short lived. The most important procedure is to ensure that the airway of the patient is open; this involves removing any debris (dentures, vomit etc) from the patient's mouth and extending the neck to make sure the tongue has not fallen back to block off the air passages. If asphyxiation or drowning is suspected, immediate mouth to mouth resuscitation is performed to ventilate the lungs. If pulses have disappeared external cardiac massage should also be commenced.

A series of observations should be started as soon after the accident as possible. The rate of respiration, the colour of the patient, the pulse rate and the level of consciousness are noted. The last is the most important and varies from fully conscious through drowsy, but rational; asleep but rousable; responds to painful stimuli only, to unresponsive. The patient should be placed in the semi-prone position so that any secretions or vomit (common after a head injury) may appear from the mouth rather than be inhaled.

A further index of neurological damage after head injury is the size of the pupils and their response to a bright light being shone into them. Normally the pupils will react equally and rapidly to stimulation by light, and they should be equal in size; any variation in size or failure to respond to light should be noted. If consciousness is not regained after 5–10 minutes it is wise to seek further advice if possible.

Bleeding. This may be revealed for example from a cut, or concealed where no blood is seen yet blood is lost from the circulation, either into a body cavity or a muscle. The signs of concealed bleeding are pale, cold and clammy skin, a rise in pulse rate, and eventually disorientation and loss of consciousness. If a patient has merely fainted the pulse rate tends to be slower than normal. The cause of concealed bleeding may not be obvious but evidence of a blow to a particular area of the body may be helpful. There is, however, little to be done except keep the patient in a moderately warm, quiet area and seek further help.

The treatment of cuts is first and foremost to stop the bleeding. This may be achieved in almost all cases by elevation of the affected part and the application of direct pressure with a thick dressing. The length of time needed for this compression may be several minutes, and remember that to overcome the pressure of blood from a cut may require such pressure that actual pain is caused to the person applying the pressure.

The use of a tourniquet should be avoided in all situations except when blood loss is so great that life may be endangered.

Once blood flow has been stopped the cut should be cleaned with Cetrimide solution and then dried. The edges of the wound are then brought together with adhesive paper strips (Steristrips) rather than sutures. If bleeding still persists a pressure bandage may be applied for a short time. By avoiding sutures the use of local anaesthetic and instruments is by-passed.

Bruises are local collections of blood below the skin or in muscles; whilst not dangerous they are often the cause of a dull ache and stiffness. There is no specific treatment for bruises, except to keep the part moving rather than immobilising it; the bruise will then clear more rapidly.

Burns. Fire on a yacht is a much dreaded and fortunately rare occurrence. However several sorts of burn are common at sea. First, sunburn is very painful even if judged self-inflicted. Slow exposure to the sun is imperative. Only in the most severe cases should a mild antihistamine such as Piriton (4 mg 8 hourly) be needed. Burns and scalds in the galley are also common and for this reason even in the hottest climates a long apron or oilskin trousers should be worn when cooking. Rope burns, from desperate effort to secure a loose halyard or wild sheet, may cause severe damage to the palms of the hands. Both galley and rope burns may be treated with a paste of sodium bicarbonate applied to a wet tissue placed over the affected area. This cools the burn and to a certain extent prevents blistering.

Broken Bones. Fractures at sea are not uncommon. The signs are local tenderness and/or bruising, loss of function of the affected bone and usually some degree of deformity. Whilst it is not possible to give a detailed account of the treatment of fractures, the principles are similar in most cases.

The fracture may be associated with severe pain requiring the use of Papaveratum (15 mg intramuscularly). The deformity should be corrected as far as possible without causing undue pain and then the bone immobilised using a series of splints (sail battens are good for this). The colour of the limb beyond the fracture should be noted and care taken to ensure that the blood supply to this area is intact. If the limb becomes pale, excessively painful and paralysed, urgent advice should be sought as this implies that the blood supply is embarrassed.

'First Aid For Yachtsmen' by Dr R. Howarth gives a particularly good account of the treatment of fractures and may be a worthwhile addition to the medical chest.

Indigestion and Abdominal Pain. A change in the motion of the yacht may cause stomach acid to regurgitate into the lower gullet especially after some hours lying in a bunk. This causes an unpleasant burning feeling behind the breast bone and a sour taste in the mouth, which may also be experienced after the excesses of a stay in port; it may be remedied by taking Asilone or Gelusil tablets every few hours.

One of the fears of long ocean voyages is that one of the crew may develop appendicitis, but this is no more likely than on dry land. Given that most cases of appendicitis occur during the early and middle teens and that most ocean yachtsmen are older than this, it is an unlikely occurrence. However abdominal pain beginning in the centre of the abdomen and moving to the lower right side, associated with loss of appetite, mild fever and vomiting may be the early symptoms of appendicitis. If the diagnosis is fairly certain and help is not too far away further advice is best taken. However, in mid-ocean the patient is best confined to his bunk, given fluids (rectally if necessary), pain killers and antibiotics (Metronidazole suppositories 1 every 6 hours). This is certainly safer than attempting one's first appendicectomy under local anaesthetic on a rolling yacht, and there are many recorded cases of appendicitis being successfully treated without surgery.

Colicky abdominal pains associated with vomiting and diarrhoea are usually the signs of a gastro intestinal infection rather than appendicitis. Opinions vary slightly upon the best treatment, but plenty of fluids and a fat-free diet plus an antispasmodic such as Buscopan (20 mg every 4 hours) relieves symptoms reasonably quickly. Persistent diarrhoea may be stopped using Immodium. If large amounts of fluid are lost, especially in hot climates, salt supplements should be added to the convalescent diet.

Intermittent colicky pains radiating from the loin down to the groin and testis which cause the patient to writhe about in agony are seen with renal colic. Buscopan is very effective in treating this complaint but the severe pain may need Papveratum (or better Pethidine). Fluids should be taken in large amounts in order to try and flush out the cause of the pain, usually a stone passing from the kidney to the bladder.

Constipation. If possible the crew of all yachts should be taking a high fibre diet to give them one or two bulky motions per day each. In practice low residue reconstitutable foods are commonly used for convenience and space saving. Dulcodos or Dorbanex is effective in relieving constipation which should not be allowed to reoccur.

Aches and pains. Headaches, sprains, muscular pains and toothache are best treated with Paracetamol tablets 2 every 4 hours.

Infections. These are rare at sea and are most commonly seen after a stay in port. Mild epidemics of bacterial or viral infections may sweep through whole crews. Sore throats are best treated with Penicillin V 250 mg every 6 hours for one week. Urinary infections occur most commonly in women and can be treated with Septrin 2 tablets every 12 hours for one week.

If an abscess has formed (a local collection of pus) this cannot be treated with antibiotics and the pus must be released surgically. Depending upon the site of the abscess local anaesthetic (1% Lignocaine) may be useful before incision. The pus should be freely drained with a large incision or else there may be a possibility of reformation.

Skin Problems. These are perhaps the most common complaints on long sea voyages. The continuous soaking of the skin with salt water removes natural oils and cracks appear at the finger tips. Small scratches enlarge and may heal very slowly. It has been found effective to apply Lanoline cream to the hands twice a day which makes the hard dry skin more maleable and less uncomfortable.

Some fair-skinned people are prone to cold sores when exposed to bright sunlight. If Uvistat cream is applied before exposure ultraviolet light is absorbed and cannot activate the virus which causes the cold sores.

Occasionally noxious chemicals are used as thinners or anti-fouling material and these may cause allergic reactions on the skin if bright sunlight is also present. Even in the hottest climates gloves and protective clothing should always be used when anti-fouling. If a reaction is acquired use Piriton tablets with or without the local application of calamine lotion.

SEASICKNESS

After the doctor's excellent advice we go back to the lay seaman's point of view for the most common ailment at sea, and one which doctors can rarely cure—seasickness. There is, of course, a natural cure, which is to stay at sea until it passes; it will eventually go, and often takes only a day or two. Some sailors find that after a long trip they are cured forever, others find the first few days of every voyage bad. There are a few ways to minimise seasickness.

At the first hint of an ill feeling either stay on deck, watch the sea, and if possible steer the yacht; or much better than this, lie down below. Many sufferers will say 'Oh no, I can't go below', and will then sit freezing on deck all night. The secret of going below is to get from the deck to lying down in as short a time as possible—certainly less than 30 seconds. Throw off boots and foul weather gear, leap into the bunk, sleeping bag over the top, and *relax*. It is important not to brace against every movement of the yacht; lie flat on your back and move with the boat; this works well, especially if you can sleep for a short while. Try some hot tea and dry biscuits when you wake; ideally, persuade someone to bring them to you in bed so you can take them without standing up. The worst thing you can do is to sit on the edge of the bunk, deciding what to do next; the answer will be a visit to the lee rail.

There are numerous seasick tablets on the market; find one that suits your system. Some people find the newer tablets recently developed to be the answer, others find that the old style travel sickness pills work best. If one can do without pills, so much the better, as they do tend to cause drowsiness. If they must be taken at sea, the best time is just before coming off watch.

11 Breakages, Repairs and Maintenance

It would be impossible to cover all there is to know about sail repairs, rigging repairs, mechanics, plumbing and electricity in anything less than five complete books. However 90% of all problems at sea can be handled with 10% of all knowledge. I hope this chapter will help.

Sails

These are the driving force behind any voyage, and hence very important. Sails tend to be damaged in two ways, either by chafe or by blow-outs. Typical chafe points include: the genoa on the spreader ends, the mainsail on the leeward running backstay, the foot of the light spinnaker on the forestay; and there are many others. Damage thus caused usually amounts to a few broken stitches or small holes; regular checks and repairs can prevent these developing into severe weaknesses that may then cause blow-outs. Further areas of possible trouble are hanks on a jib and clew, head and tack attachments. This section deals with ways of handling all these problems on board.

Hand Sewing. A palm and needle is the only way to fix a sail if the cloth is too heavy for a sewing machine, or of course if a sewing machine is not carried. On large yachts it is a good idea to keep the sewing machine tuned for spinnaker and light genoa repairs, and to repair any heavier sail by hand. Enough palms and needles should be carried so that several crew can work simultaneously on a large job. When using a palm, make sure that the eye of the needle is in the centre of the palm before pushing, otherwise, as pressure is applied, the needle may slip and spear your hand. For most hand sewing jobs waxed whipping thread is the thing to use.

A small chafe hole of only a few centimetres long can be repaired by using herringbone stitching (see diagram 59), but this will only be strong enough in an area of minimal strain. To improve the mend, a small patch of similar material can be handsewn on top; for a patch 5 cm by 5 cm use a piece of cloth 7 cm by 7 cm, cut off the corners, fold over the edges and sew it down as shown in diagram 60. The stitches could be about 6 or 7 mm long.

Fortunately most damage to heavy sails is along seams, as the thread, especially if at all

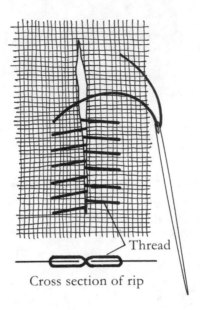

59. *Simple herring-bone stitches for rip.*

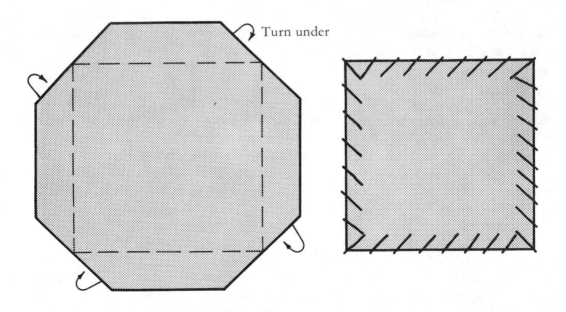

60. *A small patch sewn by hand.*

chafed, is the weak link. Such rips are easy, if tedious, to repair: first remove all the broken bits of thread from both sides of the rip. The precise line up of the repair, both lengthwise and crosswise, can be achieved by accurately picking up the old machine holes; this line-up has to be correct if the sail is to set properly again as if it is wrong the sail will probably rip again when all the strain comes on one point. As the hand sewing thread is stronger than the original it is not necessary to make the stitches so small. See diagram 61. Using this system on two complete seams of an old mainsail, we were able to sail *British Steel* 5,000 miles from Rio back to England without further sail repair.

If a seam or larger patch has to be hand sewn, and there are no convenient holes to be picked up, it is a good idea to hold the repair in place during the operation; this is best done using ordinary domestic contact adhesive—even if the cloth is wet, it will help.

Machine Sewing. When cruising, a sewing machine is probably counted as a space wasting, low priority luxury. When racing, it is an essential item of equipment, that amply rewards the loving care needed to keep it in order. J. J. Reed make a machine specifically designed for use on board yachts; it is reliable and rugged. It is also reasonably priced, as a lot of the fancy gadgets available on domestic machines are left out. Zigzag is the stitch used in most sail repairs as it allows stretch in both directions.

It is essential to be well prepared for the use of the machine; somewhere, probably the saloon table, there should be a place where it can be wedged securely during use. On *Great Britain II* the saloon was refitted with priority given to ease of sail repairs. A rectangular box 1.5 metres long, .75 metres wide and .5 metres high was bolted to the saloon floor. The box was designed with a flat top onto which the sewing machine fitted exactly; when not in use the machine and the sail repair kit (cloth, thread, needles etc.) lived inside the box. The table/box was no use for eating off, but then one eats off one's lap at sea nearly all the time.

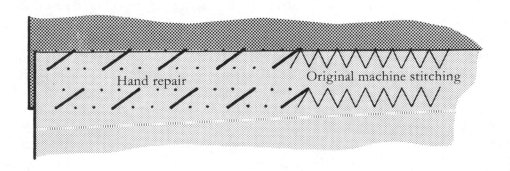

Hand repair · · · Original machine stitching

61. *Hand repair of a seam. Pick up every third hole.*

The secret of sewing a good seam with a machine is to get the tensions on the top and bottom threads correct; too little on both and the stitches will be loose, too much and they will bunch the cloth. Worse than this is uneven tension top and bottom; for example, diagram 62 shows what happens if the top thread is relatively too tight. Study of the manual is recommended.

As mentioned earlier, the machine will probably only be used for light genoas and spinnakers. A genoa seam repair can be sewn, but care must be taken with the lengthwise line-up—see section on spinnakers. A large rip in the light genoa cloth is best repaired by replacing part of the sail; this involves sewing on a new panel and cutting out the old. This system is also described in detail in the section on spinnakers.

Spinnaker Blow-outs. The hardest part of any repair is the lining up of the seam or rip; this has to be done as accurately as possible if the repair is to be successful. Most spinnaker blow-outs are a combination of rips along a seam, rips along the cloth and rips up the edge of the luff tape. When a spinnaker goes it really goes, and yet it is surprising just how extensive a repair can be achieved, even in the cramped conditions in a yacht.

The spinnaker probably ended up in the water after blowing out, so the first thing to do is to try and dry it. It can probably not be left on deck because of the wind, so pile it down the hatch; then try to follow down either side of the rip; this will give some indication of how the rip runs, and also pulls it to the top of the pile to dry off. It will obviously be impossible to lay the sail out, as a sailmaker would do; instead it is necessary to repair a bit at a time; for instance, the rip may appear as indicated in diagram 63. It could be repaired in any order, but the individual jobs are: repair along a seam, repair a long cloth rip, repair a small cloth rip and repair along a luff tape. The only time the whole repair is seen together is when the sail is next hoisted.

Spinnaker Luff Tape Repair. A luff tape repair is an easy special case, as there is no line-up problem. The luff tape itself overlaps the cloth by a few centimetres; when it goes, it usually rips up the edge of the tape. The neatest and easiest way to fix this is to unpick the sewing on the luff tape, remove the strip of sail that has ripped off, and resew the tape onto what is left of the spinnaker. The result is a sail a few centimetres narrower, which is better than nothing. Getting the luff tape at the correct tension is not vital; if it is sewn on freely—i.e. without forcing either sail or tape through the machine—it should be O.K. It will not, of course, go back on exactly as before. If at the end of sewing there is a surfeit of luff tape, cut it and keep on machine, so that the surplus overlaps the luff tape on the good part of the sail. If it is too short, use a piece of strong material—similar to the luff tape—to lengthen it. Make sure any luff tape to luff tape join is very strong indeed, as a weak link here will let the sail blow again. When machining luff tapes, especially near reinforced clews, the number of thicknesses of cloth may cause difficulties for the machine; I have found the way to handle these heavy sections is to fool the machine by starting sewing on a thinner section and hit the thicker part at speed. It usually works. Zigzag stitch should be used. See diagram 64.

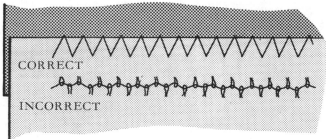

CORRECT

INCORRECT

62. *Machine repair. Take care to correct thread tension top and bottom.*

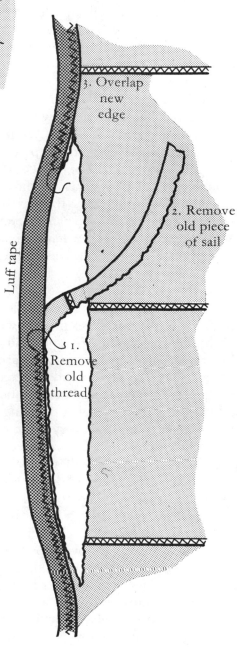

3. Overlap new edge

2. Remove old piece of sail

1. Remove old thread

Luff tape

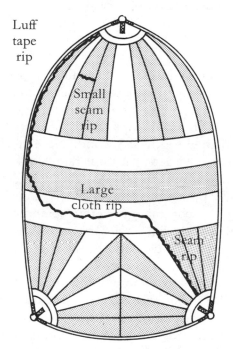

Luff tape rip

Small seam rip

Large cloth rip

Seam rip

63. *A tri-radial cut spinnaker showing a typical 'blow-out'.*

64. *Repairing a luff tape rip.*

A Small Cloth Rip. A small rip of less than a metre—such as across one panel of cloth—can be repaired in either of two ways. The quickest, but least satisfactory way, is to use tape, bought in rolls of sticky-backed spinnaker material, 5 cm wide, with a covering of protective paper. Cut two pieces of the tape, each the length of the rip plus 10 cm; lay out the rip on a board or table top but if the rip is too long to be laid out, it should be treated as a long rip and dealt with as described later. The sides of the rip should just butt together, and must certainly not overlap, otherwise a hard spot will result; peel the paper from the tape and stick it along the tear, taking care not to put any tension on the tape as it is laid—in fact it should deliberately be kept very loose to match the sail lying on the table. Turn the cloth over and place the second piece of tape on the other side; sew the tape down with the machine. again using a zigzag stitch.

A neater way of doing this repair is to replace a part of the sail; for a rip across an 18 inch (45 cm) panel, cut out a new piece of similar cloth about 15 cm wide and long enough to overlap the panel and the seams on either side of it; lay this patch over the rip, stick it in place (gluing just the perimeter), and zigzag round its edge. Now turn the sail over and cut out from the panel a rectangle which is smaller by 2 cm all round than the patch just sewn on. This rectangle takes out the damaged part of the sail. Sew down the edge of the cloth just cut. See diagram 65.

A Long Rip. Whether a long rip is along a seam or across the cloth, the major problem is the same; if the two edges of a rip were simply sewn together, after 10 metres or so of machining one would probably find one side of the repair 20 cm or more longer than the other. This happens for two reasons; firstly, when a cloth rips the chances are that one side will be permanently stretched more than the other; secondly, the sewing machine is unlikely to feed the top and bottom cloths at exactly the same rate. Unlike the luff tape case, there is no way of losing this excess. To avoid this problem the two sides of the rip must be marked every half metre or so. The possibility of uneven stretch means that this cannot be done by measurement alone, so the whole length of the repair must be pulled out tight with both sides under tension. If the rip is 15 metres long, then 15 metres have to be stretched out; this often takes several hands, with the sail fed from the sail locker, through the saloon, down aft and back again. Once pulled taut, a line-up mark can be drawn (felt tip pen is best) on both edges somewhere in the middle of the rip; the sail is then stretched out between this mark and one end and more line-up marks drawn. Continue in this way until the whole tear is marked; occasionally, with careful examination, a positive, natural line-up mark can be found—look for a kink in the rip or a seam crossing it; if one is identified it will shorten the length of the initial stretch-out. This line-up must be done as accurately as possible if the repair is to be a success.

The sail is now ready for sewing. If the rip was along a seam it can be sewn back with the same overlap as it originally had, but make sure while machining that the line-up marks match up. To achieve this it will probably be necessary to force-feed one of the sides through the machine. There is a temptation to ignore the marks, as the sewn sail may look so perfect. However, they must be kept in line, even if minute tucks are required in one edge every few centimetres to line up the marks. Provided the marking was accurate to begin with, and they are adhered to, the repaired sail will set perfectly—even if the repaired seam looks rough on close examination.

If the long rip is straight through the cloth, rather than on a seam, there will be a problem of transverse, as well as longitudinal line-up. This is made still more difficult by the likelihood of frayed edges. There are two ways of repairing such a rip; the first uses sticky tape and is achieved following these steps:

 1. Mark the sail as described above.
 2. Pass the rip across a board or table top, with the edges just butting together, and the longitudinal marks lining up.
 3. Stick the tape over the rip as it is fed past.
 4. Complete one side, turn over and repeat on the other.
 5. Machine sew two rows of stitching down each edge of the tape. If the tape on either side does not match up exactly, six rows of stitching may be required altogether.

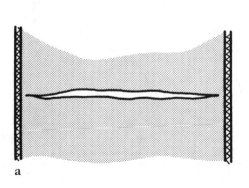

a

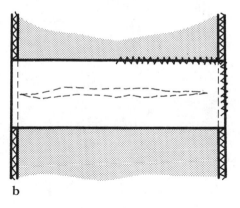

b

65. *a. Lay out rip.*
    b. Sew patch over.
    c. On the other side
       cut out damaged
       part of sail and sew
       down edge.

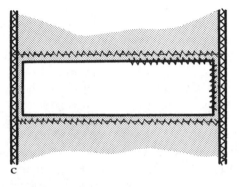

c

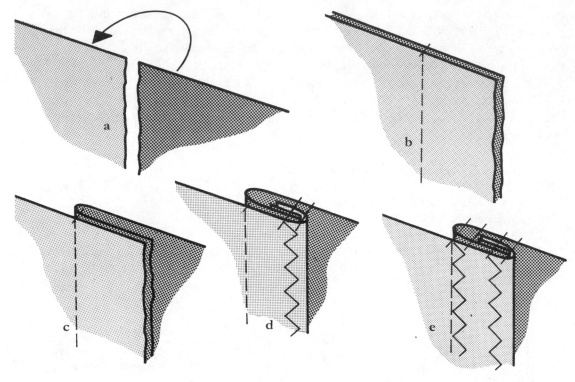

66. *The stages of sewing a long rip in the cloth.*

There are a few problems with this system; it uses a lot of tape, the sail has to be dry, there is a lot of stitching and the result is not very neat. The second system is much quicker and neater:

1. Mark the sail as described above.
2. Fold one side of the rip round, so that it lies on top of the other with the ripped edges level. See diagram 66a.
3. Sew a line of straight stitching 2 cm in from the edges, all the way down the rip, lining up the marks as you go. See diagram 66b.
4. Unfold the two sides. Diagram 66c.
5. Tuck under the end third (7 mm) of the flange formed by step 4, and sew down with zigzag stitching. Diagram 66d.
6. Optionally, and a good idea if the sail is not needed immediately, sew a second row of zigzags on top of the first straight stitched seam. Diagram 66e.

The beauty of this system is that even with a wavy rip, a good transverse line-up is obtained, provided the first row of stitches is always 2 cm in from the edge. The result is a repair with no tape, no patches, just an extra seam in the sail. The fact that 4 cm of cloth is lost throughout the rip is not noticeable if the ends are tapered in.

Head and Clew Repairs. The corners of all sails take a tremendous amount of punishment, and despite complex reinforcing are occasionally damaged. If the cloth rips through a reinforced clew, the only satisfactory way to repair it is to unpick all the individual layers of cloth, repair them individually and rebuild it as accurately as possible. This is quite a difficult task. Fortunately the majority of blow-outs terminate when reinforcing is met.

More common, and easier to fix, is the failure of a clew of head ring. There are several methods employed by sailmakers to put corners in sails and each has potential problems which may be brought out by the continual stress and chafe of long distance sailing. One of the worst problems is found when the head of a spinnaker is made by setting an eye in the cloth panel at the head; these eyes are often brass and chafe quickly if a shackle is used on the halyard. I favour using an all-rope spinnaker halyard and tying it on to the sail with a bowline in all cases—it is certainly necessary in this case.

A better system is a stainless steel triangular or D ring fixed to the sail with strong tape. This can still fail if the ring chafes through the tapes, or if a weld on the ring goes, allowing it to open out. When a sailmaker fixes a ring to a sail he often finishes the job off with a leather cover for neatness; it pays to remove this occasionally to see that all is well underneath. Regardless of how the eye or ring was fixed originally, it can only be repaired or replaced in one way:

> Cut away any damaged material at the corner and hand-sew a D ring or equivalent to the sail; this is done using three or more lengths of strong terylene webbing, as shown in diagram 67. Rings and tape should be carried on board specifically for this purpose. Due

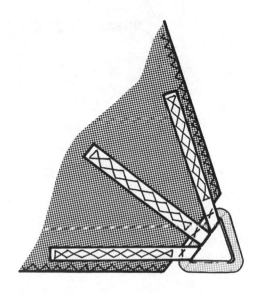

67. *A clew, head or tack repair.*

to the thickness of the webbing and the corner of the sail it will be very difficult, if not impossible, to palm a needle through it. In this case the holes can be pre-punched: stick the webbing in place with adhesive and then, using a sharpened screwdriver and a hammer (and a wooden board underneath), punch the holes. Sewing is then easy. See diagram 68.

Hanks. There are several types of jib hank on the market. For fixing the hank to the jib luff there are two common systems—the knock- and the sew-on. The sew-on is much superior in that, though the stitching needs replacing occasionally, at least it does not chafe through the jib, a disadvantage with the knock-on type. Another disadvantage is that a knock-on cannot be knocked-off, but has to be cut off. One advantage to it is that if a jib needs a quick hank replacement at sea, a knock-on is the answer. See diagram 69a.

The next choice is the way in which the plunger is operated: the piston with a knob on the end (diagram 69b) is easier to use, especially with cold, wet hands, than the piston with a knob on the side (diagram 69c). However, the side knob version is less prone to damage. Running with a boomed out jib the hanks with end knobs tend to punch holes in the sail, which in turn can snag the hanks undone and occasionally break them; it is not unusual to have to replace 3 or 4 a day under these circumstances.

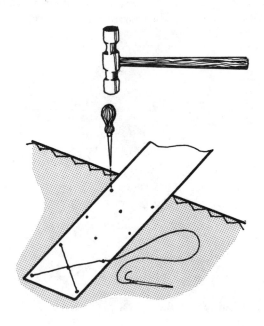

68. *Pre-punch the holes.*

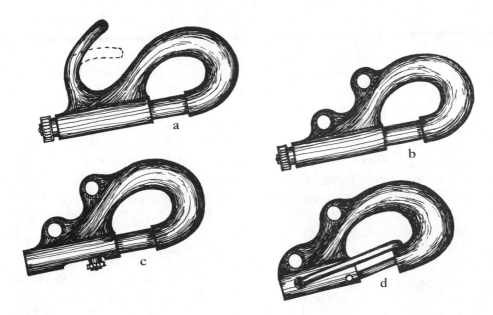

69. *Hanks:— (a) Knock-on. (b) End pull. (c) Side pull plunger. (d) Dog lead.*

A completely different type of hank is that similar to a dog's lead clip. They are nice to use, as only one hand is needed to operate them. The yacht *33 Export* used them in the 1977/78 world race and found them excellent. However, some hanks of this type are made of stainless steel, which is dangerous, as the hank may then chafe the forestay rather than the other way round.

To summarise, use end piston sew-ons for all sails except those which may be boomed out, in which case use side piston sew-ons. Carry spares for these, at least a dozen for an Atlantic crossing, and also a few knock-ons for emergency replacements.

The Rig

Running Rigging and Chafe. One of the biggest differences between inshore and deep sea sailing is the degree of seriousness of chafe. On a four mile leg of an inshore race a badly led sheet will survive, while on a four day leg offshore that same sheet will chafe through a dozen times. It is important continually to check all sheets and halyards for signs of wear. Genoa sheets are usually chafe free, but look out for the guard rails and also make sure that any lead block lines up with the natural angle of the sheet. Spinnaker sheets are also safe provided they are correctly Barber-hauled clear of the boom, as described earlier. Spinnaker guys can be a problem, especially at the pole end; chafe is minimised if the guy is never allowed to 'work' through the jaws of the pole. This 'working' is avoided if the clew of the spinnaker is always kept hard up against the pole end, and the pole guy and lazy sheet are kept slack. Even so, there will be some wear and it is a good idea to cut off a partly worn guy end and retie it before it breaks. By using wire spinnaker guys the problem is solved; a wire guy also stretches less and hence is better for sail control when reaching. However, wire is nasty to handle and for this reason I have always been against its use. Wire guys should never be seen on a cruising yacht, but I now believe that the standard of deep sea racing is such that the slight advantage they give makes it necessary to live with them.

Halyards also reward anti-chafe care with longer life. Spinnaker halyard exits at the masthead will always chafe slightly. On long runs a man should go aloft each day to check for any signs of wear; if there is, he can change halyards on the sail, and bring down the damaged one for inspection. An all rope spinnaker halyard can be end-for-ended if it starts to chafe. Once done, if the halyard chafes again, it will be necessary to cut a metre or so off the end to remove the bad part; a new spinnaker halyard should be long enough to allow for this.

Wire halyards are in general strong enough to resist chafe: galvanised wire should be checked regularly; it may look rusty and yet still be sound. To check this, bend the wire in a tight loop and if any strands break, the halyard should be replaced immediately. The weak joints are near the wire to rope tail splice and near the eye in the end. Stainless halyards won't rust, but should be checked for broken strands, which could cut up a crewman's hands.

To change a halyard use a messenger, a thin line twice the length of the mast: sew the messenger on to the end of the rope tail of the halyard to be removed. See diagram 70.

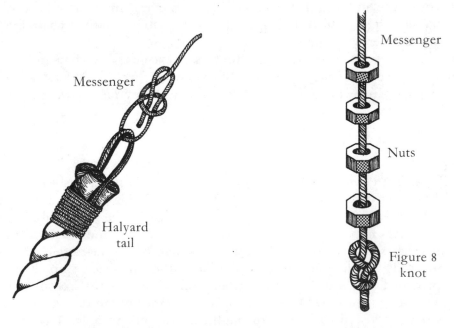

70. *A messenger/halyard join.*   71. *A messenger 'mouse'.*

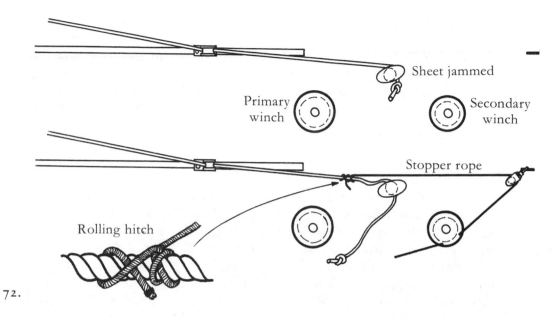

Sheet jammed

Primary winch

Secondary winch

Stopper rope

Rolling hitch

72.

Draw the halyard out and the messenger in; when the messenger has been drawn up inside the mast, out of the sheave at the head and back down to the deck, disconnect the old halyard and sew on the new. The messenger can now be used to draw the new halyard back into the mast.

If an internal halyard breaks while in use, the chances are that it will pull out of the mast. It can be replaced at sea with a little care and a lot of luck. First winch all the other halyards up tight to reduce the chance of a tangle or a twist inside the mast. Make the end of the messenger into a 'mouse' by using a series of nuts. See diagram 71. A man at the masthead then feeds this 'mouse' over the exit sheave and dangles it down inside. With patience it can be hooked out of the entry sheave at or near the foot of the mast; to do this use a wire coathanger or a piece of wire that riggers supply specifically for this purpose. Once the messenger is in a new halyard can be rove.

Careful anti-chafe patrols can save a lot of gear; in 134 days of racing on *G.B.II* we used only one spare halyard and two spare spinnaker guys. The sheets lasted the voyage and are still in use. Naomi James on her nine months' circumnavigation used the same sheets and halyards all the way round, finally breaking one halyard ten miles from the finish.

While on the subject of enemies to sheets, halyards and guys, there is nothing worse than a trigger happy crewman with a knife. I once sailed on a long trip with just such a person; any problem or snarl-up, out came his knife, slash, problem solved, and a new sheet needed. While in some cases a knife is the only cure, there are more seamanlike ways of getting out of trouble. I shall illustrate one by describing a hypothetical situation: a sheet has been let go in error and has run out through the turning block, until brought up by the figure of 8 knot in its end. See diagram 72, top drawing. There is a lot of weight in the sheet, so it can neither be pulled back nor let go. The solution is to take a rope of a slightly smaller diameter and tie it on to the sheet using a rolling hitch, as shown in diagram 72. This stopper rope is then led to a spare winch and taken up. As the rolling hitch grips the sheet it will pull it in until there is enough slack for it to be replaced on its own winch. Incidentally, the rolling hitch is one of the few knots a yachtsman should be able to tie. The only others are the bowline, reef and figure of eight knots.

Standing Rigging. 19-Strand stainless steel wire rigging is very strong, and unless a yacht has been ridiculously lightly rigged, is unlikely to break. What can, and does, happen is that one or more of the 19 strands breaks, either at the end of, or somewhere down the length of the stay. If this happens the broken strand should be taped back in place. The fact that one wire breaks is not necessarily a signal that the remainder are going to follow suit. A difficulty arises if a strand breaks in the forestay; if the break is at, or very near, the end of the stay it can be taped down as before; but if a wire goes in the middle of the stay this will not work, as the tape would be chafed by the hanks of the jib and the broken ends would prevent the sail from being hoisted or lowered. This problem occurred on board *Second Life* ten days out from England at the end of the first round-the-world race. Fearing for the strength of the stay, we taped up the broken strand and then ceased to use the forestay altogether. Needless to say our progress was very slow. As the break was in the middle of the stay, we should have completely unravelled both ends of the broken wire. They could then have been cut away, leaving a forestay of 18/19th its original strength. This could then have been used as usual. When *Pen Duick VI* arrived in Auckland in December 1977 to join the round-the-world race, her forestay had four strands missing; Eric Tabarly seemed quite unconcerned and was only just beginning to consider its replacement.

Solid rod rigging cannot strand. If it fails at all it will probably go where the rod is fixed to the end terminal; this is very unlikely to happen if it is properly made to begin with.

A more likely, and equally serious, problem is the failure of the standing rigging attachment points to either the deck or the mast. It is very difficult to check the integrity of these fittings, as cracks can develop in mast bolts, mast tangs or chainplates without becoming visible to the naked eye. Before a long voyage all mast fittings should be inspected very carefully—especially the bolts which are normally hidden inside the mast.

If a stay breaks the helmsman should immediately alter course to take the weight away from the weakened area—i.e. run off if the forestay breaks, luff up if the backstay breaks, or tack if a windward shroud breaks. (If the mast comes down turn back to chapter 6.) Once the helmsman has completed the manoeuvre the stay should be quickly replaced with a halyard which can be winched up to provide temporary support. Having done this, a slightly more permanent solution can be worked out and hopefully the yacht will sail on. The types of failure that may occur and the way in which they can be fixed, are illustrated by a few examples.

Sailing *British Steel* northwards from the equator, one windy morning we hit a large Atlantic swell; crashing into a wave, the forestay chainplate broke from the deck. The jib luff held the mast up while we replaced the forestay on a spare chainplate. Fortunately the yacht had been designed to carry three forestays for short-handed sailing.

A few days later, on the same yacht, the mast bolt holding the lower shrouds broke; the mast, totally unsupported in the middle, bowed violently from side to side. We ran down wind and I instructed all hands to stand well clear. After a few seconds, as the mast was still standing, we ventured down the deck and lowered the mainsail. We then took both spinnaker halyards from forward, back under the spreaders, crossed over behind the mast and out to either side-deck; when they were winched up tight, the movement of the spar was reduced. Temporary rigging was set up by taking some spare halyard wire and securing it in loops around the mast above the spreaders; the lower shrouds were fixed to these loops. By the time this operation was complete the mast was badly damaged at a point just above deck level, where there was a join in the mast tube; the internal sleeve had buckled, allowing the mast to move aft 1 cm. Despite extra bolts tapped through to the sleeve the mast slowly compressed at the join. However, with reduced sail we completed the race.

The lower shrouds of *Express Crusader* were lost on one side when the tang—the plate that fixes the rigging to the bolt in the mast—broke. Naomi James rigged temporary shrouds in the same way as we had done on *British Steel*. Then, being resourceful, she constructed a tang substitute from D rings and shackles and got the lowers back up again.

The last example is an experience I had on the trimaran *Great Britain IV* during the round Britain race in 1978: the starboard cap shroud chain plate broke from the deck of the float; we tacked before the mast came down. The only alternative chain plate was right at the stern of the float, which had once taken the running backstay; we had to lengthen the shroud with a metre of chain from the anchor so that it would reach, and went on to finish the race successfully.

The Mast. Any mast repairs or maintenance is difficult at sea, because the area of work is gyrating about the sky. As the yacht rolls, a movement of 30 cm at head height becomes 3 metres at the top of a 15 metre mast. Even in the calmest weather, and with a good harness and bosun's chair, it is rare that two hands can be employed on a job for more than a few seconds. Therefore a mast must be well prepared. As well as the areas mentioned already, the sheaves, mainsail track and any mast joins should be inspected.

The sheaves must be free running and yet be a good fit in the sheave box; a sheave which has worn sides and a worn centre bush can lie at a slight angle, which may allow the halyard to jump the sheave—when this happens the halyard falls between the side of the sheave and its box and jams immovably. Should this occur at sea the best bet is to cut the halyard as near the sheave as possible (this gets the sail down) and then try to winch out the remainder of the halyard. Another trick that sheaves are prone to is seizing up; the halyard will still run, but there will be a lot of friction and chafe: the sheave should be knocked out and freed-up.

The mainsail track should be strengthened before a long voyage: hoist the mainsail and mark the area of track at which the head of the sail rests; repeat the procedure with first one, then two, then three reefs in the sail. These marked areas come under a lot of strain, as they have to support the tension on the leech of the sail when it is sheeted hard in. The track should be strengthened at those points; if rivetted to the mast, add more rivets or put in larger ones; if it is an integral part of the mast, consult the mast maker.

The majority of masts are made in sections of about 10 metres each; these are joined by butting the two tubes together and rivetting or set-screwing them through an internal sleeve. The compression load is taken by the friction between the tubes and the sleeve and by the rivets or screws. A join should be checked for any sign of movement; if there is it should be taken apart and rebuilt.

During the Cape Town to Auckland leg of the 1977 world race *Great Britain II*'s mast showed signs of all the above ailments. The mast had by then raced two and a half times round the world. In Auckland we had it virtually completely rebuilt and it was as good as new—except for the main track reinforcing, which somehow got left out. Sure enough, ten days later, as we sheeted in after putting in a second reef, part of the track ripped off the mast. It was out of the question to replace it at sea, and for the rest of the leg we had to set the mainsail shackled to a jackstay up the back of the mast.

The Boom and Spinnaker Poles. There is not much that can go wrong with a boom except for it breaking. This is unlikely to happen, unless it dips into the water at high speed and the vang is not released. While racing along a heavy weather reach it is a good idea to have a crewman playing the vang in and out, to avoid boom damage.

Should the boom break it can only be repaired if a sleeve is carried for the purpose; this also applies to spinnaker pole breakages. As sleeves take up a lot of space, and as neither a broken boom or pole is disabling, I would only bother to carry spares if on a serious trans-ocean race; there is no need for a cruising yacht to repair a broken boom at sea. The mainsail can easily be set loose-footed by taking two sheets from the clew to the quarters of the yacht (as for a trysail) and a third from the clew straight down to the mainsheet track; this way a perfect set can be obtained, except perhaps when running dead down wind, which is not too important.

Spinnaker pole fittings can work loose; if this happens they can usually be strengthened with extra rivets or bolts. The jaws at the outboard end (diagram 24) can suffer from weak springs, which allows them to open unintentionally. There are few things more annoying than to be running along under spinnaker and suddenly have the jaws open and the sail flying free. If this happens, put the best man on the helm and hopefully he will keep the sail full. Meanwhile, lower the outboard end of the pole and let it swing forward to the foredeck; on the windward side take the weight on the lazy sheet, ease the spinnaker guy, taking a bight of it forward, which is then replaced in the jaws; hoist the pole, tightening the spinnaker guy as it rises. If it happens again, repeat the procedure, but this time turn the pole upside down; this way the spinnaker guy, which is pulling upwards, pulls into the fitting instead of out of it.

The author aloft fixing temporary rigging.

Using a pole upside down complicates spinnaker gybing; whether dip-pole or two-pole gybing (see chapter 5), it will not be possible to clear the old spinnaker guy from the pole end. Even if the jaws are snapped open the spinnaker guy will be reluctant to fall out—and if it does it will be under the pole, preventing it from being lowered. The way round this for a two-pole gybe is to proceed as normal to move 7 (see chapter 5 page 84). Then:

8. Take the weight on the port sheet.
9. Completely slacken the port spinnaker guy.
10. Ease the topping lift and port pole guy and take in the fore-guy; the pole comes down and in to the foredeck with the port spinnaker guy still through its end.
11. Clear the port spinnaker guy from the pole end by hand.
12. Stow the pole.

For a dip-pole gybe moves 8 to 11 as described here replace moves 3 to 5 (see page 86).

Down Below

Auxiliary engines on yachts tend to be badly treated. They are ignored for months on end, kept in a damp environment, seldom used, often abused, and still expected to be reliable. Unless one of the crew is an engineer all a skipper can do before setting off on a long trip is to get the engine professionally checked, take spares as recommended by the manufacturer, the workshop manual, and hope for the best. There are a few wrinkles (some of which won't be found in the book of instructions) that may help the amateur. With a diesel engine the most likely cause of a stopping, or non-starting is the fuel system. Neither air nor water ignite under compression. Study the fuel system and see how it passes from the tank to the water trap, to the lift pump, to the filter, to the injector pump (or pumps) and finally to the injectors. The extra fuel lines that do not appear to make any sense are those taking excess fuel from the injector heads back into the system at the filter. Make sure that someone on board knows how to bleed the fuel system to get rid of any air; this air gets into the system either when one runs out of fuel or if there is any crack or leak in a fuel line. A contributory factor to this latter problem is that the fuel pump on the engine has to pull the diesel up from a tank below engine level. If it can pull air in through a crack instead, it will. To avoid this it is a good idea to fit a header tank from which the fuel can gravity feed to the lift pump; this tank need only contain a few gallons and can be filled by hand pump from the main tank. See diagram 73. Incidentally, if caught at sea with a broken fuel line, try repairing it with plastic tape. I have had an engine in commission for four weeks with a perfectly airtight plastic tape join in a fuel line; we changed the tape every few days.

If the engine refuses to turn over at all, it could be for two reasons; either the batteries are low or the starter motor is not as fit as it should be. A starter motor can jam, especially if bilge water has got in the bell housing, splashed up to the drive end of the starter motor and rusted it up. If this is the case, try hitting it with a hammer as the starter key is turned; this often manages to free it. If this fails, try more battery power; switch in the domestic batteries and try again. As a last resort, there is one trick that never fails: rewire the batteries in series instead of in parallel and give the starter motor extra volts. For instance if an engine starter motor is 12 volts it may be powered by two 12-volt batteries in parallel, i.e. their positive terminals connected together, their negative terminals connected together, and power taken off them as a single unit. To wire them in series connect the negative terminal of one to the positive of the other, and then take the power from the two free terminals. This will put out 24 volts.

I have used this system for five or more starts over a period of a week when caught out with a sticky starting motor. Of course, the starter motor should be replaced as soon as the yacht reaches port. Any problem, other than those described above, will need professional attention; if none is available on board, forget the noisy, smelly thing and with a sigh of relief, sail on.

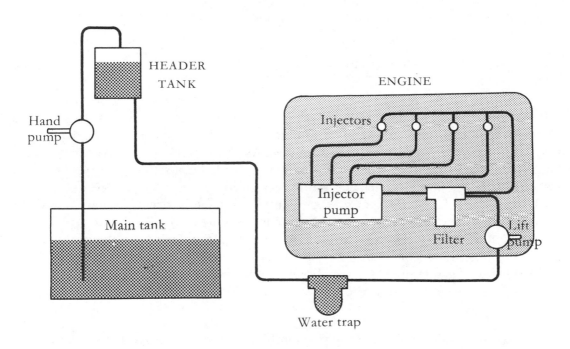

73. *Fitting a header tank to the fuel system reduces chances of air leaks.*

Electrics. As a generating system is not running all the time, the electrical system on a yacht must rely on batteries. For this reason the voltage used is 12 or 24. 24 volts is better, especially on larger yachts, as the higher the voltage, the less the power loss in the wires leading to the lights etc. The whole system has to be in balance; that is, whatever power (normally expressed in amps per hour, or amphours) is taken out must be replaced by battery charging. If the main engine is the only charging system it is important to set it up with its own starting batteries; this way, even if the domestic batteries are run flat by excessive use of lights or radio transmitting, for instance, the situation can still be saved. An extra hand starting generator must be carried if electrical systems have to be relied upon.

To calculate how much the charger will have to be used, first study the daily consumption. For example, for a typical 24 volt system, using the formula Watts $=$ Volts $\times$ Amps, we find:

Lighting

For the saloon	Two	12 watt bulbs for 3 hours $=$	3	amp-hrs
For the navigation table	One	6 watt bulb for 6 hours $=$	$1\frac{1}{2}$	amp-hrs
Navigation lights	Three	20 watt bulbs for 8 hours $=$	20	amp-hrs
Compass light	One	3 watt bulb for 8 hours $=$	1	amp-hrs

Radio

Receive	Takes	7 amps for 1 hour	$=$	7	amp-hrs
Transmit	Takes	24 amps for 10 minutes	$=$	4	amp-hrs
				$36\frac{1}{2}$	amp-hrs

If the engine or generator indicates that it is charging at 20 amps, say, it will be necessary to charge for 1 hour and 50 minutes per day; without the use of navigation lights this figure would be only 50 minutes. As the batteries will probably have a combined capacity of more than 200 amphours, it would be possible to last several days without charging, and then charge for a longer period.

Electrics and salt water do not go together well, and every attempt must be made to keep electrical connections dry. Most electrical failures on a yacht are caused by corrosion at a join or a terminal in the wire. Navigation lights set on the pulpit suffer from continual immersions—and the occasional clout with the spinnaker pole—and I favour putting them in the hull at the bow, behind small windows. On a small yacht a combined mast-head lantern is the best system.

Plumbing. Fortunately, unlike electricity, plumbing does not suffer from the damp. From a maintenance point of view the difficulty lies in all pipes and fittings being hidden underneath the floor boards. As with all other aspects of a yacht, prevention is better than cure; regular checks should be made to see that pipe junctions are in good condition—plastic is better than copper—and the pipes fit tightly, are leak free and are securely fixed with jubilee clips; make sure no pipe suffers too tight a bend in its path through the bilges. A diagram should be drawn of the three systems—fresh water, sea water and waste—and the pipes should be easily identifiable. By checking the whole system out before sailing it will be discovered whether or not it is all easily accessible. If not, the floor boards should be reorganised or more inspection hatches fitted. Provided the access is easy, there is no repair beyond the scope of the amateur plumber armed with a few pieces of spare pipe and some stainless steel jubilee clips.

Special attention should be paid to bilge pumps; at least one should be fitted and plumbed in and one should be portable. The fitted pumps must be where they are easy to use and where there is sufficient space around them for the sides to be opened for possible unblocking. Ideally a pump should be operable from on deck when the hatch is closed, and another operable from below.

12   Multihull Sailing

There is much mystique surrounding multihulls and the way they are sailed. This is built up by some multihull enthusiasts who have rather extreme views. It is unjustified, as in most respects a multihull is the same as a monohull and should be sailed in much the same way. There are, of course, some differences and it is important to know how to make these work for you, rather than against you.

Multihulls are faster than monohulls of a similar size. Why is this so? The answer lies in their high power-to-weight ratio and their canoe bodies. To appreciate this it is necessary to look at stability. All craft need stability, otherwise they will fall over. A monohull achieves this stability by the creation of a righting moment as it heels. The moment is caused by buoyancy acting upwards, gravity acting downwards, and the lever arm between the centre of buoyancy and the centre of gravity. See diagram 74. A deep, heavy keel lengthens the lever by lowering the centre of gravity, and also increases the magnitude of the two forces acting on the lever. A broad beam lengthens the lever arm by causing the centre of buoyancy to move well to leeward as the yacht heels; thus a stable monohull has a broad beam and a heavy keel. The heavy keel obviously reduces the sail power-to-hull weight ratio of the yacht; the broad beam is even more damaging.

As the speed of the craft increases, so does the wave making resistance of its wide hull. This occurs to such an extent that when a displacement vessel reaches a speed in knots equal to $2\frac{1}{2}$ times the square root of its water-line length in metres, it can accelerate no more. For instance a 14-metre yacht with an 11-metre water-line cannot sail faster than $8\frac{1}{2}$ knots. The only way a wide hulled yacht can break this barrier is by lifting clear of the water and planing. Unfortunately the yacht is held in the water by its keel weight and remains a displacement craft. With wave assistance a monohull may surf and, for a few seconds only, achieve higher speeds.

A multihull's stability is created in the same way—i.e. a righting moment. However, as a multihull heels, the centre of buoyancy moves immediately to the leeward outrigger. See diagram 75. Because of the length of the beams connecting the hulls, this righting arm is automatically very long and hence there is no need for a lot of weight (such as a keel) to increase the moment. The individual hulls can be narrow, as stability comes from the total beam of the multihull; so a stable multihull is light and narrow-hulled. The lightness gives a good power-to-weight ratio, and the narrow hulls (provided their water-line beam is less than one ninth of their water-line length) are not subject to a speed limitation from wave making resistance.

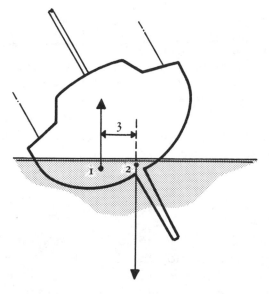

74. *A monohull heeling to the wind.*
    1. Centre of buoyancy.
    2. Centre of gravity.
    3. Righting arm.

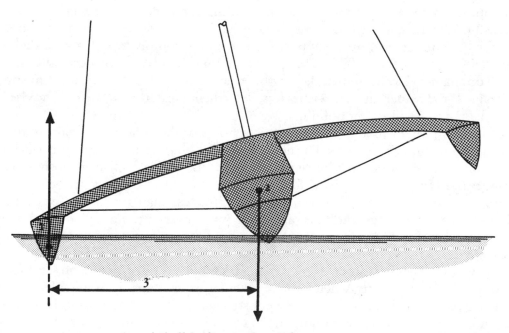

75. *A multihull heeling to the wind.*
    1. Centre of buoyancy, 2. Centre of gravity. 3. Righting arm.

By studying the two diagrams 75 and 80 it will be easy to see the one disadvantage of a multihull. As a monohull heels, its righting moment increases and is at its maximum when the yacht is heeled nearly 90°; it is still positive when the craft is nearly upside down. A multihull, on the other hand, has its maximum righting moment when heeled only a few degrees. From this point the moment decreases until it is zero at 90° of heel, and then becomes increasingly negative until the craft is upside down—where she stays. The high initial stability of a catamaran or trimaran is an advantage, as it means they sail with little or no heel. That it decreases to zero and beyond is of course dangerous, and is discussed further in the survival section of this chapter.

Multihull Construction

Because of their high initial stability and their large water plane area the strains on a multihull are very large; construction therefore has to be very strong. In cruising multihulls this strength can easily be achieved, as weight is not an important factor. With racing multihulls though, this weight factor is important; as weight is not needed for stability, one tries to build them as light as possible; they have to be built strong enough, but only just. Too strong is too heavy. As a result they tend to be built using complex and exotic construction techniques. Kevlar and Carbon Fibre are used extensively.

It appears that no amount of skilled engineering can make a large racing catamaran successful. The difficulty is in the cross beams having to be strong enough, not only to hold the hulls together, but to support the enormous compression loads of the mast. Since *British Oxygen/Kriter III* broke up in 1976 there has been no successful offshore racing catamaran. In the remainder of this chapter I shall therefore refer mainly to trimarans. If the reader sails, or wishes to sail, a cruising catamaran, I would advise him to handle it exactly like a monohull.

In the design of a trimaran there are two schools of thought with regard to the big question of outrigger buoyancy. The floats should be built with two or more watertight compartments. The question is, what percentage of the craft's displacement should each outrigger be? If it is 100% or more, the main hull can lift clear of the water before the lee outrigger submerges completely; conversely, if it is less than 100%, the lee outrigger will press into the water and the main hull will never lift. For all normal sailing conditions it makes little difference whether an outrigger is 80% or 120% of total displacement. What is more important is that the outrigger is long and has plenty of buoyancy at each end in order to give diagonal stability. For this reason, and for the added stability and security when lying ahull, a figure of 120% is preferable.

The rig on a trimaran also has to be very strong; the cap shrouds especially have to take a lot of weight; unlike a monohull, the tri will not heel and give to a wind squall. They should be stronger than the rigging on an equivalent one-hulled craft, unless they are led to the floats, when the resulting wider angle of support at the mast-head will

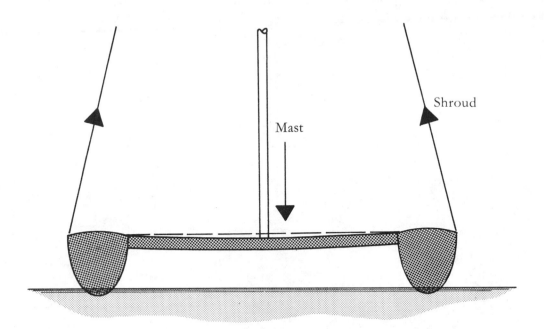

76. The problem of stepping a mast on a large catamaran.

make up for the extra load they have to bear. A disadvantage of taking the shrouds to the floats is that the stiffness of the rig then depends on the stiffness of the beams holding the hulls together. There are two ways of obtaining a stiff trimaran rig: one is to step the mast on one of the cross-beams where it crosses the main hull; the cap shrouds are then led out to the ends of the beam. If the shroud divides, via a link plate, into two parts, a leg can be taken to each beam. Underneath, the beam wires are led into the hull just above the water-line. See diagram 77, top drawing. The alternative method is to rig the mast solely to the main hull. To do this the mast is built with spreaders in the conventional way. The rigging and chainplates must be very strong. See diagram 77, bottom drawing.

As a trimaran does not need a ballasted keel, it can be built with no keel at all; but like any other sailing vessel it must have some resistance to sideways motion. A dinghy style centre board or dagger-board can be fitted in the main hull. The advantage of a pivoting centre-board is that it will knock up if an obstruction is hit. Unfortunately, when the board is down, the water turbulence in the empty centre-board box is destructively heavy. The 24-metre *Great Britain III* was built with a centre-board, and after the top of the box had blown off a second time, she was converted to a dagger-board. A lifting dagger-board is the satisfactory answer. As it will not knock up it should be used in a slot which has an area of foam safety cushion just aft of it. See diagram 78. This cushion will absorb a great deal of the shock in the event of the vessel running aground. The rudder should also be lifting, for no better reason than that it will allow the trimaran to take the ground; however, strength must not be sacrificed to achieve this.

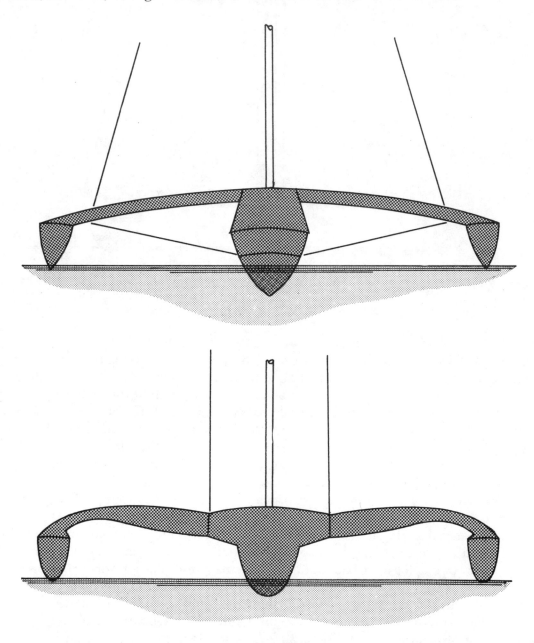

77. *Different styles of trimaran showing two ways of staying the main mast.*

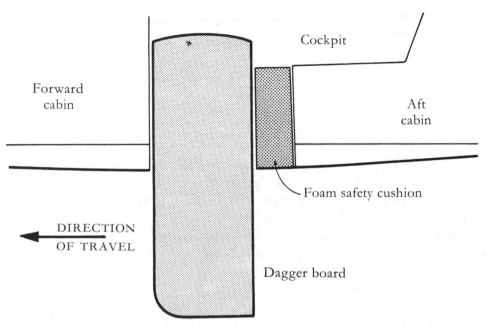

78. *A foam safety cushion behind the dagger board to prevent damage on running aground.*

Multihull Sailing

To Windward. The objective, as described in chapter 4, is to maximise v.m.g. to windward. The choice must be made of sailing close and slowly or free and fast. It is here that the multihull trap lies. Because of its high speeds a trimaran will always draw the apparent wind well ahead of the true wind, and the unwary sailor may think he is going well to windward, when he is in actual fact reaching backwards and forwards, very fast along the same line. An example will make this clear.

A fine day, 15 knots of true breeze and a flat sea; a trimaran is beating to windward with full sail; the helmsman finds that sailing at 31 degrees to the apparent wind the yacht makes 7 knots, and the wind gauge registers 20 knots. He may not realise it, but he is sailing 45 degrees to the true wind (he will tack through 90°) and his v.m.g. is 5 knots. Looking for improvement he frees off to 40 degrees apparent and finds the yacht makes 10 knots. He is delighted—9 degrees freer and 3 knots of speed gained—but in fact he is sailing at 65° to the true wind and his v.m.g. is down to 4¼ knots. Mistakenly encouraged, he tries 45° apparent and finds the yacht makes 13 knots; good speed he thinks, not too free, this is the way to go to windward. In fact speed is his enemy and he is actually sailing 83° to the true wind, with a v.m.g. of just over 1½ knots.

Examples of sailing with a 15 knots true wind are:

Apparent wind angle	Boat speed	True wind angle	V.M.G.
31°	7 knots	45°	5 knots
40°	10 knots	65°	4¼ knots
45°	13 knots	83°	1½ knots

Therefore the secret of sailing a fast craft to windward is to watch very carefully the direction of the true wind on the water. Sailing close to the wind is essential; certainly it is a mistake to tack through more than 100°. Because of the danger of following the apparent wind I find it to be easiest to sail a trimaran to windward on boat speed. With the 16-metre *Great Britain IV*, designed by Derek Kelsall, we sailed to windward at 8 knots in any reasonable amount of breeze. If the speed rose above 8 knots we were sailing too free, and below 8 meant we were too close. In very light airs the situation gets even more difficult. It is quite possible for a racing trimaran to move at 3 knots in 2 knots of true wind. In this case, if the apparent wind angle is 34°, the true wind angle is 90°— i.e. progress to windward is nil! The only way to make progress is to pinch up to 20° apparent, slow down, and hence get to windward. All these figures are quite realistic.

A lot of care is needed in tacking a multihull. It is unlikely that the vessel will tack straight from a reach. By the time she is head to the wind the boat will have lost way and will stop. A tack must be started from a close-hauled course and only a gentle degree of helm used. Sailing a trimaran single-handed from Portsmouth, England, to Cork in Ireland, I had to beat for 500 miles. I never missed a tack until, entering Cork harbour, I sailed into confined waters. Because it was then essential for each tack to be successful, I started to use a heavy hand on the helm, with the result that I missed the first important going about. Having just extricated myself without hitting a moored yacht or going aground I relaxed, took more care and all was well. On that particular vessel—a 10-metre trimaran designed by Dick Newick—the way to tack was to use about 10° of rudder, maintain speed and let the jib fly free as she came round. Backing the jib stops a light craft in its tracks and should only be resorted to if she is already stopped.

Reaching. On a beam reach a multihull is quite capable of sailing at the same speed as the true wind. Due to the effect of boat speed on the apparent wind—as just described—the sails will still be sheeted well in. Before setting off on a fast reach lift the dagger board halfway up. If it is left down there is a danger of it, or its trunk, breaking from the tremendous loads generated. After brilliantly winning the 1978 Route du Rhum race, Mike Birch went for a sail to show some of his opposition what his trimaran was like. The board broke when one of his guests reached off with it fully down.

Running. Sailing a fast yacht with the wind astern is very peaceful. The speed of the trimaran reduces the apparent wind to such an extent that most running is done in light airs. The decision on whether to dead run or to follow a series of reaches has to be made, and reaching a multihull will probably pay off in most cases. Various headings can be tried, and by consulting the v.m.g. table (Table 8 page 125), the best can be chosen.

If the wind angle allows, a spinnaker can be used to advantage. The system for spinnaker handling on a trimaran is simplified by the broad sheeting base presented by the hulls. The sail is set with three ropes on each clew. For ease of explanation I call these the fore guy, the guy and the sheet. On either side the sheet is led to the aft end of the outrigger, the guy to the forward end of the outrigger and the fore guy to the bow of the main hull; thus each clew can be controlled by the three lines and made to fly in any position within the triangle formed by the three sheeting points. No pole is needed, under normal conditions, to hold the windward clew of the spinnaker forward and/or outboard. See diagram 79.

With the apparent wind on the beam, set the windward clew with weight on the fore guy and the guy; this will stop it rising, and will hold it off the fore stay. The leeward side is controlled by the sheet only.

For a wind on the quarter the windward clew should be set with weight on the fore guy, guy and sheet. This will hold it out from the centre line and well forward. Again the leeward side is controlled by the sheet.

For dead running the sail is set using the sheets on either side and, in a breeze, a bit of weight on the guys to prevent the sail rising too high. Gybing is a simple question of taking the main over while juggling with the two sheets and guys.

On a smaller multihull (10-metre trimarans can race trans-ocean successfully) the fore guy is not necessary. If the windward clew needs to be held down for a reach, it can be done using a bight of lazy sheet straight down to a cleat on the bow of the main hull.

In very light winds a spinnaker may be reluctant to fill. When it collapses, the windward clew can drift in towards the mast, from where it is unlikely to rise; tension on the guy will hold the clew out to windward, but overdoing this will stop it rising when the sail fills. For this reason a very light-weight pole, the length of the foredeck, should be carried; it can be used to hold the windward clew up and out, ready for the breeze. *Great Britain IV* used this system to great effect in winning the 1978 round Britain race. The inboard end of the pole can clip to a fixed eye on the forward side of the mast, and the outboard end clips round the guy.

Strong Winds are handled in a perfectly normal way regardless of the point of sailing. Reduce sail by setting smaller jibs and reefing the mainsail, exactly as is done in a monohull. Take care to recognise when the trimaran is overpowered; because it sails upright it is harder to judge when sail reductions are needed. Watching the lee float and developing a 'feel' are the best bets. If the signs are missed and the wind rises further, the main hull will lift, showing that sail should have been reduced earlier.

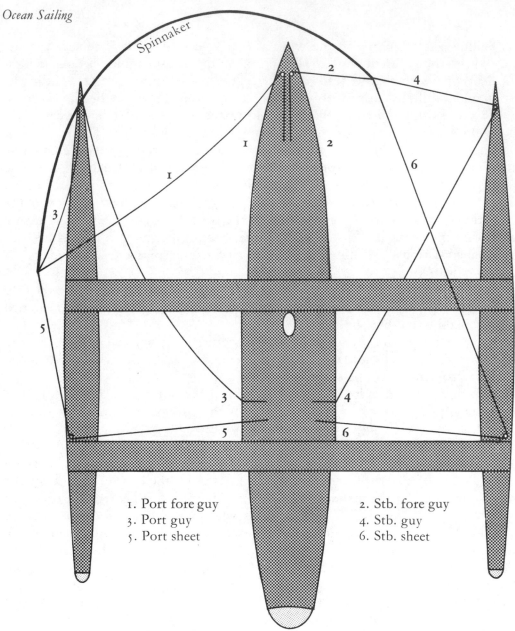

Spinnaker

1. Port fore guy	2. Stb. fore guy
3. Port guy	4. Stb. guy
5. Port sheet	6. Stb. sheet

79. *Spinnaker controls on a trimaran. With the wind on the starboard quarter weight will be on 2. 4. 6. and 5.*

Multihull Safety

During the last half of the 1970's there was a large increase in the number of trimarans racing. They were mostly built for, and sailed in, short-handed events. While their speed was undoubtedly superior to monohulls, their safety record was far worse, and in one twelve month period no fewer than six trimarans were lost in the Atlantic alone. The causes of these accidents were either capsize or structural collapse. It appears that no amount of mathematical calculation can correctly predict the forces exerted by the sea on a sailing vessel. Static forces are a matter of simple calculation, but the complex impulsive forces created by hitting waves are incomputable.

Structural damage will result if the trimaran is not strong enough for the conditions it meets. The yachtsman must hope that the designer and builder have got their sums right, but at the same time he must sail sensibly. For instance, to avoid slamming when beating, it may be necessary to slow down deliberately. Dick Newick summed it up when, to the comment that one of his designs was very strong, he replied: 'Yes, but it can be broken.'

Capsizes may be caused by wind action, wave action or a combination of the two. Although flat seas and a lot of wind simultaneously are seldom experienced offshore, they can occur in squally weather. The trimaran *Triple Arrow* was capsized in the 1974 round Britain race by wind strength alone; the weight of the wind in a squall was sufficient, when acting on full sail, to flip the tri. In a case like this, as the vessel heels, the force of the wind in the sails reduces, but so does the righting moment. Which will win?

Another factor comes into play—just as the sails are losing windage, the wind starts to act on the underside of the hulls, beams and bridge deck—and a capsize is a possibility. See diagram 80. If, in a deliberate attempt to gain speed, the sheets are not eased in a

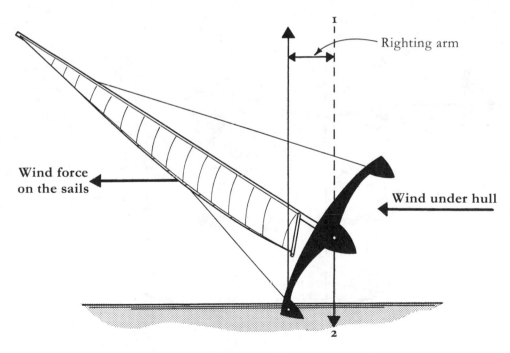

80. *A trimaran nears capsize. 1. is the buoyancy, 2. is gravity. The force of the sails is decreasing, but so is the righting moment.*

squall, the forward motion of the trimaran will bring yet more forces into play.

This is what happens when a squall hits a reaching trimaran; as she heels and accelerates, the centre of drive of the sails moves to leeward. On a monohull this would cause weather helm and possibly a broach. On a multihull there is another factor at work, as when the centre hull lifts, the centre of resistance to forward motion moves to leeward as well; in fact it moves out to the lee outrigger, which is further outboard than the centre of drive of the sails. The resulting couple causes lee helm—i.e. the trimaran tries to bear away. See diagram 81. This is safer than a broach, which might cause the vessel to trip over; instead she comes quickly upright as she turns downwind.

Big seas are not so easy to handle. Their size and steepness could throw over a multihull without any help from the wind. By the time the seas have reached this stage the crew have probably decided to stop sailing and to take survival action. The ultimate instability of a multihull necessitates a reappraisal of the tactics to be employed when sailing is no longer possible.

A catamaran or trimaran will lie a-hull comfortably in any amount of wind. The

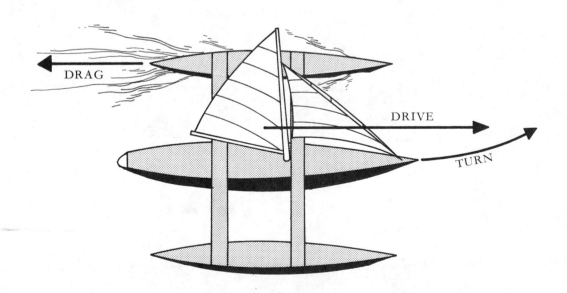

81. *At about 15° of heel, the centre hull lifts from the water leaving the forces as shown here. The trimaran bears away.*

daggerboard should be partly raised to protect it from sideways shocks. If the waves are large, there is a danger that a steep wall of water will pick up the windward float and capsize the craft. When there is a likelihood of this happening do not risk lying a-hull.

An alternative is to rig a strong, weighted sea anchor. Set it off the bow of the windward hull; the vessel is then held bow up at 30° to 45° to the wind and waves. The sea anchor, as well as holding the bows up to the seas, will also hold the windward hull down, should it be lifted by a wave. Sternway may be generated, so the rudder and skeg must be very strong. A second style of sea anchor used with great success, is a unit made from a standard military parachute. Three long lines run from the parachute to the three bows of the trimaran, which is held exactly head to wind. A trip line should be attached to the head of the chute and buoyed with a fender, to keep it clear of the main lines. To rig the system the parachute should be packed in the normal way and then thrown off the bow of the windward float while lying a-hull.

When searoom is available, and the loss of ground can be afforded, running off is the safest procedure. In fact, in extreme conditions it is the only sensible tactic to adopt. If the speed under bare poles threatens to drive the bows under, or broach the boat, then warps should be towed.

In the event of a capsize, all is not lost, provided reasonable precautions have been taken. A trimaran will not sink, because of the buoyancy in her outriggers. There will be an air pocket in the bilges (now the roof) of the main hull. A crewman trapped below when the craft goes over, is actually in quite a safe place. His first job is to get some air circulation by removing a skin fitting—such as a log or echo sounder—from the hull. If there are no skin fittings he should drill, and then cut, a hole through the hull. On board *Great Britain IV* we always sailed with a drill and bit with a saw, taped underneath the chart table ready for an emergency. Once a hatch has been cut the crew can live inside the upturned hull. The liferaft should have been stowed where it is accessible with the vessel upside down or right side up—underneath, or on the aft face of a crossbeam, for instance. But remember, as long as she stays afloat, stay with the vessel.

A recent innovation that may in the future make all multihulls safer, is the self-righting catamaran. The completely inverted craft can be righted using a very ingenious system: the crew close off a watertight bulkhead built amidships right across the two hulls and superstructure. Next, by remote control, they open two seacocks and a vent which allows the bow section to flood completely. The bows sink down and the stern rises clear of the water until it is almost vertical. At this point the buoyancy of the coachhouse causes it to flip past the vertical until it comes to rest with the bows down at 30° to the horizontal—but the right way up. The seacocks and vent can be closed and the forward section pumped dry. A total recovery has been achieved.

A good self-steering gear by Sailomat on Naomi James's 16 metre Express Crusader.

Single-handed Sailing

Alfred Johnson sailed the Atlantic alone in 1876. Since then many long single-handed voyages have been undertaken. The invention of self-steering gear and the introduction—in 1960—of regular short-handed racing, has made this side of the sport very popular. This chapter looks at some of the problems faced by the lone sailor.

Self-Steering Gear

No-one can steer for 24 hours a day. It is possible to balance most yachts on some points of sailing, but a self-steering gear will handle all points of sailing. Basically there are two systems, those activated by wind and water, and those activated by electricity. The latter are small versions of the automatic pilots fitted to all commercial craft.

Wind and water driven gears are totally self-sufficient. They get their power from the motion of the yacht through the water. There are numerous different designs afloat—a lot home made. They mainly fall into the following categories:

   1. A wind vane connected straight to the yacht's tiller. To obtain the power needed to steer the yacht a disproportionately large wind vane is needed. This system is unlikely to be of any use except on the smallest yachts.
   2. A wind vane connected to a trim tab on the aft edge of the rudder. The movement of the wind vane, as the yacht goes off course, angles the trim tab to the opposite side to the desired course correction; the tab in turn causes the rudder to move. If the tab turns to starboard the water flow will force the rudder to port and vice-versa. This system is in common use, but is unsophisticated compared with later innovations.
   3. A wind vane and servo oar influencing the yacht's rudder. The wind vane moves as the yacht goes off course. This movement causes the servo oar to angle itself to the fore and aft line of the vessel. The flow of the water on the angled oar causes it to swing like a pendulum. Lines from the swinging servo oar pull on the tiller to restore the yacht to its original heading.
   4. A wind vane and servo oar influencing the self-steering gear's own rudder. This unit works in a similar way to the one above, except that the servo oar drives a rudder (about $\frac{1}{4}$ the size of the yacht's rudder) 'tuned' to it as part of the gear.

An example illustrates the use of this type of equipment. Diagrams 82a, b and c, plus the flow chart will facilitate understanding.

The single-handed sailor wishes to steer south. Using the main helm he comes on course and sets the sails to the apparent wind, which he finds is on the starboard beam. During this manoeuvring the wind vane and rudder of the self-steering gear are allowed to feather. When the yacht has settled down the main helm is locked or lashed in place.

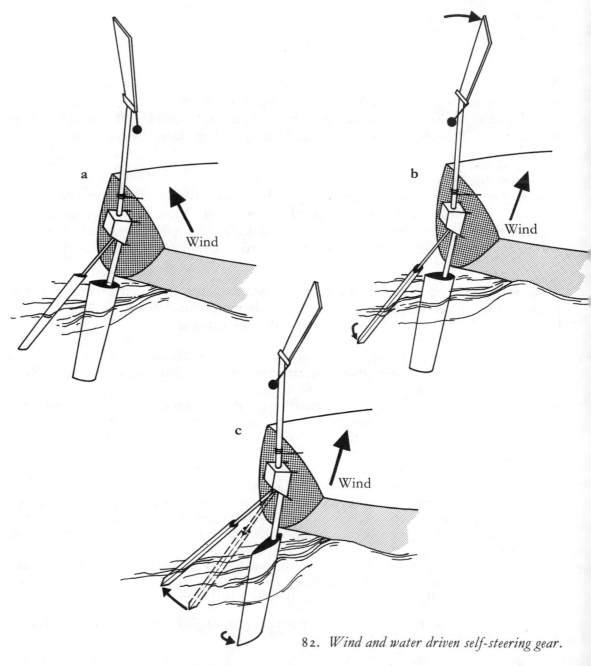

82. *Wind and water driven self-steering gear.*

The wind vane mast is now adjusted until the vane is lined up with the wind. The gear is set in motion by releasing the wind vane, so that it is free to pivot, and by letting go the control line that allowed the rudder to feather. The yacht is on course, the main helm is locked, the wind vane, servo oar and self-steering rudder are centred and the wind is on the beam. See diagram 82a.

The yacht drifts off course to port. The effect is a movement of the apparent wind aft, which in turn causes the wind vane to pivot. A connection from the vane acts on the servo oar, turning it to starboard about its vertical axis. See diagram 82b.

The forward motion of the yacht causes the water flow to push on the angled servo oar, forcing it to swing out to port; the gear linkage from the head of the swinging oar makes the self-steering rudder turn to starboard. See diagram 82c. The rudder turns the yacht to starboard until the wind is again on the beam and the vane, oar and rudder are once more centred. The yacht is back to the position shown in diagram 82a.

FLOW CHART OF SELF-STEERING

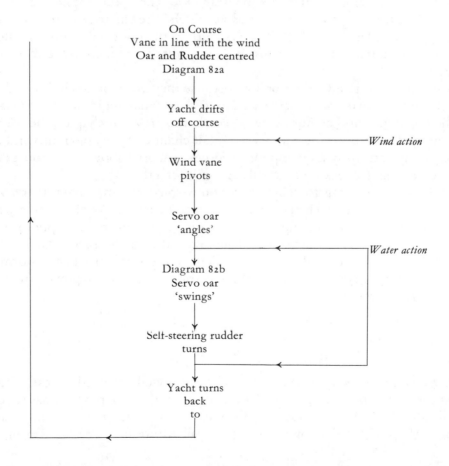

Any wind driven self-steering gear will always maintain the yacht on a steady course relative to the apparent wind. This means that a wind shift will automatically cause the vessel to alter course. The boat follows the wind, so although it is under control of the self-steering gear, the yachtsman knows his sails are set correctly; he must regularly check that the yacht is still on the desired compass heading. To alter course is a simple matter of re-aligning the wind vane mast with the new estimated direction of the apparent wind. The gear will then bring the boat round and settle it down on the new heading. Tacking is done in this way.

Electric autopilots are a good alternative to self-steering gears, provided electric power is available. Small units for handling monohulls up to 11 metres and multihulls up to 15 metres use less than one amp on a 12-volt system—about the same as a cabin light. The autopilot consists of a compass and a motor driven arm. The course to be steered is set on the dial at the top of the compass unit. Any alteration in the yacht's heading is picked up electronically and the signal given to the motor drive to pull or push on the arm attached to the boat's tiller. See diagram 83. The more sophisticated gears can be adjusted in three ways: (a) the speed at which it reacts to a course deviation, (b) the amount of rudder with which it reacts, and (c) the course deviation it allows before it considers reacting. These controls allow the unit to be tuned to the yacht and to the sea conditions.

Multihull sailors favour autopilots because they are a lot less bulky and much lighter than their wind driven counterparts. There is also a danger in steering a fast craft relative to the apparent wind because, as was seen in the previous chapter, the course sailed can change considerably with only a very small change in the apparent wind direction.

A yachtsman using an autopilot need never worry about his compass heading, but should regularly check that his sails are set correctly.

Large craft wishing to self-steer a compass course may have to resort to a large autopilot—some of which take up to 15 amps of current. An alternative is to use a wind and water driven self-steering gear, but with a low powered autopilot rigged to act on the servo oar. The wind vane is disconnected and the servo oar is angled by the electronic device; the rudder is controlled by the servo oar in the normal way. This system gets its instructions from the electric compass, but power from the forward motion of the yacht.

Sail Handling

A Single-hander's rig must be easy to handle and well balanced. These requirements are most easily met by a ketch, a yawl, or a cutter-rigged sloop which has several relatively small sails. The larger number of sails will make it easier to find a combination that will balance the yacht well enough to help, or substitute for, the self-steering gear.

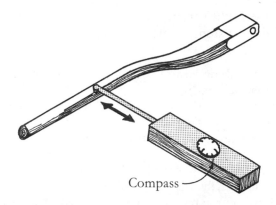

Compass —

83. *A small autopilot.*

The mainsail should be rigged with slab rather than roller-reefing. (See chapter 4). On the other hand a roller furling jib is a good idea, as it reduces the time for a single-handed jib change from 30 minutes to 30 seconds.

If a spinnaker is used there must be an efficient system for handling it; getting it down is the problem. An entrant in the 1976 single-handed trans-Atlantic race proposed to hoist his spinnaker in stops and when the time came to take the sail down, he would simply let the guys, sheets and halyards run. The sail would be lost, but with two spinnakers two halyards and two guys and sheets, he would at least enjoy two spinnaker runs. Fortunately his theory was never put to the test. A more tidy system is to use a spinnaker squeezer, as described in the next section.

It is relatively unimportant whether the halyards are controlled at the mast, or led back to the cockpit. Foredeck work is necessary when lowering sails, so it is probably best to have the halyards at the mast. The trimaran *Quest*, designed by Paul Weychan, has the halyards led forward to a small cockpit on the foredeck. Lowering headsails is made easier, but the general inaccessibility of the winches slows down all other sail handling manoeuvres.

Main and Headsail Handling. The single-hander should handle his mainsail in exactly the same way as a full crew. Slab reefing is performed stage by stage and is still a quick system. Bear in mind the difficulty of hoisting or lowering a mainsail off the wind, reefs should be put in the sail in good time.

Changing headsails in the conventional way, with hanked jib luffs, is bound to be an untidy operation. In very light airs it may be possible to lower a jib and gather it at the same time, but this will not be possible in a breeze, so an alternative solution must be found. There are two possibilities. One method when on the wind is to tack, leaving the jib aback; without easing the sheet, the halyard can be let go completely and the sail hauled down on the windward side of the foredeck. The friction from the sail blowing onto the mast and rigging will prevent it falling freely and yet it is easy to overcome.

Once the jib is down the yacht can be tacked back and a new jib hoisted.

A second and far better system is this.

1. Hoist the staysail if it is not already set.
2. Hank on the new jib underneath the bottom hank of the one in use.
3. Leave the jib sheeted in.
4. Adjust the helm so that the yacht will be balanced on mainsail and staysail alone—this will help the self-steering gear.
5. Release the jib halyard. The sail will fall halfway down. Leave one turn of halyard on the winch.
6. Go forward and pull down the luff of the sail, keeping it clear of the water if possible. The single turn on the halyard winch will slide smoothly.
7. Take the halyard off the head of the sail and make it up to a strop fixed to the bow specifically for this purpose.
8. Haul the sail inboard and put a temporary tie on it.
9. Back at the mast take in any slack in the halyard and make it fast.
10. Unhank the old jib and stow it.
11. Re-lead the sheets and tie them to the new jib.
12. Set the leeward sheet so that it will prevent the sail from excessive flogging as it is hoisted. If it is set too tight it will prevent the sail from rising. Trial and error is needed here.
13. Put the halyard on the head of the new headsail.
14. Hoist as quickly as possible and winch the luff up tight.
15. Start sheeting in.
16. Readjust the helm to balance the yacht with a jib set.
17. Complete sheeting in.

If the headsail falls over the side at stages 5 and 6, no harm will come to it, as the luff is still hanked on the forestay and the clew is held in by the sheet. Although it is a tiring nuisance to have a wet sail to heave inboard, there is no realistic alternative. The whole operation will probably take half an hour, even if nothing goes wrong.

Unless it is part of a furler headsail system, a luff groove jib is very tricky to use alone. A lowered sail is uncontrollable, as it is not attached to the forestay except at the tack. A way round this difficulty is to fit the luff of the jib with lugs which slide up the luff groove. When the bottom of the groove is closed off, the lugs will act like hanks to keep a lowered sail attached to the yacht.

A roller furling jib completely does away with the complexities and problems of headsail changing. The basis of the system is a forestay, or an aluminium extrusion round the forestay, which rotates to roll up the sail from the luff. See diagram 84. As the luff has to turn, there must be a system of bearings to allow this to happen. One system has a normal forestay with an aluminium extrusion round it. This extrusion carries the luff of the sail and can turn on small bearings placed every metre or so round the stay. See diagram 85a. The other system incorporates a swivel terminal at either end of the forestay which allows the stay itself to rotate. In this case the forestay is an aluminium extrusion with luff grooves, see diagram 85b. In both cases the rotation—and hence the

84. *A furler jib.*

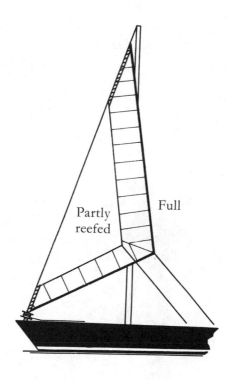

85. *Roller forestay systems.*

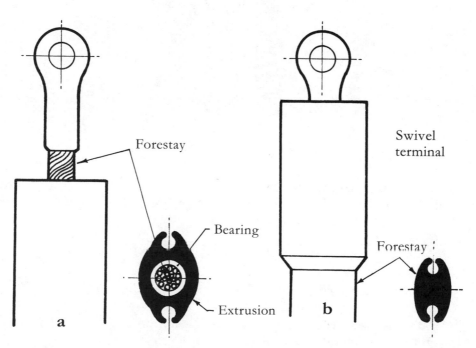

reefing of the jib—is controlled by a drum at the foot of the stay, with a rope or wire from the drum led aft to the cockpit. In order to prevent the halyard twisting round the stay as it rolls up, a swivel is employed. This swivel fits round the aluminium extrusion, on which it is free to slide up and down. The halyard is attached to the outer part and the head of the jib to the inner, see diagram 86. When the headsail is fully hoisted the swivel should be within 30 cm of the halyard sheave, then the halyard will hold the outer part of the swivel stationary while the inner part, along with the extrusion and jib luff, turns inside it.

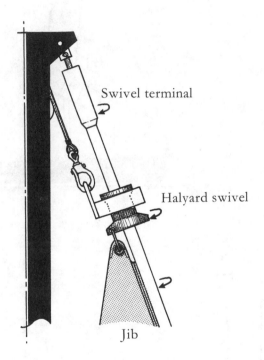

86. *Furler halyard arrangement.*

As the headsail is reefed, so the position of the sheet lead has to be moved forward—see diagram 84. The lower the clew of the sail, the more the movement. Consequently a roller jib should be cut with a fairly high clew.

Reducing sail with a roller furling jib is as follows:

    1. Adjust the self-steering gear so that the yacht bears away slightly. This reduces the weight of wind on the sail.
    2. Let go the leeward jib sheet.

3. Pull in the drum line until the sail is the required size.
4. Move the sheet lead forward.
5. Sheet in and put the yacht back on course.

On a large yacht it is dangerous to fiddle with the sheet lead of a flogging sail. A slower but safer alternative is:

4. Sheet in as much as possible with the sheet at the old lead position and put the yacht back on course.
5. Bring a bight of the windward sheet round to leeward and make it up temporarily on a spare winch.
6. Ease the leeward sheet, change the lead, and sheet in again.
7. Take the windward sheet back to its proper place.

Increasing sail with a roller furling jib is done as follows:

1. Ease the sheet which takes the weight off the jib luff.
2. Ease the drum line and the jib unfurls; in light airs it may be necessary to pull the sheet to help it out.
3. Move the sheet lead aft.
4. Sheet in.

A partly reefed headsail is unlikely to be as well shaped as a normal jib of the same size. However, the speed and simplicity of changing sails more than makes up for this.

Spinnaker Handling. A lone yachtsman will have little difficulty hoisting a spinnaker that has been well 'stopped', and if he could stop it again while it was set, it would also be easy to lower. Towards this end several systems have been designed, all of which are similar to the one described here, which is the spinnaker squeezer. The spinnaker is stowed, hoisted and lowered wrapped in a cloth tube. At the bottom of the tube there is a fibreglass bell-shaped cylinder. An endless line is led from this bell, up inside the tube, out through a special fitting at the head and down outside in a long loop, back to the bell. See diagram 87. This line can be pulled from deck level to raise or lower the bell. The effect is to unstop and stop the spinnaker. When the bell is completely raised it concertinas the cloth tube above the head of the setting sail. The routine for hoisting a spinnaker is as follows:

1. Rig the pole with the outboard end at head height and against the forestay.
2. Place the spinnaker guy in the pole end.
3. Lay out the spinnaker in its tube on the foredeck, making sure it is not twisted (a vertical stripe sewn on the tube helps here).
4. Slide the bell by hand about three metres up the sail; this allows one clew to be lifted to the guy at the pole end, and the other to reach the sheet.

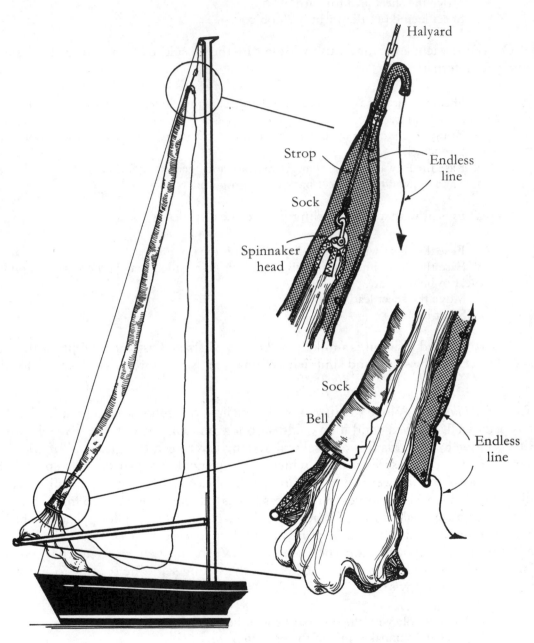

Halyard

Strop

Sock

Spinnaker
head

Endless
line

Sock

Bell

Endless
line

87. *A spinnaker in its squeezer.*

5. Check that the endless line is not tangled.
6. Attach the halyard and hoist the sail, keeping the endless line looped over your arm, so that it is not lost.
7. Lower the headsail. The situation is now as depicted in diagram 87.
8. Haul on the endless line to raise the bell about a quarter of the way up the spinnaker.
9. Pull the spinnaker pole aft and up until it is in the correct position.
10. Sheet in partly.
11. Hoist the bell to the head of the sail.
12. Sheet in to trim the spinnaker.

Meanwhile it is hoped that the self-steering is maintaining a course down wind. To lower the spinnaker follow the reverse procedure:

1. Ease the pole forward and down so that its outboard end is in reach.
2. Let go the spinnaker sheet.
3. Haul down the bell; this requires considerable effort and in a breeze a winch may have to be employed.
4. When the bell is within three metres of the foot of the sail, release the windward clew from the guy.
5. Complete the haul down of the bell to the foot of the sail and onto the foredeck.
6. Lower the halyard and gather in the tube.
7. Hoist the jib.

The headsail can be hoisted before step 1, but this will make it almost impossible to haul down the bell because of the friction of the endless line on the lee side of the sail.

There is no reason why the spinnaker cannot be gybed single-handed. The two-pole method, as described in chapter 5 should be used.

Physically the hardest job when sailing alone is hoisting the spinnaker poles. Even if a spinnaker is not used a pole is sure to be needed to boom out a jib. The easiest way to hoist the pole is as follows:

1. Pre-set the heel fitting on the mast to shoulder height.
2. Fix the pole guy, topping lift and fore guy to the pole end.
3. Make the pole guy fast with enough slack to allow the pole end to reach the forestay.
4. Make the topping lift fast with a very small amount of slack in it.
5. Make the fore guy fast with a metre or more slack.
6. Pick up the inboard end of the pole and push it forward. The outboard end lifts off the deck as weight comes on the topping lift.
7. With the pole on your shoulder push forward until it can be placed on the mast in the heel fitting.
8. Adjust the pole as required.

Heavy Weather
The one factor that may change the tactics discussed in chapter 6 is that at times there will be no helmsman or self-steering gear controlling the yacht.

When sailing to windward the self-steering gear can handle quite bad conditions—with a well balanced yacht it is not doing very much work. However, the time will come when there is danger of the gear being damaged by a wave and consequently it has to be taken inboard. At this stage, if the yacht will sail herself, progress can still be made. When the wind gets so strong that it is no longer possible to sail, survival tactics must be adopted. If sea conditions allow, the single-hander should lie a-hull; no-one is needed on deck and the lone sailor can rest. In severe seas it is essential to run downwind and this is where the lack of a helmsman can cause serious problems.

Sailing off the wind a self-steering gear has to do a lot of work. By the time the wind has reached force 7 the prudent sailor will have taken in the gear. He then steers downwind until he is tired. What does he do now? The best thing to try is to lower the mainsail and sheet the storm jib flat fore and aft, with equal weight on each sheet. To do this the windward sheet must be led aft of the inner forestay. This sail, combined with a helm lashed amidships, will take the yacht straight down the wind and waves. If the boat starts to veer to starboard the storm jib will fill on the starboard side and push the bows back on course. Exactly the same happens when the vessel veers to port. The storm jib will come in for a heavy battering and there is a good case for carrying a small, completely flat sail to be used instead. Naomi James used this system many times during her circumnavigation and found it worked perfectly.

Should the wind rise to force 9 or above, the yacht may start to surf and threaten to broach. This can be prevented by trailing heavy warps, still leaving the jib up; directional stability is maintained and no helmsman is needed. There is no doubt that the safest place for a lone sailor is down below.

Sleep

Single-handed sailing is, in the maritime sense, illegal, as a 'seamanlike lookout' is not kept at all times. There are several ways round this problem. One is to stay up all night and sleep during the day when other shipping is more alert. A better plan is to keep a regular lookout, day and night; in busy shipping lanes, such as the English Channel, this means 20 minute intervals. An alarm clock will be needed to keep up this tiring routine. Once well away from shipping lanes the interval can be increased to an hour, or an hour and a half. Not only does this allow reasonable lookout to be kept, it also means the sails and self-steering are frequently trimmed—especially important when racing. Provided the total sleep per day is sufficient, it will not matter that it is in small doses.

There is another school of thought, which applies to racing multihulls single-handed. With these craft there is a big difference between the speed obtainable when they are driven hard and that which can be made under autopilot. Consequently the way to get the highest average speed is to sail flat out for 18 hours a day and then jog along for the next 6 hours while one sleeps.

This may be the best course of action for racing a multihull, but it does nothing to minimise the chances of being hit by a ship.

14 Special Hazards

There are a few unusual hazards encountered at sea. I have left them till last because they tend to form the least of a yachtman's worries as he prepares for and undertakes, a trans-ocean voyage. Never-the-less we should consider two of them—lightning strike and collision with whales.

Lightning Strike

Like a lot of yachtsmen I never thought about the possibility of being hit by lightning until it actually happened to me. Even then, on subsequent voyages, I failed to take any precautionary measures, secure in the mistaken belief that it couldn't happen twice. It did. A description of both incidents is followed by some advice on prevention.

Struck on a Steel Yacht. Approaching Rio de Janeiro towards the end of the 1976 Cape—Rio race we ran into some very squally weather. *British Steel* was running fast as the first squall approached. We changed to the storm spinnaker and lowered the mizzen just before the pitch black cloud bore down on us. The wind climbed to near gale force and the weight on the spinnaker halyard ripped its winch off the mast. The sail fell into the water ahead, from where we quickly recovered it. Suddenly the rain poured down and we could see lightning all around us. It appeared to be striking the water—sometimes within yards of the yacht. A few seconds later there was a flash and a hissing noise. I thought we had been struck—or maybe had a near miss—and as I turned round to tell the crew to stand clear of the rigging, I saw the watch leader flat on his back. Stuart Oakeley was on the deck with his hands pressed over his ears. We manoeuvred his unconscious form down to the saloon where, to our relief, he came to, none the worse for the experience. However, we treated him for normal shock, as instructed by our first aid manual.

The lightning must have earthed down through the steel hull straight into the sea. Stuart had been stowing the mizzen at the time and obviously got a small side shock from the mast or rigging. There was no damage to the yacht or its electrics and the compass was unaffected. The good path to earth afforded by the steel hull and the fact that the discharge was probably fairly small, saved us. Other than a general reluctance of the crew to go near the rigging until the squall was over the horizon, there were no after effects.

Struck on a G.R.P. Foam Sandwich Yacht. This incident occurred on board *Great Britain II*, sailing between Cape Horn and Rio de Janeiro during the third leg of the 1977/78 round-the-world race.

At noon on the 18th January 1978, 25 days out from Auckland, we were in a position 50° South, 62° West. We were doing well in the race, as my log for the day indicated:—

> 'The wind went south westerly during the early hours and we have the storm spinnaker up again. The sailing is good and our day's run (258 miles) is the best since Auckland, which shows how slow this leg has been'.
>
> 'Great excitement at the inter-yacht radio schedule. Our two main rivals, *Condor* and *Flyer*, are both 190 miles behind us. Only 1,900 miles to Rio!'

The next day we had a shock which shattered our optimistic frame of mind. We had reduced sail to a blast reacher, reefed main and mizzen, with the wind on our port quarter. A storm cloud came up behind us and we were soon enveloped by a dark and driving rain storm. As we struggled to get the mizzen down there was an almightly flash and bang—lightning! Simultaneously several things happened: the top of the mast appeared to be on fire—we could see small lumps of red hot metal dropping off it; from the chart area there was a blinding flash, which made me think we were on fire; the helmsman, Henry Zulueta, was shaking his head and arms—he had received a shock from the wheel; two other crew, touching the mizzen mast, were also shocked—one was thrown on his back.

It only took a few seconds for all this to happen. Quickly I checked that there was no fire below, turned off all the electrics and isolated the batteries. The yacht had broached, but Henry was not keen to touch the wheel again.

'Keep away from the rigging, get some gloves for Henry!' I shouted.

The crew were all O.K., even if a bit frightened—we could still see lightning all around us. The mast looked undamaged. As we came back on course it put the wind on the port bow, so obviously the wind had shifted in the squall. When we started to adjust the sails I realised that the waves were also on the port bow, and they could not have changed immediately with the wind. It dawned on me that perhaps the wind was still in the same direction and the compass had been affected. I decided to steer by the wave direction while I tried to sort out what had happened. Henry was now gloved and happy at the wheel. I began to assess the damage.

Switching on the electronics I could see that all the navigation instruments were broken. Wind speed, wind direction, boat speed, water depth and radio direction finding were all dead. The wind instrument control unit in the chart room was a blackened mess, which accounted for the flash from below. The other instruments, most of which had been turned off at the time of the strike, were found on inspection to have burnt out components. Most of the domestic fuses had blown, and the battery charge-meters indicated flat batteries. In fact the batteries were all right, but the meters were damaged. The radio telephone was unharmed because the set was well earthed and the aerial was disconnected. Through binoculars I could see that the wind vane and anemometer at the masthead had disappeared, and the 50 cm rod on which they were mounted, had melted.

A short while later I got a glimpse of the sun and took a bearing. Calculation showed that the compass had an error of 70° to 75°. By taking the spare compass round the yacht and recording its totally erratic behaviour, I could see that the whole yacht was completely magnetised.

I was very concerned about the situation we found ourselves in—not from the safety aspect, but rather from the racing point of view. While the wind stayed strong all was well—even without instruments we recorded a 304 mile run on the day after the strike. But the compass problem was a difficult one. All through the day of the strike I took bearings of the sun. Before nightfall I calculated, for half hourly intervals, the expected bearing of the moon. Thus we could keep a continual check on compass error.

Twenty four hours after the strike the error was down to 50°. We hoped for clear skies and steady winds. Our lead in the race was up to 240 miles with 800 to go, when the wind went ahead and very light. Steering was difficult without instruments, but far worse, the compass error was varying between 50° East on one tack and 50° West on the other. See diagram 88a. It was very tricky to tell if we were on the 'headed' or the 'lifted' tack. An

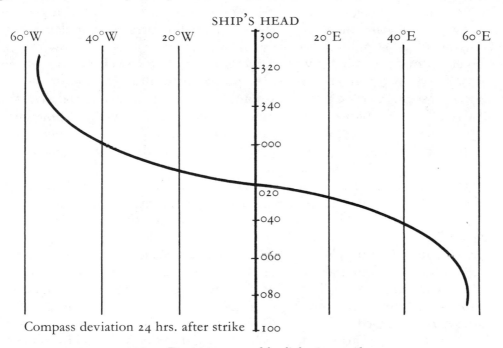

SHIP'S HEAD

Compass deviation 24 hrs. after strike

88a. *Deviation caused by lightning strike.*

alteration of course of 20° true could cause the compass to alter 60°. Slowly our lead was eroded, until with 50 miles to go we were only five miles ahead of *Condor* which was visible right astern.

Approaching the finish was one of the few times when radio D.F. would have paid. The horizon was hazy, visibility only a few miles, and there was a D.F. beacon just by the finishing line. As our D.F. set was blown, I had to rely on Leslie Williams navigation on *Condor*: when they altered course, so did we. After 7000 miles of sailing we won by less than half an hour.

In Rio we were advised that the magnetism induced in all the steel fixtures and fittings of the yacht would soon dissipate. Three weeks later, just before the start of the last leg of the race, we swung the compass; the error was still up to 20° and the deviation card produced is shown in diagram 88b. Four months later there was still 10° of deviation on some headings.

Lightning Conduction and Prevention. Lightning is a high frequency positive electrical discharge and as such is a dangerous and unpredictable commodity to try and conduct. However, sailing, as we did on *Great Britain II*, with no form of lightning conduction or prevention, was foolhardy. The theory behind lightning conductors is that a connection by a highly conductive material—such as metal—from the mast and rigging down to the water, will provide an easy path to earth in the event of a strike. The discharge will not necessarily follow one path and is quite capable of jumping from one conductor to another (perhaps a crewman). For this reason the best place for a conductor is right forward. A strip of metal running down the bow from the forestay chainplate to several feet below the waterline will do. See diagram 89.

The great advantage of a lightning conductor is that it acts as a lightning preventer. This preventive property can be improved by proper installation. Thunderstorms occur in conditions of strong electric fields. Any pointed piece of metal connected to earth (the sea) will give off a stream of positively charged particles—the sharper the point the more intense the stream. The effect of these particles is to neutralise—or balance out—the charge in the air. The lightning will be diverted away from the point. Thus if a spike is mounted at the masthead and connected to earth it will provide an umbrella of protection for the whole yacht. The Ocean 71 type *Smuggler of Abersoch* has the ideal arrangement, a 15 mm diameter spike mounted at the masthead and connected to the forestay. A stainless steel strip runs down the outside of the boat to four feet below the waterline.

A most important point is that the rigging must be connected to the water outside the yacht. G.R.P. is a good insulator—in the *G.B.II* strike the charge probably found its way to earth via the mast step to the keel bolts. We were fortunate that no-one on deck—or down below—was hurt.

If a radio aerial is rigged it must be lowered in thundery weather. Where this is not possible, a facility must be arranged whereby the aerial can be switched from the radio directly to an earth plate outside the hull.

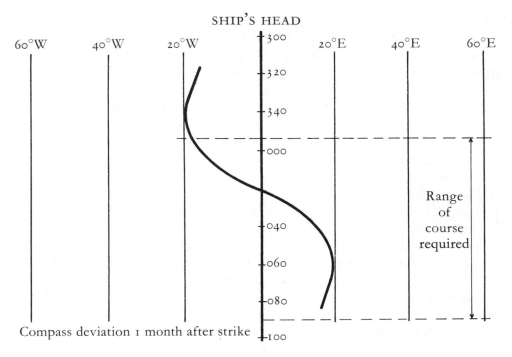

SHIP'S HEAD

60°W 40°W 20°W

300
320
340
000
040
060
080
100

20°E 40°E 60°E

Range of course required

Compass deviation 1 month after strike

88b. *Deviation caused by lightning strike.*

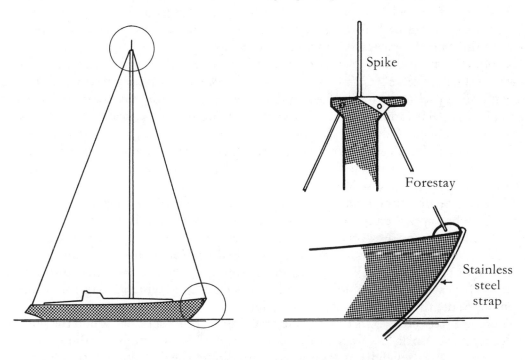

Spike

Forestay

Stainless steel strap

89. *Lightning conductor/protector.*

Whales

The incidence of yachts colliding with whales is on the increase, probably because the number of yachts at sea is also increasing. Even so, there have been a number of disturbing incidents over the last few years.

Dolphins and pilot whales delight in the company of yachts. The faster the vessel is moving, the more the creatures like it. They are very careful in their play and very rarely touch the hull. On the other hand, larger whales do not appear to be attracted to, or provoked by, boats intruding into their natural environment. In a total of 20 or more sightings of whales I have experienced only two 'close encounters'. On one occasion it was entirely our fault. Sailing at top speed down wind we sighted a large whale just beyond the next wave ahead, swimming slowly across our bows. We were too close to alter course. Just before the expected collision the mammal sounded and we passed harmlessly over the top of it. The second encounter was a deliberate attempt by a whale to 'investigate' us. We were sailing very slowly past a pair of whales, when one of them turned and swam forward to within 20 metres of us before losing interest and turning away.

Other yachtsmen have been less lucky. The Bailey's were sunk by a whale near the Galapagos Islands. Their wooden yacht sank quite quickly after a surprise collision. Whether the whale was aggressive or also surprised is difficult to tell. The Bailey's survived an incredible 118 days in a liferaft before being rescued.

In the 1976 Cape-Rio race the French yacht *Postulat*—a lightweight wooden craft—hit a whale with her keel. The yacht stopped and appeared to bounce two or three times against the obstruction before it finally moved away and was recognised for what it was. *Postulat* finished the race with only minor damage.

Another yacht in the same race was not so fortunate. After a successful Cape-Rio race, in which she won class I, *Guia III* set out for the race from Rio back to Portsmouth. *Guia* was an Italian yacht with a French skipper and an English radio operator. Before the race I arranged regular radio schedules between *Guia* and my entry, *British Steel*. For several days all went well and I enjoyed talking to them. One day, as we sailed across the equator, they failed to come on the air. Three days later the crew of *Guia* were again in touch with the rest of the fleet—but the radio they were using was on the bridge of a cargo ship bound for New York!

They had been sailing in clear weather and had seen a whale swimming fast towards them. In what appeared to be a deliberate attack it hit them in the bow, splitting the wooden hull over an area of a metre. After attempts to stop the water flow failed, they abandoned ship. From the life-raft they watched the yacht sink, 12 minutes after the collision, but they were picked up within 24 hours. The rescue ship was quite a distance off when it saw their flares; luckily the ship was passing to windward of them and, as so often happens, the lookout was facing to leeward.

There are two sides to this story, one amusing and one serious. When the crew were landed in New York, the owner of *Guia* telegraphed instructions for them to stay in a smart hotel. This they did. On coming down to dinner the first evening they were turned away from the restaurant, as their yachting gear—their only attire—did not include the mandatory jackets. Nothing daunted the intrepid crew returned a few minutes later wearing their foul weather tops. Needless to say they were admitted.

The more serious aspect of the story concerns their life-raft. The three legs of the Atlantic triangle race (of which this was the final part) were run by different clubs. The Royal Naval Sailing Association was handling the Rio–Portsmouth leg and consequently was responsible for scrutinising the yachts in Rio. The R.N.S.A. committee were not happy with *Guia's* life-raft. The skipper claimed that a raft good enough for the previous leg of the race was good enough for the last, but he was overruled by the R.N.S.A. and forced to buy a new raft. After their rescue the crew cabled the committee to express their thanks and pointed out that they need not have gone to such extremes to prove their point!

A final incident worth looking at. Commander Erroll Bruce, while sailing a yacht under spinnaker, found himself steering between a large whale and her calf. There was no time to alter course to avoid coming between parent and young. The large whale was swimming aggressively towards the yacht, but sheered off as soon as the engine was started.

Having studied several examples, can we come to any conclusions? From the research done, marine biologists can find no conclusive evidence to support any possible theories. It is felt, however, that any attack by a whale is more likely to be an attempt to remove a rival mammal than an attempt to damage alien craft. For this reason any activity that identifies one as a non-whale, such as hitting the hull, starting the engine or switching on the echo sounder, is worth a try.

Is there a common denominator in the yachts sunk? Certainly not the colour of their anti-fouling paint. One thing does come up—most, if not all, of them had wooden hulls. Is this coincidence? Is it because there are more wooden yachts around the oceans? Both unlikely. Is it because wood is more susceptible to damage from this type of collision than other building materials? Or do the whales know what a hull is made of and prefer wood?

The Final Hazard

The greatest hazard an ocean sailor has to face is ashore. A yacht and crew sailing for weeks on end with no difficulties and lacking nothing become, on entering port, the largest sink of time and money imaginable. While nothing is needed at sea, there will be a list of jobs and requirements a mile long when landfall is made. There will be worries, work, telephone calls and bills to pay. Not until harbour is left behind will the yacht and her crew be relaxed and fit again. Admiral Nelson was right when he said:

'It is ports that rot both ships and men'. My advice, and his, is: 'Get to sea as soon as possible.'

Sailing up the North Atlantic on Second Life.

Appendix 1—Apparent Wind Formulae

Code:
a is the apparent wind speed in knots
A is the apparent wind angle from the bow (0° to 180°)
t is the true wind speed in knots
T is the true wind angle from the bow (0° to 180°)
b is the boat speed in knots

Problem 1.
Given a, A and b (i.e. the instrument readings while sailing), find t and T.

$$t = \sqrt{b^2 + a^2 - 2ba \cos A}$$
$$T = \cos^{-1}[(a^2 + t^2 - b^2)/2at] + A$$

Problem 2.
Given t, T and b (i.e. the instrument readings while stationary, plus an estimate of boat speed), find a and A.

$$a = \sqrt{b^2 + t^2 + 2bt \cos T}$$
$$A = \cos^{-1}[(a^2 + b^2 - t^2)/2ab]$$

Mathematical note
If $\cos A = x$ then $A = \cos^{-1}[x]$

Appendix II   Nautical Almanac—G.H.A. and DEC.

1980 NOVEMBER 23, 24, 25 (SUN., MON., TUES.)

G.M.T.	SUN G.H.A.	SUN Dec.	MOON G.H.A.	v	Dec.	d	H.P.	Lat.	Twilight Naut.	Twilight Civil	Sunrise	Moonrise 23	Moonrise 24	Moonrise 25	Moonrise 26
	° '	° '	° '		° '			°	h m	h m	h m	h m	h m	h m	h m
23 00	183 24.4	S20 19.8	352 05.9	5.2	N17 39.2	6.5	60.5	N 72	07 31	09 18	▬	☐	☐	15 27	17 34
01	198 24.2	20.3	6 30.1	5.1	17 45.7	6.3	60.4	N 70	07 17	08 47	11 13	14 28	☐	15 27	17 34
02	213 24.0	20.8	20 54.2	5.2	17 52.0	6.2	60.4	68	07 06	08 24	09 58	15 17	15 48	16 51	18 20
03	228 23.9 ··	21.4	35 18.4	5.1	17 58.2	6.1	60.4	66	06 56	08 06	09 22	15 48	16 28	17 30	18 50
04	243 23.7	21.9	49 42.5	5.1	18 04.3	5.9	60.4	64	06 48	07 51	08 56	16 11	16 55	17 57	19 12
05	258 23.5	22.4	64 06.7	5.1	18 10.2	5.8	60.3	62	06 41	07 39	08 36	16 30	17 16	18 17	19 30
06	273 23.3	S20 22.9	78 30.8	5.1	N18 16.0	5.7	60.3	60	06 34	07 28	08 20	16 45	17 34	18 34	19 44
07	288 23.2	23.4	92 54.9	5.1	18 21.7	5.5	60.3	N 58	06 29	07 19	08 06	16 58	17 48	18 49	19 57
08	303 23.0	24.0	107 19.0	5.1	18 27.2	5.4	60.3	56	06 24	07 11	07 55	17 10	18 01	19 01	20 08
S 09	318 22.8 ··	24.5	121 43.1	5.1	18 32.6	5.3	60.2	54	06 19	07 03	07 44	17 20	18 11	19 11	20 17
U 10	333 22.6	25.0	136 07.2	5.1	18 37.9	5.1	60.2	52	06 14	06 56	07 35	17 29	18 21	19 21	20 26
N 11	348 22.5	25.5	150 31.3	5.1	18 43.0	5.0	60.2	50	06 10	06 50	07 27	17 37	18 30	19 29	20 33
D 12	3 22.3	S20 26.0	164 55.4	5.1	N18 48.0	4.9	60.1	45	06 01	06 37	07 10	17 54	18 48	19 47	20 49
A 13	18 22.1	26.5	179 19.5	5.1	18 52.9	4.7	60.1	N 40	05 53	06 26	06 55	18 08	19 03	20 02	21 03
Y 14	33 21.9	27.0	193 43.6	5.1	18 57.6	4.6	60.1	35	05 45	06 16	06 43	18 20	19 16	20 14	21 14
15	48 21.7 ··	27.6	208 07.7	5.1	19 02.2	4.5	60.1	30	05 38	06 07	06 33	18 30	19 27	20 25	21 24
16	63 21.6	28.1	222 31.8	5.2	19 06.7	4.3	60.0	20	05 24	05 51	06 14	18 48	19 46	20 44	21 41
17	78 21.4	28.6	236 56.0	5.1	19 11.0	4.2	60.0	N 10	05 10	05 36	05 58	19 04	20 02	21 00	21 55
18	93 21.2	S20 29.1	251 20.1	5.1	N19 15.2	4.0	60.0	0	04 55	05 21	05 43	19 18	20 18	21 15	22 09
19	108 21.0	29.6	265 44.2	5.2	19 19.2	3.9	59.9	S 10	04 39	05 05	05 28	19 33	20 33	21 30	22 23
20	123 20.9	30.1	280 08.4	5.1	19 23.1	3.8	59.9	20	04 19	04 48	05 11	19 49	20 50	21 46	22 37
21	138 20.7 ··	30.6	294 32.5	5.2	19 26.9	3.6	59.9	30	03 54	04 26	04 52	20 07	21 09	22 05	22 54
22	153 20.5	31.1	308 56.7	5.2	19 30.5	3.5	59.8	35	03 38	04 13	04 41	20 18	21 20	22 16	23 04
23	168 20.3	31.6	323 20.9	5.2	19 34.0	3.4	59.8	40	03 18	03 57	04 28	20 30	21 33	22 28	23 15
24 00	183 20.1	S20 32.1	337 45.1	5.2	N19 37.4	3.2	59.8	45	02 52	03 38	04 13	20 45	21 48	22 43	23 28
01	198 20.0	32.6	352 09.3	5.2	19 40.6	3.1	59.7	S 50	02 17	03 13	03 54	21 03	22 07	23 00	23 44
02	213 19.8	33.1	6 33.5	5.3	19 43.7	2.9	59.7	52	01 58	03 01	03 45	21 11	22 16	23 09	23 51
03	228 19.6 ··	33.7	20 57.8	5.3	19 46.6	2.8	59.7	54	01 33	02 47	03 35	21 20	22 26	23 18	24 00
04	243 19.4	34.2	35 22.1	5.3	19 49.4	2.7	59.6	56	00 57	02 30	03 24	21 31	22 37	23 29	24 09
05	258 19.2	34.7	49 46.4	5.3	19 52.1	2.5	59.6	58	////	02 10	03 11	21 43	22 49	23 41	24 19
06	273 19.1	S20 35.2	64 10.7	5.4	N19 54.6	2.4	59.6	S 60	////	01 44	02 55	21 57	23 04	23 55	24 31

G.M.T.	SUN G.H.A.	SUN Dec.	MOON G.H.A.	v	Dec.	d	H.P.	Lat.	Sunset	Twilight Civil	Twilight Naut.	Moonset 23	Moonset 24	Moonset 25	Moonset 26
07	288 18.9	35.7	78 35.1	5.4	19 57.0	2.3	59.5	°	h m	h m	h m	h m	h m	h m	h m
08	303 18.7	36.2	92 59.5	5.4	19 59.3	2.1	59.5	N 72	▬	14 15	16 02	☐	☐	☐	☐
M 09	318 18.5 ··	36.7	107 23.9	5.4	20 01.4	2.0	59.5	N 70	12 20	14 46	16 16	11 29	☐	14 37	14 24
O 10	333 18.3	37.2	121 48.3	5.5	20 03.4	1.8	59.4	68	13 35	15 09	16 27	10 41	12 14	13 12	13 38
N 11	348 18.1	37.7	136 12.8	5.5	20 05.2	1.7	59.4	66	14 11	15 27	16 37	10 10	11 35	12 33	13 08
D 12	3 18.0	S20 38.2	150 37.3	5.6	N20 06.9	1.6	59.4	64	14 37	15 42	16 45	09 48	11 08	12 06	12 45
A 13	18 17.8	38.7	165 01.9	5.6	20 08.5	1.4	59.3	62	14 57	15 54	16 52	09 29	10 46	11 45	12 27
Y 14	33 17.6	39.2	179 26.5	5.6	20 09.9	1.3	59.3	60	15 13	16 05	16 59	09 14	10 29	11 28	12 12
15	48 17.4 ··	39.7	193 51.1	5.7	20 11.2	1.2	59.3	N 58	15 27	16 14	17 04	09 02	10 15	11 14	11 59
16	63 17.2	40.2	208 15.8	5.7	20 12.4	1.0	59.2	56	15 38	16 23	17 10	08 51	10 03	11 02	11 48
17	78 17.0	40.6	222 40.5	5.7	20 13.4	0.9	59.2	54	15 49	16 30	17 14	08 41	09 52	10 51	11 38
18	93 16.8	S20 41.1	237 05.2	5.8	N20 14.3	0.7	59.1	52	15 58	16 37	17 19	08 32	09 42	10 41	11 29
19	108 16.7	41.6	251 30.0	5.8	20 15.0	0.6	59.1	50	16 06	16 43	17 23	08 24	09 34	10 33	11 21
20	123 16.5	42.1	265 54.8	5.9	20 15.6	0.5	59.1	45	16 24	16 56	17 32	08 08	09 16	10 15	11 05
21	138 16.3 ··	42.6	280 19.7	5.9	20 16.1	0.4	59.0	N 40	16 38	17 08	17 41	07 55	09 01	10 00	10 51
22	153 16.1	43.1	294 44.6	6.0	20 16.5	0.2	59.0	35	16 50	17 17	17 48	07 43	08 48	09 47	10 39
23	168 15.9	43.6	309 09.6	6.0	20 16.7	0.1	59.0	30	17 01	17 26	17 56	07 33	08 37	09 36	10 29
25 00	183 15.7	S20 44.1	323 34.6	6.1	N20 16.8	0.1	58.9	20	17 19	17 43	18 10	07 16	08 19	09 17	10 11
01	198 15.5	44.6	337 59.7	6.1	20 16.7	0.3	58.9	N 10	17 35	17 58	18 23	07 01	08 02	09 01	09 56
02	213 15.3	45.1	352 24.8	6.2	20 16.6	0.3	58.8	0	17 50	18 13	18 38	06 47	07 47	08 45	09 41
03	228 15.2 ··	45.6	6 50.0	6.2	20 16.3	0.5	58.8	S 10	18 06	18 28	18 55	06 33	07 32	08 30	09 27
04	243 15.0	46.1	21 15.2	6.3	20 15.8	0.5	58.8	20	18 22	18 46	19 15	06 18	07 15	08 13	09 11
05	258 14.8	46.5	35 40.5	6.4	20 15.2	0.7	58.7	30	18 41	19 08	19 40	06 01	06 56	07 54	08 53
06	273 14.6	S20 47.0	50 05.9	6.4	N20 14.5	0.8	58.7	35	18 53	19 21	19 57	05 51	06 45	07 43	08 43
07	288 14.4	47.5	64 31.3	6.4	20 13.7	0.9	58.6	40	19 06	19 37	20 16	05 40	06 33	07 30	08 31
08	303 14.2	48.0	78 56.7	6.6	20 12.8	1.1	58.6	45	19 21	19 57	20 42	05 27	06 18	07 15	08 16
T 09	318 14.0 ··	48.5	93 22.3	6.6	20 11.7	1.2	58.6	S 50	19 40	20 21	21 18	05 11	06 00	06 57	07 59
U 10	333 13.8	49.0	107 47.9	6.6	20 10.5	1.3	58.5	52	19 49	20 34	21 38	05 03	05 51	06 48	07 51
E 11	348 13.6	49.5	122 13.5	6.7	20 09.1	1.4	58.5	54	19 59	20 48	22 03	04 55	05 42	06 38	07 41
S 12	3 13.4	S20 49.9	136 39.2	6.8	N20 07.7	1.6	58.5	56	20 11	21 05	22 41	04 45	05 31	06 27	07 31
D 13	18 13.2	50.4	151 05.0	6.8	20 06.1	1.7	58.4	58	20 24	21 26	////	04 35	05 19	06 14	07 19
A 14	33 13.0	50.9	165 30.8	6.9	20 04.4	1.8	58.4	S 60	20 40	21 53	////	04 22	05 04	05 59	07 06
Y 15	48 12.9 ··	51.4	179 56.7	7.0	20 02.6	2.0	58.3								
16	63 12.7	51.9	194 22.7	7.1	20 00.6	2.1	58.3								
17	78 12.5	52.3	208 48.8	7.1	19 58.5	2.2	58.3								
18	93 12.3	S20 52.8	223 14.9	7.1	N19 56.3	2.3	58.2								
19	108 12.1	53.3	237 41.0	7.3	19 54.0	2.4	58.2								
20	123 11.9	53.8	252 07.3	7.3	19 51.6	2.5	58.1								
21	138 11.7 ··	54.2	266 33.6	7.4	19 49.1	2.7	58.1								
22	153 11.5	54.7	281 00.0	7.5	19 46.4	2.8	58.1								
23	168 11.3	55.2	295 26.5	7.5	19 43.6	2.9	58.0								

	SUN			MOON			
Day	Eqn. of Time 00ʰ	Eqn. of Time 12ʰ	Mer. Pass.	Mer. Pass. Upper	Mer. Pass. Lower	Age	Phase
	m s	m s	h m	h m	h m	d	
23	13 38	13 29	11 47	00 33	13 03	16	
24	13 21	13 12	11 47	01 33	14 02	17	◖
25	13 03	12 54	11 47	02 32	15 00	18	

S.D. 16.2	d 0.5		S.D. 16.4		16.2	15.9	

4ᵐ — INCREMENTS AND CORRECTIONS — 5ᵐ

4	SUN PLANETS	ARIES	MOON	v or d	Corrⁿ	v or d	Corrⁿ	v or d	Corrⁿ
s	° ′	° ′	° ′	′	′	′	′	′	′
00	1 00·0	1 00·2	0 57·3	0·0	0·0	6·0	0·5	12·0	0·9
01	1 00·3	1 00·4	0 57·5	0·1	0·0	6·1	0·5	12·1	0·9
02	1 00·5	1 00·7	0 57·7	0·2	0·0	6·2	0·5	12·2	0·9
03	1 00·8	1 00·9	0 58·0	0·3	0·0	6·3	0·5	12·3	0·9
04	1 01·0	1 01·2	0 58·2	0·4	0·0	6·4	0·5	12·4	0·9
05	1 01·3	1 01·4	0 58·5	0·5	0·0	6·5	0·5	12·5	0·9
06	1 01·5	1 01·7	0 58·7	0·6	0·0	6·6	0·5	12·6	0·9
07	1 01·8	1 01·9	0 58·9	0·7	0·1	6·7	0·5	12·7	1·0
08	1 02·0	1 02·2	0 59·2	0·8	0·1	6·8	0·5	12·8	1·0
09	1 02·3	1 02·4	0 59·4	0·9	0·1	6·9	0·5	12·9	1·0
10	1 02·5	1 02·7	0 59·7	1·0	0·1	7·0	0·5	13·0	1·0
11	1 02·8	1 02·9	0 59·9	1·1	0·1	7·1	0·5	13·1	1·0
12	1 03·0	1 03·2	1 00·1	1·2	0·1	7·2	0·5	13·2	1·0
13	1 03·3	1 03·4	1 00·4	1·3	0·1	7·3	0·5	13·3	1·0
14	1 03·5	1 03·7	1 00·6	1·4	0·1	7·4	0·6	13·4	1·0
15	1 03·8	1 03·9	1 00·8	1·5	0·1	7·5	0·6	13·5	1·0
16	1 04·0	1 04·2	1 01·1	1·6	0·1	7·6	0·6	13·6	1·0
17	1 04·3	1 04·4	1 01·3	1·7	0·1	7·7	0·6	13·7	1·0
18	1 04·5	1 04·7	1 01·6	1·8	0·1	7·8	0·6	13·8	1·0
19	1 04·8	1 04·9	1 01·8	1·9	0·1	7·9	0·6	13·9	1·0
20	1 05·0	1 05·2	1 02·0	2·0	0·2	8·0	0·6	14·0	1·1
21	1 05·3	1 05·4	1 02·3	2·1	0·2	8·1	0·6	14·1	1·1
22	1 05·5	1 05·7	1 02·5	2·2	0·2	8·2	0·6	14·2	1·1
23	1 05·8	1 05·9	1 02·8	2·3	0·2	8·3	0·6	14·3	1·1
24	1 06·0	1 06·2	1 03·0	2·4	0·2	8·4	0·6	14·4	1·1
25	1 06·3	1 06·4	1 03·2	2·5	0·2	8·5	0·6	14·5	1·1
26	1 06·5	1 06·7	1 03·5	2·6	0·2	8·6	0·6	14·6	1·1
27	1 06·8	1 06·9	1 03·7	2·7	0·2	8·7	0·7	14·7	1·1
28	1 07·0	1 07·2	1 03·9	2·8	0·2	8·8	0·7	14·8	1·1
29	1 07·3	1 07·4	1 04·2	2·9	0·2	8·9	0·7	14·9	1·1
30	1 07·5	1 07·7	1 04·4	3·0	0·2	9·0	0·7	15·0	1·1
31	1 07·8	1 07·9	1 04·7	3·1	0·2	9·1	0·7	15·1	1·1
32	1 08·0	1 08·2	1 04·9	3·2	0·2	9·2	0·7	15·2	1·1
33	1 08·3	1 08·4	1 05·1	3·3	0·2	9·3	0·7	15·3	1·1
34	1 08·5	1 08·7	1 05·4	3·4	0·3	9·4	0·7	15·4	1·2
35	1 08·8	1 08·9	1 05·6	3·5	0·3	9·5	0·7	15·5	1·2
36	1 09·0	1 09·2	1 05·9	3·6	0·3	9·6	0·7	15·6	1·2
37	1 09·3	1 09·4	1 06·1	3·7	0·3	9·7	0·7	15·7	1·2
38	1 09·5	1 09·7	1 06·3	3·8	0·3	9·8	0·7	15·8	1·2
39	1 09·8	1 09·9	1 06·6	3·9	0·3	9·9	0·7	15·9	1·2
40	1 10·0	1 10·2	1 06·8	4·0	0·3	10·0	0·8	16·0	1·2
41	1 10·3	1 10·4	1 07·0	4·1	0·3	10·1	0·8	16·1	1·2
42	1 10·5	1 10·7	1 07·3	4·2	0·3	10·2	0·8	16·2	1·2
43	1 10·8	1·10·9	1 07·5	4·3	0·3	10·3	0·8	16·3	1·2
44	1 11·0	1 11·2	1 07·8	4·4	0·3	10·4	0·8	16·4	1·2
45	1 11·3	1 11·4	1 08·0	4·5	0·3	10·5	0·8	16·5	1·2
46	1 11·5	1 11·7	1 08·2	4·6	0·3	10·6	0·8	16·6	1·2
47	1 11·8	1 11·9	1 08·5	4·7	0·4	10·7	0·8	16·7	1·3
48	1 12·0	1 12·2	1 08·7	4·8	0·4	10·8	0·8	16·8	1·3
49	1 12·3	1 12·4	1 09·0	4·9	0·4	10·9	0·8	16·9	1·3
50	1 12·5	1 12·7	1 09·2	5·0	0·4	11·0	0·8	17·0	1·3
51	1 12·8	1 12·9	1 09·4	5·1	0·4	11·1	0·8	17·1	1·3
52	1 13·0	1 13·2	1 09·7	5·2	0·4	11·2	0·8	17·2	1·3
53	1 13·3	1 13·5	1 09·9	5·3	0·4	11·3	0·8	17·3	1·3
54	1 13·5	1 13·7	1 10·2	5·4	0·4	11·4	0·9	17·4	1·3
55	1 13·8	1 14·0	1 10·4	5·5	0·4	11·5	0·9	17·5	1·3
56	1 14·0	1 14·2	1 10·6	5·6	0·4	11·6	0·9	17·6	1·3
57	1 14·3	1 14·5	1 10·9	5·7	0·4	11·7	0·9	17·7	1·3
58	1 14·5	1 14·7	1 11·1	5·8	0·4	11·8	0·9	17·8	1·3
59	1 14·8	1 15·0	1 11·3	5·9	0·4	11·9	0·9	17·9	1·3
60	1 15·0	1 15·2	1 11·6	6·0	0·5	12·0	0·9	18·0	1·4

5	SUN PLANETS	ARIES	MOON	v or d	Corrⁿ	v or d	Corrⁿ	v or d	Corrⁿ
s	° ′	° ′	° ′	′	′	′	′	′	′
00	1 15·0	1 15·2	1 11·6	0·0	0·0	6·0	0·6	12·0	1·1
01	1 15·3	1 15·5	1 11·8	0·1	0·0	6·1	0·6	12·1	1·1
02	1 15·5	1 15·7	1 12·1	0·2	0·0	6·2	0·6	12·2	1·1
03	1 15·8	1 16·0	1 12·3	0·3	0·0	6·3	0·6	12·3	1·1
04	1 16·0	1 16·2	1 12·5	0·4	0·0	6·4	0·6	12·4	1·1
05	1 16·3	1 16·5	1 12·8	0·5	0·0	6·5	0·6	12·5	1·1
06	1 16·5	1 16·7	1 13·0	0·6	0·1	6·6	0·6	12·6	1·2
07	1 16·8	1 17·0	1 13·3	0·7	0·1	6·7	0·6	12·7	1·2
08	1 17·0	1 17·2	1 13·5	0·8	0·1	6·8	0·6	12·8	1·2
09	1 17·3	1 17·5	1 13·7	0·9	0·1	6·9	0·6	12·9	1·2
10	1 17·5	1 17·7	1 14·0	1·0	0·1	7·0	0·6	13·0	1·2
11	1 17·8	1 18·0	1 14·2	1·1	0·1	7·1	0·7	13·1	1·2
12	1 18·0	1 18·2	1 14·4	1·2	0·1	7·2	0·7	13·2	1·2
13	1 18·3	1 18·5	1 14·7	1·3	0·1	7·3	0·7	13·3	1·2
14	1 18·5	1 18·7	1 14·9	1·4	0·1	7·4	0·7	13·4	1·2
15	1 18·8	1 19·0	1 15·2	1·5	0·1	7·5	0·7	13·5	1·2
16	1 19·0	1 19·2	1 15·4	1·6	0·1	7·6	0·7	13·6	1·2
17	1 19·3	1 19·5	1 15·6	1·7	0·2	7·7	0·7	13·7	1·3
18	1 19·5	1 19·7	1 15·9	1·8	0·2	7·8	0·7	13·8	1·3
19	1 19·8	1 20·0	1 16·1	1·9	0·2	7·9	0·7	13·9	1·3
20	1 20·0	1 20·2	1 16·4	2·0	0·2	8·0	0·7	14·0	1·3
21	1 20·3	1 20·5	1 16·6	2·1	0·2	8·1	0·7	14·1	1·3
22	1 20·5	1 20·7	1 16·8	2·2	0·2	8·2	0·8	14·2	1·3
23	1 20·8	1 21·0	1 17·1	2·3	0·2	8·3	0·8	14·3	1·3
24	1 21·0	1 21·2	1 17·3	2·4	0·2	8·4	0·8	14·4	1·3
25	1 21·3	1 21·5	1 17·5	2·5	0·2	8·5	0·8	14·5	1·3
26	1 21·5	1 21·7	1 17·8	2·6	0·2	8·6	0·8	14·6	1·3
27	1 21·8	1 22·0	1 18·0	2·7	0·2	8·7	0·8	14·7	1·3
28	1 22·0	1 22·2	1 18·3	2·8	0·3	8·8	0·8	14·8	1·4
29	1 22·3	1 22·5	1 18·5	2·9	0·3	8·9	0·8	14·9	1·4
30	1 22·5	1 22·7	1 18·7	3·0	0·3	9·0	0·8	15·0	1·4
31	1 22·8	1 23·0	1 19·0	3·1	0·3	9·1	0·8	15·1	1·4
32	1 23·0	1 23·2	1 19·2	3·2	0·3	9·2	0·8	15·2	1·4
33	1 23·3	1 23·5	1 19·5	3·3	0·3	9·3	0·9	15·3	1·4
34	1 23·5	1 23·7	1 19·7	3·4	0·3	9·4	0·9	15·4	1·4
35	1 23·8	1 24·0	1 19·9	3·5	0·3	9·5	0·9	15·5	1·4
36	1 24·0	1 24·2	1 20·2	3·6	0·3	9·6	0·9	15·6	1·4
37	1 24·3	1 24·5	1 20·4	3·7	0·3	9·7	0·9	15·7	1·4
38	1 24·5	1 24·7	1 20·7	3·8	0·3	9·8	0·9	15·8	1·4
39	1 24·8	1 25·0	1 20·9	3·9	0·4	9·9	0·9	15·9	1·5
40	1 25·0	1 25·2	1 21·1	4·0	0·4	10·0	0·9	16·0	1·5
41	1 25·3	1 25·5	1 21·4	4·1	0·4	10·1	0·9	16·1	1·5
42	1 25·5	1 25·7	1 21·6	4·2	0·4	10·2	0·9	16·2	1·5
43	1 25·8	1 26·0	1 21·8	4·3	0·4	10·3	0·9	16·3	1·5
44	1 26·0	1 26·2	1 22·1	4·4	0·4	10·4	0·9	16·4	1·5
45	1 26·3	1 26·5	1 22·3	4·5	0·4	10·5	1·0	16·5	1·5
46	1 26·5	1 26·7	1 22·6	4·6	0·4	10·6	1·0	16·6	1·5
47	1 26·8	1 27·0	1 22·8	4·7	0·4	10·7	1·0	16·7	1·5
48	1 27·0	1 27·2	1 23·0	4·8	0·4	10·8	1·0	16·8	1·5
49	1 27·3	1 27·5	1 23·3	4·9	0·4	10·9	1·0	16·9	1·5
50	1 27·5	1 27·7	1 23·5	5·0	0·5	11·0	1·0	17·0	1·6
51	1 27·8	1 28·0	1 23·8	5·1	0·5	11·1	1·0	17·1	1·6
52	1 28·0	1 28·2	1 24·0	5·2	0·5	11·2	1·0	17·2	1·6
53	1 28·3	1 28·5	1 24·2	5·3	0·5	11·3	1·0	17·3	1·6
54	1 28·5	1 28·7	1 24·5	5·4	0·5	11·4	1·0	17·4	1·6
55	1 28·8	1 29·0	1 24·7	5·5	0·5	11·5	1·1	17·5	1·6
56	1 29·0	1 29·2	1 24·9	5·6	0·5	11·6	1·1	17·6	1·6
57	1 29·3	1 29·5	1 25·2	5·7	0·5	11·7	1·1	17·7	1·6
58	1 29·5	1 29·7	1 25·4	5·8	0·5	11·8	1·1	17·8	1·6
59	1 29·8	1 30·0	1 25·7	5·9	0·5	11·9	1·1	17·9	1·6
60	1 30·0	1 30·2	1 25·9	6·0	0·6	12·0	1·1	18·0	1·7

Appendix IV Sight Reduction Tables

LATITUDE **CONTRARY** NAME TO DECLINATION — L.H.A. 33°, 327°

Dec.	45° Hc	45° d	45° Z	46° Hc	46° d	46° Z	47° Hc	47° d	47° Z	48° Hc	48° d	48° Z	Dec.
°	° ′	′	°	° ′	′	°	° ′	′	°	° ′	′	°	°
0	36 22.3	−52.7	137.4	35 38.0	−53.2	137.9	34 53.3	−53.6	138.4	34 08.2	−53.9	138.9	0
1	35 29.6	53.0	138.0	34 44.8	53.3	138.5	33 59.7	53.7	138.9	33 14.3	54.1	139.4	1
2	34 36.6	53.1	138.6	33 51.5	53.5	139.0	33 06.0	53.9	139.5	32 20.2	54.2	139.9	2
3	33 43.5	53.2	139.2	32 58.0	53.7	139.6	32 12.1	53.9	140.0	31 26.0	54.3	140.4	3
4	32 50.3	53.4	139.7	32 04.3	53.7	140.1	31 18.2	54.1	140.5	30 31.7	54.4	140.9	4
5	31 56.9	−53.6	140.3	31 10.6	−53.9	140.6	30 24.1	−54.2	141.0	29 37.3	−54.5	141.4	5
6	31 03.3	53.6	140.8	30 16.7	54.0	141.2	29 29.9	54.3	141.5	28 42.8	54.6	141.9	6
7	30 09.7	53.8	141.3	29 22.7	54.1	141.7	28 35.6	54.5	142.0	27 48.2	54.7	142.3	7
8	29 15.9	53.9	141.8	28 28.6	54.2	142.2	27 41.1	54.5	142.5	26 53.5	54.9	142.8	8
9	28 22.0	54.0	142.3	27 34.4	54.3	142.6	26 46.6	54.6	142.9	25 58.6	54.8	143.2	9
10	27 28.0	−54.1	142.8	26 40.1	−54.4	143.1	25 52.0	−54.7	143.4	25 03.8	−55.0	143.7	10
11	26 33.9	54.2	143.3	25 45.7	54.5	143.6	24 57.3	54.7	143.9	24 08.8	55.1	144.1	11
12	25 39.7	54.3	143.8	24 51.2	54.6	144.0	24 02.6	54.9	144.3	23 13.7	55.1	144.6	12
13	24 45.4	54.4	144.2	23 56.6	54.6	144.5	23 07.7	54.9	144.8	22 18.6	55.2	145.0	13
14	23 51.0	54.4	144.7	23 02.0	54.8	145.0	22 12.8	55.0	145.2	21 23.4	55.2	145.4	14
15	22 56.6	−54.6	145.2	22 07.2	−54.8	145.4	21 17.8	−55.1	145.6	20 28.2	−55.3	145.8	15
16	22 02.0	54.6	145.6	21 12.4	54.8	145.8	20 22.7	55.1	146.0	19 32.9	55.4	146.3	16
17	21 07.4	54.7	146.1	20 17.6	55.0	146.3	19 27.6	55.2	146.5	18 37.5	55.4	146.7	17
18	20 12.7	54.7	146.5	19 22.6	55.0	146.7	18 32.4	55.2	146.9	17 42.1	55.4	147.1	18
19	19 18.0	54.8	146.9	18 27.6	55.0	147.1	17 37.2	55.3	147.3	16 46.7	55.5	147.5	19
20	18 23.2	−54.9	147.4	17 32.6	−55.1	147.5	16 41.9	−55.3	147.7	15 51.2	−55.6	147.9	20
21	17 28.3	54.9	147.8	16 37.5	55.2	148.0	15 46.6	55.4	148.1	14 55.6	55.6	148.2	21
22	16 33.4	55.0	148.2	15 42.3	55.1	148.4	14 51.2	55.4	148.5	14 00.0	55.6	148.6	22
23	15 38.4	55.0	148.6	14 47.2	55.3	148.8	13 55.8	55.4	148.9	13 04.4	55.7	149.0	23
24	14 43.4	55.1	149.0	13 51.9	55.3	149.2	13 00.4	55.5	149.3	12 08.7	55.6	149.4	24
25	13 48.3	−55.1	149.4	12 56.6	−55.3	149.6	12 04.9	−55.5	149.7	11 13.1	−55.8	149.8	25
26	12 53.2	55.1	149.9	12 01.3	55.3	150.0	11 09.4	55.6	150.1	10 17.3	55.7	150.2	26
27	11 58.1	55.2	150.3	11 06.0	55.4	150.4	10 13.8	55.6	150.5	9 21.6	55.8	150.5	27
28	11 02.9	55.2	150.7	10 10.6	55.4	150.8	9 18.2	55.6	150.8	8 25.8	55.8	150.9	28
29	10 07.7	55.2	151.1	9 15.2	55.4	151.1	8 22.6	55.6	151.2	7 30.0	55.8	151.3	29
30	9 12.5	−55.3	151.5	8 19.8	−55.5	151.5	7 27.0	−55.6	151.6	6 34.2	−55.8	151.7	30
31	8 17.2	55.2	151.9	7 24.3	55.4	151.9	6 31.4	55.7	152.0	5 38.4	55.8	152.0	31
32	7 22.0	55.3	152.2	6 28.9	55.5	152.3	5 35.7	55.7	152.3	4 42.6	55.9	152.4	32
33	6 26.7	55.4	152.6	5 33.4	55.5	152.7	4 40.0	55.6	152.7	3 46.7	55.8	152.8	33
34	5 31.3	55.3	153.0	4 37.9	55.6	153.1	3 44.4	55.7	153.1	2 50.9	55.9	153.1	34
35	4 36.0	−55.3	153.4	3 42.3	−55.5	153.4	2 48.7	−55.7	153.5	1 55.0	−55.9	153.5	35
36	3 40.7	55.4	153.8	2 46.8	55.5	153.8	1 53.0	55.7	153.8	0 59.1	55.9	153.9	36
37	2 45.3	55.4	154.2	1 51.3	55.5	154.2	0 57.3	55.7	154.2	0 03.2	−55.8	154.2	37
38	1 49.9	55.3	154.6	0 55.8	55.6	154.6	0 01.6	−55.7	154.6	0 52.6	+55.9	25.4	38
39	0 54.6	−55.4	155.0	0 00.2	−55.5	155.0	0 54.1	+55.8	25.0	1 48.5	55.9	25.1	39
40	0 00.8	+55.4	24.7	0 55.3	+55.6	24.7	1 49.9	+55.7	24.7	2 44.4	+55.8	24.7	40
41	0 56.2	55.3	24.3	1 50.9	55.5	24.3	2 45.6	55.6	24.3	3 40.2	55.9	24.3	41
42	1 51.5	55.4	23.9	2 46.4	55.5	23.9	3 41.2	55.7	23.9	4 36.1	55.8	24.0	42
43	2 46.9	55.4	23.5	3 41.9	55.5	23.5	4 36.9	55.7	23.6	5 31.9	55.8	23.6	43
44	3 42.3	55.3	23.1	4 37.4	55.5	23.1	5 32.6	55.7	23.2	6 27.7	55.9	23.2	44
45	4 37.6	+55.3	22.7	5 32.9	+55.5	22.8	6 28.3	+55.6	22.8	7 23.6	+55.8	22.9	45
46	5 32.9	55.4	22.3	6 28.4	55.5	22.4	7 23.9	55.6	22.4	8 19.4	55.7	22.5	46
47	6 28.3	55.3	22.0	7 23.9	55.5	22.0	8 19.5	55.6	22.0	9 15.1	55.8	22.1	47
48	7 23.6	55.2	21.6	8 19.4	55.4	21.6	9 15.1	55.6	21.7	10 10.9	55.7	21.7	48
49	8 18.8	55.3	21.2	9 14.8	55.4	21.2	10 10.7	55.5	21.3	11 06.6	55.7	21.4	49
50	9 14.1	+55.2	20.8	10 10.2	+55.4	20.8	11 06.2	+55.6	20.9	12 02.3	+55.6	21.0	50
51	10 09.3	55.2	20.4	11 05.6	55.3	20.4	12 01.8	55.5	20.5	12 57.9	55.7	20.6	51
52	11 04.5	55.2	20.0	12 00.9	55.3	20.0	12 57.3	55.4	20.1	13 53.6	55.6	20.2	52
53	11 59.7	55.1	19.6	12 56.2	55.3	19.7	13 52.7	55.4	19.7	14 49.2	55.5	19.8	53
54	12 54.8	55.1	19.2	13 51.5	55.2	19.3	14 48.1	55.4	19.3	15 44.7	55.5	19.4	54
55	13 49.9	+55.1	18.8	14 46.7	+55.2	18.8	15 43.5	+55.3	18.9	16 40.2	+55.5	19.0	55
56	14 45.0	55.0	18.4	15 41.9	55.2	18.4	16 38.8	55.3	18.5	17 35.7	55.4	18.6	56
57	15 40.0	55.0	17.9	16 37.1	55.1	18.0	17 34.1	55.2	18.1	18 31.1	55.4	18.2	57
58	16 35.0	54.9	17.5	17 32.2	55.0	17.6	18 29.3	55.2	17.7	19 26.5	55.3	17.8	58
59	17 29.9	54.9	17.1	18 27.2	55.0	17.2	19 24.5	55.1	17.3	20 21.8	55.2	17.4	59
60	18 24.8	+54.8	16.7	19 22.2	+55.0	16.8	20 19.6	+55.1	16.9	21 17.0	+55.2	17.0	60
61	19 19.6	54.7	16.2	20 17.2	54.8	16.4	21 14.7	55.0	16.5	22 12.2	55.2	16.6	61
62	20 14.3	54.7	15.8	21 12.0	54.8	15.9	22 09.7	54.9	16.0	23 07.4	55.0	16.1	62
63	21 09.0	54.6	15.4	22 06.8	54.8	15.5	23 04.6	54.9	15.6	24 02.4	55.0	15.7	63
64	22 03.6	54.5	14.9	23 01.6	54.6	15.0	23 59.5	54.8	15.1	24 57.4	54.9	15.3	64
65	22 58.1	+54.5	14.5	23 56.2	+54.6	14.6	24 54.3	+54.7	14.7	25 52.3	+54.8	14.8	65
66	23 52.6	54.4	14.0	24 50.8	54.5	14.1	25 49.0	54.6	14.2	26 47.1	54.7	14.4	66
67	24 47.0	54.3	13.6	25 45.3	54.4	13.7	26 43.6	54.5	13.8	27 41.8	54.7	13.9	67
68	25 41.3	54.2	13.1	26 39.7	54.3	13.2	27 38.1	54.4	13.3	28 36.5	54.5	13.4	68
69	26 35.5	54.1	12.6	27 34.0	54.2	12.7	28 32.5	54.3	12.8	29 31.0	54.4	13.0	69
70	27 29.6	+54.0	12.1	28 28.2	+54.1	12.2	29 26.8	+54.2	12.4	30 25.4	+54.4	12.5	70
71	28 23.6	53.8	11.6	29 22.3	54.0	11.7	30 21.0	54.1	11.9	31 19.8	54.2	12.0	71
72	29 17.4	53.8	11.1	30 16.3	53.9	11.2	31 15.1	54.0	11.4	32 14.0	54.0	11.5	72
73	30 11.2	53.7	10.6	31 10.2	53.7	10.7	32 09.1	53.9	10.8	33 08.0	54.0	11.0	73
74	31 04.9	53.5	10.1	32 03.9	53.7	10.2	33 03.0	53.7	10.3	34 02.0	53.8	10.4	74
75	31 58.4	+53.4	9.6	32 57.6	+53.4	9.7	33 56.7	+53.6	9.8	34 55.8	+53.7	9.9	75
76	32 51.8	53.2	9.0	33 51.0	53.4	9.1	34 50.3	53.4	9.2	35 49.5	53.5	9.4	76
77	33 45.0	53.1	8.5	34 44.4	53.2	8.6	35 43.7	53.3	8.7	36 43.0	53.4	8.8	77
78	34 38.1	53.0	7.9	35 37.6	53.0	8.0	36 37.0	53.1	8.1	37 36.4	53.2	8.2	78
79	35 31.1	52.8	7.3	36 30.6	52.8	7.4	37 30.1	52.9	7.5	38 29.6	53.0	7.6	79
80	36 23.9	+52.6	6.7	37 23.4	+52.7	6.8	38 23.0	+52.7	6.9	39 22.6	+52.8	7.0	80
81	37 16.5	52.4	6.1	38 16.1	52.5	6.2	39 15.7	52.6	6.3	40 15.4	52.6	6.4	81
82	38 08.9	52.2	5.5	39 08.6	52.3	5.6	40 08.3	52.3	5.7	41 08.0	52.4	5.8	82
83	39 01.1	52.0	4.9	40 00.9	52.0	5.0	41 00.6	52.1	5.0	42 00.4	52.2	5.1	83
84	39 53.1	51.8	4.3	40 52.9	51.8	4.3	41 52.7	51.9	4.4	42 52.6	51.9	4.5	84
85	40 44.9	+51.5	3.6	41 44.7	+51.6	3.6	42 44.6	+51.7	3.7	43 44.5	+51.7	3.8	85
86	41 36.4	51.3	2.9	42 36.3	51.4	3.0	43 36.3	51.3	3.0	44 36.2	51.4	3.1	86
87	42 27.7	51.1	2.2	43 27.7	51.0	2.3	44 27.6	51.1	2.3	45 27.6	51.1	2.3	87
88	43 18.8	50.7	1.5	44 18.7	50.8	1.5	45 18.7	50.8	1.5	46 18.7	50.8	1.6	88
89	44 09.5	50.5	0.8	45 09.5	50.5	0.8	46 09.5	50.5	0.8	47 09.5	50.5	0.8	89
90	45 00.0	+50.2	0.0	46 00.0	+50.2	0.0	47 00.0	+50.2	0.0	48 00.0	+50.1	0.0	90
	45°			46°			47°			48°			

Dec.	49° Hc	49° d	49° Z	50° Hc	50° d	50° Z	51° Hc	51° d	51° Z	52° Hc	52° d	52° Z	Dec.
°	° ′	′	°	° ′	′	°	° ′	′	°	° ′	′	°	°
0	33 22.9	−54.3	139.3	32 37.3	−54.6	139.7	31 51.4	−55.0	140.1	31 05.2	−55.2	140.5	0
1	32 28.6	54.4	139.8	31 42.7	54.8	140.2	30 56.4	55.0	140.6	30 10.0	55.4	141.0	1
2	31 34.2	54.5	140.3	30 47.9	54.8	140.7	30 01.4	55.2	141.0	29 14.6	55.4	141.4	2
3	30 39.7	54.6	140.8	29 53.1	55.0	141.1	29 06.2	55.2	141.5	28 19.2	55.5	141.8	3
4	29 45.1	54.8	141.3	28 58.1	55.0	141.6	28 11.0	55.3	141.9	27 23.7	55.6	142.3	4
5	28 50.3	−54.8	141.7	28 03.1	−55.1	142.1	27 15.7	−55.4	142.4	26 28.1	−55.7	142.7	5
6	27 55.5	54.9	142.2	27 08.0	55.2	142.5	26 20.3	55.5	142.8	25 32.4	55.7	143.1	6
7	27 00.6	55.0	142.6	26 12.8	55.3	142.9	25 24.8	55.5	143.2	24 36.7	55.8	143.5	7
8	26 05.6	55.1	143.1	25 17.5	55.4	143.4	24 29.3	55.7	143.7	23 40.9	55.9	143.9	8
9	25 10.5	55.2	143.5	24 22.1	55.4	143.8	23 33.6	55.6	144.1	22 45.0	55.9	144.3	9
10	24 15.3	−55.2	144.0	23 26.7	−55.5	144.2	22 38.0	−55.8	144.5	21 49.1	−56.0	144.7	10
11	23 20.1	55.3	144.4	22 31.2	55.5	144.6	21 42.2	55.8	144.9	20 53.1	56.0	145.1	11
12	22 24.8	55.4	144.8	21 35.7	55.6	145.0	20 46.4	55.8	145.3	19 57.1	56.1	145.5	12
13	21 29.4	55.4	145.2	20 40.1	55.7	145.4	19 50.6	55.9	145.7	19 01.0	56.1	145.9	13
14	20 34.0	55.5	145.6	19 44.4	55.7	145.8	18 54.7	56.0	146.0	18 04.9	56.2	146.2	14
15	19 38.5	−55.5	146.0	18 48.7	−55.8	146.2	17 58.7	−56.0	146.4	17 08.7	−56.2	146.6	15
16	18 43.0	55.6	146.4	17 52.9	55.8	146.6	17 02.7	56.0	146.8	16 12.5	56.2	147.0	16
17	17 47.4	55.7	146.8	16 57.1	55.9	147.0	16 06.7	56.1	147.2	15 16.3	56.3	147.3	17
18	16 51.7	55.7	147.2	16 01.2	55.9	147.4	15 10.6	56.1	147.5	14 20.0	56.3	147.7	18
19	15 56.0	55.7	147.6	15 05.3	55.9	147.8	14 14.5	56.1	147.9	13 23.7	56.4	148.0	19
20	15 00.3	−55.7	148.0	14 09.4	−56.0	148.1	13 18.4	−56.2	148.3	12 27.3	−56.3	148.4	20
21	14 04.6	55.8	148.4	13 13.4	56.0	148.5	12 22.2	56.2	148.6	11 31.0	56.4	148.7	21
22	13 08.8	55.9	148.8	12 17.4	56.0	148.9	11 26.0	56.2	149.0	10 34.6	56.4	149.1	22
23	12 12.9	55.8	149.1	11 21.4	56.1	149.2	10 29.8	56.2	149.3	9 38.2	56.5	149.4	23
24	11 17.1	55.9	149.5	10 25.3	56.0	149.6	9 33.6	56.3	149.7	8 41.7	56.4	149.8	24
25	10 21.2	−55.9	149.9	9 29.3	−56.1	150.0	8 37.3	−56.3	150.0	7 45.3	−56.5	150.1	25
26	9 25.3	56.0	150.3	8 33.2	56.2	150.3	7 41.0	56.3	150.4	6 48.8	56.5	150.5	26
27	8 29.3	55.9	150.6	7 37.0	56.1	150.7	6 44.7	56.3	150.7	5 52.3	56.5	150.8	27
28	7 33.4	56.0	151.0	6 40.9	56.2	151.0	5 48.4	56.4	151.1	4 55.8	56.5	151.1	28
29	6 37.4	56.0	151.3	5 44.7	56.1	151.4	4 52.0	56.3	151.4	3 59.3	56.5	151.5	29
30	5 41.4	−56.0	151.7	4 48.6	−56.2	151.7	3 55.7	−56.4	151.8	3 02.8	−56.5	151.8	30
31	4 45.4	56.0	152.1	3 52.4	56.2	152.1	2 59.3	56.3	152.1	2 06.3	56.5	152.1	31
32	3 49.4	56.0	152.4	2 56.2	56.2	152.5	2 03.0	56.4	152.5	1 09.8	56.5	152.5	32
33	2 53.4	56.1	152.8	2 00.0	56.2	152.8	1 06.6	56.3	152.8	0 13.3	−56.6	152.8	33
34	1 57.3	56.0	153.1	1 03.8	56.2	153.2	0 10.3	−56.4	153.2	0 43.3	+56.5	26.8	34
35	1 01.3	−56.0	153.5	0 07.6	−56.2	153.5	0 46.1	+56.4	26.5	1 39.8	+56.5	26.5	35
36	0 05.3	−56.1	153.9	0 48.6	+56.2	26.1	1 42.5	56.3	26.2	2 36.3	56.5	26.2	36
37	0 50.8	+56.0	25.8	1 44.8	56.2	25.8	2 38.8	56.4	25.8	3 32.8	56.5	25.8	37
38	1 46.8	56.1	25.4	2 41.0	56.2	25.4	3 35.2	56.3	25.5	4 29.3	56.5	25.5	38
39	2 42.9	56.0	25.1	3 37.2	56.2	25.1	4 31.5	56.4	25.1	5 25.8	56.5	25.2	39
40	3 38.9	+56.0	24.7	4 33.4	+56.2	24.7	5 27.9	+56.3	24.8	6 22.3	+56.5	24.8	40
41	4 34.9	56.0	24.4	5 29.6	56.1	24.4	6 24.2	56.3	24.4	7 18.8	56.5	24.5	41
42	5 30.9	56.0	24.0	6 25.7	56.2	24.0	7 20.5	56.3	24.1	8 15.3	56.4	24.1	42
43	6 26.9	56.0	23.6	7 21.9	56.1	23.7	8 16.8	56.3	23.7	9 11.7	56.4	23.8	43
44	7 22.9	55.9	23.3	8 18.0	56.1	23.3	9 13.1	56.2	23.4	10 08.1	56.4	23.5	44
45	8 18.8	+56.0	22.9	9 14.1	+56.1	23.0	10 09.3	+56.3	23.0	11 04.5	+56.4	23.1	45
46	9 14.8	55.9	22.5	10 10.2	56.0	22.6	11 05.6	56.2	22.7	12 00.9	56.4	22.8	46
47	10 10.7	55.9	22.2	11 06.2	56.1	22.2	12 01.8	56.1	22.3	12 57.3	56.3	22.4	47
48	11 06.6	55.9	21.8	12 02.3	56.0	21.9	12 57.9	56.2	22.0	13 53.6	56.3	22.1	48
49	12 02.5	55.8	21.5	12 58.3	56.0	21.5	13 54.1	56.1	21.6	14 49.9	56.2	21.7	49
50	12 58.3	+55.8	21.1	13 54.3	+55.9	21.1	14 50.2	+56.1	21.2	15 46.1	+56.2	21.3	50
51	13 54.1	55.8	20.7	14 50.2	55.9	20.8	15 46.3	56.0	20.9	16 42.3	56.2	21.0	51
52	14 49.9	55.7	20.3	15 46.1	55.9	20.4	16 42.3	56.1	20.5	17 38.5	56.2	20.6	52
53	15 45.6	55.7	19.9	16 42.0	55.8	20.0	17 38.4	55.9	20.1	18 34.7	56.1	20.2	53
54	16 41.3	55.6	19.5	17 37.8	55.8	19.6	18 34.3	55.9	19.7	19 30.8	56.0	19.9	54
55	17 36.9	+55.6	19.1	18 33.6	+55.7	19.2	19 30.2	+55.9	19.4	20 26.8	+56.0	19.5	55
56	18 32.5	55.6	18.7	19 29.3	55.7	18.8	20 26.1	55.8	19.0	21 22.8	56.0	19.1	56
57	19 28.1	55.5	18.3	20 25.0	55.7	18.5	21 21.9	55.8	18.6	22 18.8	55.9	18.7	57
58	20 23.6	55.4	17.9	21 20.7	55.5	18.1	22 17.7	55.7	18.2	23 14.7	55.8	18.3	58
59	21 19.0	55.4	17.5	22 16.2	55.5	17.6	23 13.4	55.6	17.8	24 10.5	55.8	17.9	59
60	22 14.4	+55.3	17.1	23 11.7	+55.5	17.2	24 09.0	+55.6	17.4	25 06.3	+55.7	17.5	60
61	23 09.7	55.3	16.7	24 07.2	55.4	16.8	25 04.6	55.5	16.9	26 02.0	55.6	17.1	61
62	24 05.0	55.1	16.3	25 02.6	55.3	16.4	26 00.1	55.4	16.5	26 57.6	55.5	16.7	62
63	25 00.1	55.2	15.8	25 57.9	55.2	16.0	26 55.5	55.4	16.1	27 53.1	55.5	16.2	63
64	25 55.3	55.0	15.4	26 53.1	55.1	15.5	27 50.9	55.2	15.7	28 48.6	55.4	15.8	64
65	26 50.3	+54.9	14.9	27 48.2	+55.1	15.1	28 46.1	+55.2	15.2	29 44.0	+55.3	15.4	65
66	27 45.2	54.9	14.5	28 43.3	54.9	14.6	29 41.3	55.1	14.8	30 39.3	55.2	14.9	66
67	28 40.1	54.7	14.0	29 38.2	54.9	14.2	30 36.4	55.0	14.3	31 34.5	55.1	14.5	67
68	29 34.8	54.7	13.6	30 33.1	54.8	13.7	31 31.4	54.9	13.8	32 29.6	55.0	14.0	68
69	30 29.5	54.5	13.1	31 27.9	54.6	13.2	32 26.3	54.7	13.4	33 24.6	54.9	13.5	69
70	31 24.0	+54.4	12.6	32 22.5	+54.6	12.7	33 21.0	+54.7	12.9	34 19.5	+54.8	13.0	70
71	32 18.4	54.3	12.1	33 17.1	54.4	12.2	34 15.7	54.5	12.4	35 14.3	54.6	12.5	71
72	33 12.7	54.2	11.6	34 11.5	54.3	11.7	35 10.2	54.4	11.9	36 08.9	54.5	12.0	72
73	34 06.9	54.1	11.1	35 05.8	54.2	11.2	36 04.6	54.3	11.4	37 03.4	54.4	11.5	73
74	35 01.0	53.9	10.6	36 00.0	54.0	10.7	36 58.9	54.1	10.8	37 57.8	54.3	11.0	74
75	35 54.9	+53.8	10.0	36 54.0	+53.9	10.2	37 53.0	+54.0	10.3	38 52.1	+54.0	10.4	75
76	36 48.7	53.6	9.5	37 47.9	53.7	9.6	38 47.0	53.8	9.7	39 46.1	53.9	9.9	76
77	37 42.3	53.4	8.9	38 41.6	53.5	9.0	39 40.8	53.6	9.2	40 40.0	53.8	9.3	77
78	38 35.7	53.3	8.3	39 35.1	53.4	8.4	40 34.4	53.5	8.6	41 33.8	53.5	8.7	78
79	39 29.0	53.1	7.7	40 28.5	53.1	7.9	41 27.9	53.2	8.0	42 27.3	53.3	8.1	79
80	40 22.1	+52.9	7.1	41 21.6	+53.0	7.2	42 21.1	+53.1	7.4	43 20.6	+53.2	7.5	80
81	41 15.0	52.7	6.5	42 14.6	52.8	6.6	43 14.2	52.8	6.7	44 13.8	52.9	6.8	81
82	42 07.7	52.4	5.9	43 07.4	52.5	6.0	44 07.0	52.6	6.1	45 06.7	52.7	6.2	82
83	43 00.1	52.3	5.2	43 59.9	52.3	5.3	44 59.6	52.4	5.4	45 59.4	52.4	5.5	83
84	43 52.4	52.0	4.5	44 52.2	52.0	4.6	45 52.0	52.1	4.7	46 51.8	52.1	4.8	84
85	44 44.4	+51.7	3.8	45 44.2	+51.8	3.9	46 44.1	+51.8	4.0	47 43.9	+51.9	4.0	85
86	45 36.1	51.4	3.1	46 36.0	51.5	3.2	47 35.9	51.5	3.2	48 35.8	51.6	3.3	86
87	46 27.5	51.2	2.4	47 27.5	51.1	2.4	48 27.4	51.2	2.5	49 27.4	51.2	2.5	87
88	47 18.7	50.8	1.6	48 18.6	50.9	1.6	49 18.6	50.9	1.7	50 18.6	50.9	1.7	88
89	48 09.5	50.5	0.8	49 09.5	50.5	0.8	50 09.5	50.5	0.9	51 09.5	50.5	0.9	89
90	49 00.0	+50.1	0.0	50 00.0	+50.1	0.0	51 00.0	+50.1	0.0	52 00.0	+50.1	0.0	90
	49°			50°			51°			52°			

S. Lat. { L.H.A. greater than 180°......Zn=180°−Z; L.H.A. less than 180°............Zn=180°+Z }

LATITUDE **SAME** NAME AS DECLINATION — L.H.A. 147°, 213°

Appendix V Sight Reduction Tables

INTERPOLATION

Dec. Inc.	Tens 10'	20'	30'	40'	50'	Decimals	Units 0'	1'	2'	3'	4'	5'	6'	7'	8'	9'
16.0	2.6	5.3	8.0	10.6	13.3	.0	0.0	0.3	0.5	0.8	1.1	1.4	1.6	1.9	2.2	2.5
16.1	2.7	5.3	8.0	10.7	13.4	.1	0.0	0.3	0.6	0.9	1.1	1.4	1.7	2.0	2.2	2.5
16.2	2.7	5.4	8.1	10.8	13.5	.2	0.1	0.3	0.6	0.9	1.2	1.4	1.7	2.0	2.3	2.5
16.3	2.7	5.4	8.1	10.9	13.6	.3	0.1	0.4	0.6	0.9	1.2	1.5	1.7	2.0	2.3	2.6
16.4	2.7	5.5	8.2	10.9	13.7	.4	0.1	0.4	0.7	0.9	1.2	1.5	1.8	2.0	2.3	2.6
16.5	2.8	5.5	8.3	11.0	13.8	.5	0.1	0.4	0.7	1.0	1.2	1.5	1.8	2.1	2.3	2.6
16.6	2.8	5.5	8.3	11.1	13.8	.6	0.2	0.4	0.7	1.0	1.3	1.5	1.8	2.1	2.4	2.6
16.7	2.8	5.6	8.4	11.2	13.9	.7	0.2	0.5	0.7	1.0	1.3	1.6	1.8	2.1	2.4	2.7
16.8	2.8	5.6	8.4	11.2	14.0	.8	0.2	0.5	0.8	1.0	1.3	1.6	1.9	2.1	2.4	2.7
16.9	2.9	5.7	8.5	11.3	14.1	.9	0.2	0.5	0.8	1.1	1.3	1.6	1.9	2.2	2.4	2.7
17.0	2.8	5.6	8.5	11.3	14.1	.0	0.0	0.3	0.6	0.9	1.2	1.5	1.7	2.0	2.3	2.6
17.1	2.8	5.7	8.5	11.4	14.2	.1	0.0	0.3	0.6	0.9	1.2	1.5	1.8	2.1	2.4	2.7
17.2	2.8	5.7	8.6	11.4	14.3	.2	0.1	0.3	0.6	0.9	1.2	1.5	1.8	2.1	2.4	2.7
17.3	2.9	5.8	8.6	11.5	14.4	.3	0.1	0.4	0.7	1.0	1.3	1.5	1.8	2.1	2.4	2.7
17.4	2.9	5.8	8.7	11.6	14.5	.4	0.1	0.4	0.7	1.0	1.3	1.6	1.9	2.2	2.4	2.7
17.5	2.9	5.8	8.8	11.7	14.6	.5	0.1	0.4	0.7	1.0	1.3	1.6	1.9	2.2	2.5	2.8
17.6	2.9	5.9	8.8	11.7	14.7	.6	0.2	0.5	0.8	1.0	1.3	1.6	1.9	2.2	2.5	2.8
17.7	3.0	5.9	8.9	11.8	14.8	.7	0.2	0.5	0.8	1.1	1.4	1.7	2.0	2.2	2.5	2.8
17.8	3.0	6.0	8.9	11.9	14.9	.8	0.2	0.5	0.8	1.1	1.4	1.7	2.0	2.3	2.6	2.9
17.9	3.0	6.0	9.0	12.0	15.0	.9	0.3	0.6	0.8	1.1	1.4	1.7	2.0	2.3	2.6	2.9
18.0	3.0	6.0	9.0	12.0	15.0	.0	0.0	0.3	0.6	0.9	1.2	1.5	1.8	2.2	2.5	2.8
18.1	3.0	6.0	9.0	12.0	15.1	.1	0.0	0.3	0.6	1.0	1.3	1.6	1.9	2.2	2.5	2.8
18.2	3.0	6.0	9.1	12.1	15.1	.2	0.1	0.4	0.7	1.0	1.3	1.6	1.9	2.2	2.5	2.8
18.3	3.0	6.1	9.1	12.2	15.2	.3	0.1	0.4	0.7	1.0	1.3	1.6	1.9	2.3	2.6	2.9
18.4	3.1	6.1	9.2	12.3	15.3	.4	0.1	0.4	0.7	1.0	1.4	1.7	2.0	2.3	2.6	2.9
18.5	3.1	6.2	9.3	12.3	15.4	.5	0.2	0.5	0.8	1.1	1.4	1.7	2.0	2.3	2.6	2.9
18.6	3.1	6.2	9.3	12.4	15.5	.6	0.2	0.5	0.8	1.1	1.4	1.7	2.0	2.3	2.7	3.0
18.7	3.1	6.3	9.4	12.5	15.6	.7	0.2	0.5	0.8	1.1	1.4	1.8	2.1	2.4	2.7	3.0
18.8	3.2	6.3	9.4	12.6	15.7	.8	0.2	0.6	0.9	1.2	1.5	1.8	2.1	2.4	2.7	3.0
18.9	3.2	6.3	9.5	12.6	15.8	.9	0.3	0.6	0.9	1.2	1.5	1.8	2.1	2.4	2.7	3.1
19.0	3.1	6.3	9.5	12.6	15.8	.0	0.0	0.3	0.6	1.0	1.3	1.6	1.9	2.3	2.6	2.9
19.1	3.2	6.3	9.5	12.7	15.9	.1	0.0	0.4	0.7	1.0	1.3	1.7	2.0	2.3	2.6	3.0
19.2	3.2	6.4	9.6	12.8	16.0	.2	0.1	0.4	0.7	1.0	1.4	1.7	2.0	2.3	2.7	3.0
19.3	3.2	6.4	9.6	12.9	16.1	.3	0.1	0.4	0.7	1.1	1.4	1.7	2.0	2.4	2.7	3.0
19.4	3.2	6.5	9.7	12.9	16.2	.4	0.1	0.5	0.8	1.1	1.4	1.8	2.1	2.4	2.7	3.1
19.5	3.3	6.5	9.8	13.0	16.3	.5	0.2	0.5	0.8	1.1	1.5	1.8	2.1	2.4	2.8	3.1
19.6	3.3	6.5	9.8	13.1	16.3	.6	0.2	0.5	0.8	1.2	1.5	1.8	2.1	2.5	2.8	3.1
19.7	3.3	6.6	9.9	13.2	16.4	.7	0.2	0.6	0.9	1.2	1.5	1.9	2.2	2.5	2.8	3.2
19.8	3.3	6.6	9.9	13.2	16.5	.8	0.3	0.6	0.9	1.2	1.6	1.9	2.2	2.5	2.9	3.2
19.9	3.4	6.7	10.0	13.3	16.6	.9	0.3	0.6	0.9	1.3	1.6	1.9	2.2	2.6	2.9	3.2
20.0	3.3	6.6	10.0	13.3	16.6	.0	0.0	0.3	0.7	1.0	1.4	1.7	2.0	2.4	2.7	3.1
20.1	3.3	6.7	10.0	13.4	16.7	.1	0.0	0.4	0.7	1.1	1.4	1.7	2.1	2.4	2.8	3.1
20.2	3.3	6.7	10.1	13.4	16.8	.2	0.1	0.4	0.8	1.1	1.4	1.8	2.1	2.5	2.8	3.1
20.3	3.4	6.8	10.1	13.5	16.9	.3	0.1	0.4	0.8	1.1	1.5	1.8	2.2	2.5	2.8	3.2
20.4	3.4	6.8	10.2	13.6	17.0	.4	0.1	0.5	0.8	1.2	1.5	1.8	2.2	2.5	2.9	3.2
20.5	3.4	6.8	10.3	13.7	17.1	.5	0.2	0.5	0.9	1.2	1.5	1.9	2.2	2.6	2.9	3.2
20.6	3.4	6.9	10.3	13.7	17.2	.6	0.2	0.5	0.9	1.2	1.6	1.9	2.3	2.6	2.9	3.3
20.7	3.5	6.9	10.4	13.8	17.3	.7	0.2	0.6	0.9	1.3	1.6	1.9	2.3	2.6	3.0	3.3
20.8	3.5	7.0	10.4	13.9	17.4	.8	0.3	0.6	1.0	1.3	1.6	2.0	2.3	2.7	3.0	3.3
20.9	3.5	7.0	10.5	14.0	17.5	.9	0.3	0.6	1.0	1.3	1.7	2.0	2.4	2.7	3.0	3.4
21.0	3.5	7.0	10.5	14.0	17.5	.0	0.0	0.4	0.7	1.1	1.4	1.8	2.1	2.5	2.9	3.2
21.1	3.5	7.0	10.5	14.0	17.6	.1	0.0	0.4	0.8	1.1	1.5	1.8	2.2	2.5	2.9	3.3
21.2	3.5	7.0	10.6	14.1	17.6	.2	0.1	0.4	0.8	1.1	1.5	1.9	2.2	2.6	2.9	3.3
21.3	3.5	7.1	10.6	14.2	17.7	.3	0.1	0.5	0.8	1.2	1.5	1.9	2.3	2.6	3.0	3.3
21.4	3.6	7.1	10.7	14.3	17.8	.4	0.1	0.5	0.9	1.2	1.6	1.9	2.3	2.7	3.0	3.4
21.5	3.6	7.2	10.8	14.3	17.9	.5	0.2	0.5	0.9	1.3	1.6	2.0	2.3	2.7	3.0	3.4
21.6	3.6	7.2	10.8	14.4	18.0	.6	0.2	0.6	0.9	1.3	1.6	2.0	2.4	2.7	3.1	3.4
21.7	3.6	7.3	10.9	14.5	18.1	.7	0.3	0.6	1.0	1.3	1.7	2.0	2.4	2.8	3.1	3.5
21.8	3.7	7.3	10.9	14.6	18.2	.8	0.3	0.6	1.0	1.4	1.7	2.1	2.4	2.0	3.2	3.5
21.9	3.7	7.3	11.0	14.6	18.3	.9	0.3	0.7	1.0	1.4	1.8	2.1	2.5	2.8	3.2	3.5
22.0	3.6	7.3	11.0	14.6	18.3	.0	0.0	0.4	0.7	1.1	1.5	1.9	2.2	2.6	3.0	3.4
22.1	3.7	7.3	11.0	14.7	18.4	.1	0.0	0.4	0.8	1.2	1.5	1.9	2.3	2.7	3.0	3.4
22.2	3.7	7.4	11.1	14.8	18.5	.2	0.1	0.4	0.8	1.2	1.6	1.9	2.3	2.7	3.1	3.4
22.3	3.7	7.4	11.1	14.9	18.6	.3	0.1	0.5	0.9	1.2	1.6	2.0	2.4	2.7	3.1	3.5
22.4	3.7	7.5	11.2	14.9	18.7	.4	0.1	0.5	0.9	1.3	1.6	2.0	2.4	2.8	3.1	3.5
22.5	3.8	7.5	11.3	15.0	18.8	.5	0.2	0.6	0.9	1.3	1.7	2.1	2.4	2.8	3.2	3.6
22.6	3.8	7.5	11.3	15.1	18.8	.6	0.2	0.6	1.0	1.3	1.7	2.1	2.5	2.8	3.2	3.6
22.7	3.8	7.6	11.4	15.2	18.9	.7	0.3	0.6	1.0	1.4	1.8	2.1	2.5	2.9	3.3	3.6
22.8	3.8	7.6	11.4	15.2	19.0	.8	0.3	0.7	1.0	1.4	1.8	2.2	2.5	2.9	3.3	3.7
22.9	3.9	7.7	11.5	15.3	19.1	.9	0.3	0.7	1.1	1.5	1.8	2.2	2.6	3.0	3.3	3.7
23.0	3.8	7.6	11.5	15.3	19.1	.0	0.0	0.4	0.8	1.2	1.6	2.0	2.3	2.7	3.1	3.5
23.1	3.8	7.7	11.5	15.4	19.2	.1	0.0	0.4	0.8	1.2	1.6	2.0	2.4	2.8	3.2	3.6
23.2	3.8	7.7	11.6	15.4	19.3	.2	0.1	0.5	0.9	1.3	1.6	2.0	2.4	2.8	3.2	3.6
23.3	3.9	7.8	11.6	15.5	19.4	.3	0.1	0.5	0.9	1.3	1.7	2.1	2.5	2.9	3.3	3.6
23.4	3.9	7.8	11.7	15.6	19.5	.4	0.2	0.5	0.9	1.3	1.7	2.1	2.5	2.9	3.3	3.7
23.5	3.9	7.8	11.8	15.7	19.6	.5	0.2	0.6	1.0	1.4	1.8	2.2	2.5	2.9	3.3	3.7
23.6	3.9	7.9	11.8	15.7	19.7	.6	0.2	0.6	1.0	1.4	1.8	2.2	2.6	3.0	3.4	3.8
23.7	4.0	7.9	11.9	15.8	19.8	.7	0.3	0.7	1.1	1.4	1.8	2.2	2.6	3.0	3.4	3.8
23.8	4.0	8.0	11.9	15.9	19.9	.8	0.3	0.7	1.1	1.5	1.9	2.3	2.7	3.1	3.4	3.8
23.9	4.0	8.0	12.0	16.0	20.0	.9	0.4	0.7	1.1	1.5	1.9	2.3	2.7	3.1	3.5	3.9
	10'	20'	30'	40'	50'		0'	1'	2'	3'	4'	5'	6'	7'	8'	9'

Dec. Inc.	Double Second Diff. and Corr. (Diff. values with Corr. between them)
16.0–17.9	1.0 (0.1) 3.0 (0.2) 4.9 (0.3) 6.9 (0.4) 8.9 (0.5) 10.8 (0.6) 12.8 (0.7) 14.8 (0.8) 16.7 (0.9) 18.7 (1.0) 20.7 (1.1) 22.7 (1.2) 24.6 (1.3) 26.6 (1.4) 28.6 (1.5) 30.5 (1.6) 32.5 (1.7) 34.5
18.0–19.9	0.9 (0.1) 2.8 (0.2) 4.6 (0.3) 6.5 (0.4) 8.3 (0.5) 10.2 (0.6) 12.0 (0.7) 13.9 (0.8) 15.7 (0.9) 17.6 (1.0) 19.4 (1.1) 21.3 (1.2) 23.1 (1.3) 25.0 (1.4) 26.8 (1.5) 28.7 (1.6) 30.5 (1.7) 32.3 (1.8) 34.2
20.0–21.9	0.9 (0.1) 2.6 (0.2) 4.4 (0.3) 6.2 (0.4) 7.9 (0.5) 9.7 (0.6) 11.4 (0.7) 13.2 (0.8) 14.9 (0.9) 16.7 (1.0) 18.5 (1.1) 20.2 (1.2) 22.0 (1.3) 23.7 (1.4) 25.5 (1.5) 27.3 (1.6) 29.0 (1.7) 30.8 (1.8) 32.5 (1.9) 34.3
22.0–23.9	0.8 (0.1) 2.5 (0.2) 4.2 (0.3) 5.9 (0.4) 7.6 (0.5) 9.3 (0.6) 11.0 (0.7) 12.7 (0.8) 14.4 (0.9) 16.1 (1.0) 17.8 (1.1) 19.5 (1.2) 21.2 (1.3) 22.8 (1.4) 24.5 (1.5) 26.2 (1.6) 27.9 (1.7) 29.6 (1.8) 31.3 (1.9) 33.0 (2.0) 34.7

Dec. Inc.	Tens 10'	20'	30'	40'	50'	Decimals	Units 0'	1'	2'	3'	4'	5'	6'	7'	8'	9'
24.0	4.0	8.0	12.0	16.0	20.0	.0	0.0	0.4	0.8	1.2	1.6	2.0	2.4	2.9	3.3	3.7
24.1	4.0	8.0	12.0	16.0	20.1	.1	0.0	0.4	0.9	1.3	1.7	2.1	2.5	2.9	3.3	3.7
24.2	4.0	8.0	12.1	16.1	20.1	.2	0.1	0.5	0.9	1.3	1.7	2.1	2.5	2.9	3.3	3.8
24.3	4.0	8.1	12.1	16.2	20.2	.3	0.1	0.5	0.9	1.3	1.8	2.2	2.6	3.0	3.4	3.8
24.4	4.1	8.1	12.2	16.3	20.3	.4	0.2	0.6	1.0	1.4	1.8	2.2	2.6	3.0	3.4	3.8
24.5	4.1	8.2	12.3	16.3	20.4	.5	0.2	0.6	1.0	1.4	1.8	2.2	2.7	3.1	3.5	3.9
24.6	4.1	8.2	12.3	16.4	20.5	.6	0.2	0.7	1.1	1.5	1.9	2.3	2.7	3.1	3.5	3.9
24.7	4.1	8.3	12.4	16.5	20.6	.7	0.3	0.7	1.1	1.5	1.9	2.3	2.7	3.1	3.6	4.0
24.8	4.2	8.3	12.4	16.6	20.7	.8	0.3	0.7	1.1	1.6	2.0	2.4	2.8	3.2	3.6	4.0
24.9	4.2	8.3	12.5	16.6	20.8	.9	0.4	0.8	1.2	1.6	2.0	2.4	2.8	3.2	3.6	4.0
25.0	4.1	8.3	12.5	16.6	20.8	.0	0.0	0.4	0.8	1.3	1.7	2.1	2.5	3.0	3.4	3.8
25.1	4.2	8.3	12.5	16.7	20.9	.1	0.0	0.5	0.9	1.3	1.7	2.2	2.6	3.0	3.4	3.9
25.2	4.2	8.4	12.6	16.8	21.0	.2	0.1	0.5	0.9	1.4	1.8	2.2	2.6	3.1	3.5	3.9
25.3	4.2	8.4	12.6	16.9	21.1	.3	0.1	0.6	1.0	1.4	1.8	2.3	2.7	3.1	3.5	4.0
25.4	4.2	8.5	12.7	16.9	21.2	.4	0.2	0.6	1.0	1.4	1.9	2.3	2.7	3.1	3.6	4.0
25.5	4.3	8.5	12.8	17.0	21.3	.5	0.2	0.6	1.1	1.5	1.9	2.3	2.8	3.2	3.6	4.0
25.6	4.3	8.5	12.8	17.1	21.3	.6	0.3	0.7	1.1	1.5	2.0	2.4	2.8	3.2	3.7	4.1
25.7	4.3	8.6	12.9	17.2	21.4	.7	0.3	0.7	1.1	1.6	2.0	2.4	2.8	3.3	3.7	4.1
25.8	4.3	8.6	12.9	17.2	21.5	.8	0.3	0.8	1.2	1.6	2.0	2.5	2.9	3.3	3.7	4.2
25.9	4.4	8.7	13.0	17.3	21.6	.9	0.4	0.8	1.2	1.7	2.1	2.5	2.9	3.4	3.8	4.2
26.0	4.3	8.6	13.0	17.3	21.6	.0	0.0	0.4	0.9	1.3	1.8	2.2	2.6	3.1	3.5	4.0
26.1	4.3	8.7	13.0	17.4	21.7	.1	0.0	0.5	0.9	1.4	1.8	2.3	2.7	3.1	3.6	4.0
26.2	4.3	8.7	13.1	17.4	21.8	.2	0.1	0.5	1.0	1.4	1.9	2.3	2.7	3.2	3.6	4.1
26.3	4.4	8.8	13.1	17.5	21.9	.3	0.1	0.6	1.0	1.5	1.9	2.3	2.8	3.2	3.7	4.1
26.4	4.4	8.8	13.2	17.6	22.0	.4	0.2	0.6	1.1	1.5	1.9	2.4	2.8	3.3	3.7	4.2
26.5	4.4	8.8	13.3	17.7	22.1	.5	0.2	0.7	1.1	1.5	2.0	2.4	2.9	3.3	3.8	4.2
26.6	4.4	8.9	13.3	17.7	22.2	.6	0.3	0.7	1.1	1.6	2.0	2.5	2.9	3.4	3.8	4.2
26.7	4.5	8.9	13.4	17.8	22.3	.7	0.3	0.8	1.2	1.6	2.1	2.5	3.0	3.4	3.8	4.3
26.8	4.5	9.0	13.4	17.9	22.4	.8	0.4	0.8	1.2	1.7	2.1	2.6	3.0	3.4	3.9	4.3
26.9	4.5	9.0	13.5	18.0	22.5	.9	0.4	0.8	1.3	1.7	2.2	2.6	3.0	3.5	3.9	4.4
27.0	4.5	9.0	13.5	18.0	22.5	.0	0.0	0.5	0.9	1.4	1.8	2.3	2.7	3.2	3.7	4.1
27.1	4.5	9.0	13.5	18.0	22.6	.1	0.0	0.5	1.0	1.4	1.9	2.3	2.8	3.3	3.7	4.2
27.2	4.5	9.0	13.6	18.1	22.6	.2	0.1	0.5	1.0	1.5	1.9	2.4	2.8	3.3	3.8	4.2
27.3	4.5	9.1	13.6	18.2	22.7	.3	0.1	0.6	1.1	1.5	2.0	2.4	2.9	3.3	3.8	4.3
27.4	4.6	9.1	13.7	18.3	22.8	.4	0.2	0.6	1.1	1.6	2.0	2.5	2.9	3.4	3.8	4.3
27.5	4.6	9.2	13.8	18.3	22.9	.5	0.2	0.7	1.1	1.6	2.1	2.5	3.0	3.4	3.9	4.4
27.6	4.6	9.2	13.8	18.4	23.0	.6	0.3	0.7	1.2	1.6	2.1	2.6	3.0	3.5	3.9	4.4
27.7	4.6	9.3	13.9	18.5	23.1	.7	0.3	0.8	1.2	1.7	2.2	2.6	3.1	3.5	4.0	4.4
27.8	4.7	9.3	13.9	18.6	23.2	.8	0.4	0.8	1.3	1.7	2.2	2.7	3.1	3.6	4.0	4.5
27.9	4.7	9.3	14.0	18.6	23.3	.9	0.4	0.9	1.3	1.8	2.2	2.7	3.2	3.6	4.1	4.5
28.0	4.6	9.3	14.0	18.6	23.3	.0	0.0	0.5	0.9	1.4	1.9	2.4	2.8	3.3	3.8	4.3
28.1	4.7	9.3	14.0	18.7	23.4	.1	0.0	0.5	1.0	1.5	1.9	2.4	2.9	3.4	3.8	4.3
28.2	4.7	9.4	14.1	18.8	23.5	.2	0.1	0.6	1.0	1.5	2.0	2.5	2.9	3.4	3.9	4.4
28.3	4.7	9.4	14.1	18.9	23.6	.3	0.1	0.6	1.1	1.6	2.0	2.5	3.0	3.5	3.9	4.4
28.4	4.7	9.5	14.2	18.9	23.7	.4	0.2	0.7	1.1	1.6	2.1	2.6	3.0	3.5	4.0	4.5
28.5	4.8	9.5	14.3	19.0	23.8	.5	0.2	0.7	1.2	1.7	2.1	2.6	3.1	3.6	4.0	4.5
28.6	4.8	9.5	14.3	19.1	23.8	.6	0.3	0.8	1.2	1.7	2.2	2.7	3.1	3.6	4.1	4.6
28.7	4.8	9.6	14.4	19.2	23.9	.7	0.3	0.8	1.3	1.8	2.2	2.7	3.2	3.7	4.1	4.6
28.8	4.8	9.6	14.4	19.2	24.0	.8	0.4	0.9	1.3	1.8	2.3	2.8	3.2	3.7	4.2	4.7
28.9	4.9	9.7	14.5	19.3	24.1	.9	0.4	0.9	1.4	1.9	2.3	2.8	3.3	3.8	4.2	4.7
29.0	4.8	9.6	14.5	19.3	24.1	.0	0.0	0.5	1.0	1.5	2.0	2.5	2.9	3.4	3.9	4.4
29.1	4.8	9.7	14.5	19.4	24.2	.1	0.0	0.5	1.0	1.5	2.0	2.5	3.0	3.5	4.0	4.5
29.2	4.8	9.7	14.6	19.4	24.3	.2	0.1	0.6	1.1	1.6	2.1	2.6	3.0	3.5	4.0	4.5
29.3	4.9	9.8	14.6	19.5	24.4	.3	0.1	0.6	1.1	1.6	2.1	2.6	3.1	3.6	4.1	4.6
29.4	4.9	9.8	14.7	19.6	24.5	.4	0.2	0.7	1.2	1.7	2.2	2.7	3.1	3.6	4.1	4.6
29.5	4.9	9.8	14.8	19.7	24.6	.5	0.2	0.7	1.2	1.7	2.2	2.7	3.2	3.7	4.2	4.7
29.6	4.9	9.9	14.8	19.7	24.7	.6	0.3	0.8	1.3	1.8	2.3	2.8	3.2	3.7	4.2	4.7
29.7	5.0	9.9	14.9	19.8	24.8	.7	0.3	0.8	1.3	1.8	2.3	2.8	3.3	3.8	4.3	4.8
29.8	5.0	10.0	14.9	19.9	24.9	.8	0.4	0.9	1.4	1.9	2.4	2.9	3.3	3.8	4.3	4.8
29.9	5.0	10.0	15.0	20.0	25.0	.9	0.4	0.9	1.4	1.9	2.4	2.9	3.4	3.9	4.4	4.9
30.0	5.0	10.0	15.0	20.0	25.0	.0	0.0	0.5	1.0	1.5	2.0	2.5	3.0	3.6	4.1	4.6
30.1	5.0	10.0	15.0	20.0	25.1	.1	0.1	0.6	1.1	1.6	2.1	2.6	3.1	3.6	4.1	4.6
30.2	5.0	10.0	15.1	20.1	25.1	.2	0.1	0.6	1.1	1.6	2.1	2.6	3.2	3.7	4.2	4.7
30.3	5.0	10.1	15.1	20.2	25.2	.3	0.2	0.7	1.2	1.7	2.2	2.7	3.2	3.7	4.2	4.7
30.4	5.1	10.1	15.2	20.3	25.3	.4	0.2	0.7	1.2	1.7	2.2	2.7	3.3	3.8	4.3	4.8
30.5	5.1	10.2	15.3	20.3	25.4	.5	0.3	0.8	1.3	1.8	2.3	2.8	3.3	3.8	4.3	4.8
30.6	5.1	10.2	15.3	20.4	25.5	.6	0.3	0.8	1.3	1.8	2.3	2.8	3.4	3.9	4.4	4.9
30.7	5.1	10.3	15.4	20.5	25.6	.7	0.4	0.9	1.4	1.9	2.4	2.9	3.4	3.9	4.4	4.9
30.8	5.2	10.3	15.4	20.6	25.7	.8	0.4	0.9	1.4	1.9	2.4	2.9	3.5	4.0	4.5	5.0
30.9	5.2	10.3	15.5	20.6	25.8	.9	0.5	1.0	1.5	2.0	2.5	3.0	3.5	4.0	4.5	5.0
31.0	5.1	10.3	15.5	20.6	25.8	.0	0.0	0.5	1.0	1.6	2.1	2.6	3.1	3.7	4.2	4.7
31.1	5.2	10.3	15.5	20.7	25.9	.1	0.1	0.6	1.1	1.6	2.2	2.7	3.2	3.7	4.3	4.8
31.2	5.2	10.4	15.6	20.8	26.0	.2	0.1	0.6	1.2	1.7	2.2	2.7	3.3	3.8	4.3	4.8
31.3	5.2	10.4	15.6	20.9	26.1	.3	0.2	0.7	1.2	1.7	2.3	2.8	3.3	3.8	4.4	4.9
31.4	5.2	10.5	15.7	20.9	26.2	.4	0.2	0.7	1.3	1.8	2.3	2.8	3.4	3.9	4.4	4.9
31.5	5.3	10.5	15.8	21.0	26.3	.5	0.3	0.8	1.3	1.8	2.4	2.9	3.4	3.9	4.5	5.0
31.6	5.3	10.5	15.8	21.1	26.3	.6	0.3	0.8	1.4	1.9	2.4	2.9	3.5	4.0	4.5	5.0
31.7	5.3	10.6	15.9	21.2	26.4	.7	0.4	0.9	1.4	1.9	2.5	3.0	3.5	4.0	4.6	5.1
31.8	5.3	10.6	15.9	21.2	26.5	.8	0.4	0.9	1.5	2.0	2.5	3.0	3.6	4.1	4.6	5.1
31.9	5.4	10.7	16.0	21.3	26.6	.9	0.5	1.0	1.5	2.0	2.6	3.1	3.6	4.1	4.7	5.2
	10'	20'	30'	40'	50'		0'	1'	2'	3'	4'	5'	6'	7'	8'	9'

Dec. Inc.	Double Second Diff. and Corr. (Diff. values with Corr. between them)
24.0–25.9	0.8 (0.1) 2.5 (0.2) 4.1 (0.3) 5.8 (0.4) 7.4 (0.5) 9.1 (0.6) 10.7 (0.7) 12.3 (0.8) 14.0 (0.9) 15.6 (1.0) 17.3 (1.1) 18.9 (1.2) 20.6 (1.3) 22.2 (1.4) 23.9 (1.5) 25.5 (1.6) 27.2 (1.7) 28.8 (1.8) 30.4 (1.9) 32.1 (2.0) 33.7 (2.1) 35.4
26.0–27.9	0.8 (0.1) 2.4 (0.2) 4.0 (0.3) 5.7 (0.4) 7.3 (0.5) 8.9 (0.6) 10.5 (0.7) 12.1 (0.8) 13.7 (0.9) 15.4 (1.0) 17.0 (1.1) 18.6 (1.2) 20.2 (1.3) 21.8 (1.4) 23.4 (1.5) 25.1 (1.6) 26.7 (1.7) 28.3 (1.8) 29.9 (1.9) 31.5 (2.0) 33.1 (2.1) 34.7
28.0–29.9	0.8 (0.1) 2.4 (0.2) 4.0 (0.3) 5.6 (0.4) 7.2 (0.5) 8.8 (0.6) 10.4 (0.7) 12.0 (0.8) 13.6 (0.9) 15.2 (1.0) 16.8 (1.1) 18.4 (1.2) 20.0 (1.3) 21.6 (1.4) 23.2 (1.5) 24.8 (1.6) 26.4 (1.7) 28.0 (1.8) 29.6 (1.9) 31.2 (2.0) 32.8 (2.1) 34.4
30.0–31.9	0.8 (0.1) 2.4 (0.2) 4.0 (0.3) 5.6 (0.4) 7.2 (0.5) 8.8 (0.6) 10.4 (0.7) 12.0 (0.8) 13.6 (0.9) 15.2 (1.0) 16.8 (1.1) 18.4 (1.2) 20.0 (1.3) 21.6 (1.4) 23.2 (1.5) 24.8 (1.6) 26.4 (1.7) 28.0 (1.8) 29.6 (1.9) 31.2 (2.0) 32.8 (2.1) 34.4

The Double-Second-Difference correction (Corr.) is always to be added to the tabulated altitude.

Appendix VIA—Suggested Medical Chest

Amounts are given for a crew of 8, but when compiling the medical chests it would be wise to discuss the crew and their requirements with your own general practitioner who you will find to be interested and most helpful.

Item	Dose	Amount
Tablets		
Asilone	1–2 prn	100
Dulcodos	2 nocte	50
Septrin	2 b.d. for one week	200
Penicillin V	250 mg qds for one week	200
Imodium	2 at once then one every 6 hr	100
Lomotil	4 at once then 2 every 6 hr	100
Dramamine	1 every 4 hours	100
Sturgeron	2 tds	100
Panadol	2 every 4 hours	400
Injections		
Papaveretum	20 mg IM	16 ampoules
Lignocaine 1% Local anaesthetic		50 mls.
Benzyl penicillin	600,000 units qds	20 ampoules
Suppositories		
Metronidazole	1 qds	50
Nyastatin	2 nocte for 14 days	50
Solutions and Creams		
Dorbanex	10 mls nocte	100 mls
Chloramphenicol eye cream		12 tubes
Cetrimide sterilising solution		20 sachets
Lanolin cream		500 gms
Petroleum jelly		250 gms
Uvistat cream		6 tubes
Callomine lotion		250 mls
Bandages etc		
Slings		2
Crepe bandages 4 inch		6
Elastoplast bandages 4 inch		6
Elastoplast (assorted sizes)		4 boxes
Mellolin non adhesive dressing 4 in × 4 in		20
Gauze swabs 4 in × 4 in		40
Field dressing 4 in and 6 in		10
Steristrips (assorted sizes)		6 packets.
Scissors		2

Suggested Medical Chest (*continued*)

Miscellaneous		
Thermometer		4
Disposable scalpels		6
Syringes 5 ml + needles		10
10 ml + needles		10
Artery forcep/stitch holder		1
Sutures—assortment of silk, nylon and catgut sutures		

Abbreviations: prn = as required; nocte = before bed; bd = twice daily; qds = 4 times daily; tds = three times daily; IM = intra muscularly

Appendix VIB—Emergency Medical Box

These are required for the disaster bag

Item		*Amount*
Papaveratum		6 ampoules
Scalpel		3
Petroleum jelly		1 small pot
Uvistat cream		2
Lip salve		3 sticks
Dramamine		60 tablets
Chloramphenicol eye cream		3 tubes
Panadol		40 tablets
Assortment of sutures and elastoplasts		

Index